# FROM ECUMENISM TO COMM

# From Ecumenism to Community Relations

*Inter-Church Relationships in Northern Ireland*
*1980–2005*

## MARIA POWER

*Institute of Irish Studies,*
*The University of Liverpool*

IRISH ACADEMIC PRESS
DUBLIN • PORTLAND, OR

*First published in 2007 by*
IRISH ACADEMIC PRESS
44, Northumberland Road, Dublin 4, Ireland

*and in the United States of America by*
IRISH ACADEMIC PRESS
c/o ISBS, Suite 300, 920 NE 58th Avenue
Portland, Oregon 97213-3786

*WEBSITE*: www.iap.ie

British Library Cataloguing in Publication Data
An entry can be found on request

ISBN 0 7165 3379 0  (cloth)
ISBN 978 0 7165 3379 5
ISBN 0 7165 3380 4 (paper)
ISBN 978 0 7165 3380 1

Library of Congress Cataloging-in-Publication Data
An entry can be found on request

Printed by Biddles Ltd, King's Lynn, Norfolk

*For my Grandparents,*
*Alice and Philip McGovern*

# Contents

# Acknowledgements

This book could not have been written without the help of Professor Marianne Elliott and Professor John Turner, who provided me with much-needed, guidance and advice. Thanks are also due to Professor Roy Foster and Ian McBride for their insightful comments on the initial version of this text, John Littleton in Dublin and Michael Kirwin at Heythrop College, University of London, who provided gratefully received support on the theological aspects of this study, and the ESRC, who provided invaluable assistance through their Post-Doctoral Research Fellowship Scheme (PTA-026-27-0247).

I am extremely indebted to the participants who allowed me to interview them and in doing so provided me with the material upon which this work is based. I would also like to thank the librarians at the Linen Hall Library, the Irish School of Ecumenics Library and Martin McNeely in the Presbyterian Church's Press Office in Belfast for helping me to find additional material, the Cornerstone Community in Belfast for kindly allowing me to use their banner for the front cover and Shirley Lyman for patiently transcripting my interviews. I would not have been able to carry out my fieldwork without the help of Susan, Gemma and Carl Morgan in Dungannon and Mary Murphy in Dublin, who provided me with a home away from home during those periods.

Special thanks are due to the colleagues, friends and family that have seen me through this process: particularly Lisa Hyde at Irish Academic Press and Kevin Bean, Linda Christensen, Pat Nugent and Frank Shovlin at the Institute of Irish Studies, University of Liverpool, Keri Cronin, Dayle De Lancey, Josephine Muir, Silke Horstkotte, Kharyssa Rhodes and Heather Williams for providing a wealth of entertainment, advice and encouragement. Peggy Adler, Mahbuba Chowdhury, Neil Gavin, Maria and Veronica Gerrard, Asuka Leslie, Maxie Neff, Philip Newbold, Adrian Quinn, Sr. Mary Raphael, Ronan Wall, Amanda Thomson, Valentina Tamma, Gillian Wilesden, Diane Urquhart and Martin O'Neill, my brother and sister-in-law, Claude and Andrea, my uncle, Jim McGovern, my aunts Philomena Boyle and Brenda McConnell, and Bridie Brennan, Gabriel Conway, Michael Hubbart, Peter and Isobel McNeill, Ruth

Ohlson de Fine, Anne Prendergast, Breda and Maria Roche and Philomena Smyth, I will be forever indebted to you for the love and support that you have shown me. Finally, I will be eternally grateful to my parents, Alice and Eric, to whom I owe everything.

Maria Power
June 2006

# Introduction

Northern Ireland has one of the highest levels of religious identification and observance in Western Europe,[1] with 58 per cent of the population attending a church service more than once a month[2] and the 2001 census demonstrating that 86 per cent readily identify themselves with a religious denomination.[3] Such high levels of religious self-identification upon a census form indicate clearly the salience of religious identity in Northern Ireland, especially when one takes into account the fact that it is not compulsory to answer this question, with an average of 91 per cent of the population choosing to do so since 1971. Despite evidence of secularisation,[4] 'the great majority of people in Northern Ireland are at least nominally *members* of a Christian Church … It should be reasonable to assume, then, that religion plays an important part in the lives of the citizens of the State of Northern Ireland.'[5]

The churches in Northern Ireland provide a valuable social network and, notwithstanding the decline in attendance, 'have not been replaced by any other mass organisations. Trade unions and political parties remain small. The Orange Order no longer commands the support of previous years and membership of paramilitary groups is concentrated in geographical pockets. As a result the churches are still by far the largest institutions of civil society.'[6] The churches, both Protestant and Catholic, operate by tending to the traditional aspects of church life, such as spiritual welfare, births, marriages and deaths, whilst simultaneously participating in the maintenance of their congregations' social welfare, in the areas of education, social services, employment and healthcare. In many areas of Northern Ireland it is common to find schemes as diverse as unemployment advice centres and after-school play groups being run, and sometimes funded, by local churches. According to David Stevens 'The churches are present in every community in Northern Ireland. Much of the voluntary effort in this society is focused around churches and they contribute enormously to social capital.'[7] Finally, they also provide an identity which defines cultural and political, as well as religious values and beliefs, producing 'a popular culture which invokes religion as a boundary marker between the two communities'.[8]

Such a high level of identification combined with the churches' role in the lives of communities has led them to be the focus of much academic scrutiny. 'The question of whether the conflict is really religious, or whether religious labels simply mask a conflict over economic or political issues, has aroused endless discussion. A full spectrum of opinion can be found, ranging from those authors who accord religion a paramount importance through those who almost wholly discount it.'[9] In this comment Whyte neatly sums up the nature of academic writing on the churches and religion in Northern Ireland: the churches have generally been analysed purely in terms of the conflict in Northern Ireland, with endless articles and books devoted to the issues of identity politics and the contribution of the Protestant and Catholic Churches to their development.[10] Some of the literature surrounding the relationship between religion and the conflict within the two communities, such as Elliott's *Catholics of Ulster*,[11] has highlighted that it is a complex and ambiguous one, which intermingles, to varying degrees, with the countless other influences upon both communities. As a result of this commentary we can start to build a picture of a complex society, influenced by numerous factors, such as economics, power structures and cultural identities resulting in a conflict centred upon issues of nationality and civil rights in which the churches and religious identity play a role as 'the key ethnic marker, facilitating the residential, marital and educational segregation which helps reproduce the two ethnic\national communities'.[12] Such behaviour then on the part of the Protestant and Catholic communities leads one to question how the churches have reacted to the conflict in Northern Ireland and whether they have actually tried to work together as Christians to confront and deal with the idea that the problem in the area is one of religious difference.

In spite of this, very little research has been conducted on how the Protestant and Catholic Churches have actually engaged with each other.

> There seems at least a blind-spot, which accounts for the non-recognition of the many energetic inter-church activities in the North, ranging from Churches' Fora, interchurch youth structures, and ecumenical adult education programmes enthusiastically supported by Christians of different persuasions, which actually find meaning in theologically reflecting with others on matters of religion, violence and peace; on inclusive justice, religious experience and political ideology; on the biblical challenge of welcoming those of other world religions and other neglected minorities in our midst.[13]

What research has been produced suffers from an over concentration upon a series of particular issues: it either centres upon the dialogue that has occurred between the church leaders and an analysis of the theological problems involved or has been written by those directly involved in the ecumenical movement in Ireland. Three studies have been undertaken in this form. The first, *Christians in Ulster*,[14] examines ecumenical relations in the initial decade of the troubles and takes a wide-ranging approach to the issue, with chapters covering all the main forms of inter-church activity taking place in the 1970s. The second, *Vision and Reality*,[15] provides a survey of inter-church relations between 1904 and 1984, concentrating mainly upon the activities of the churches' heirarchies. Finally, *Conflict, Controversy and Co-operation*[16] provides what the author himself calls 'a personal perspective on the role and influence of the Irish Council of Churches between 1968 and 1972'.[17] Apart from these three surveys, relationships between the churches in Northern Ireland are generally relegated to either biographies of the major figures involved,[18] footnotes or two or so pages of text within book chapters on religion in Northern Ireland.[19]

In the early 1990s the importance of inter-church work within local communities became apparent, prompting the Community Relations Council to undertake research on churches and community relations in Northern Ireland. This provides snapshots of the way in which ecumenical relations have operated within the local communities rather than just looking at the dialogue that has been occurring between the church leaders. Radford and Morrow[20] tell us a little of how local inter-church relations work within Northern Ireland but do not provide a chronological narrative of their development or an assessment of how such relationships have reacted to events external to the religious such as the paramilitary ceasefires or the political process. The overwhelming tone of such commentary is either that whilst these relationships have had some positive consequences for those involved they have been the exception rather than the rule in the lives of the churches.

This material demonstrates that some form of interaction has been taking place between the Protestant and Catholic Churches in Northern Ireland since the 1960s – the structure and development of which remains unclear. This book aims to rectify this gap and examine the way in which inter-church relations in Northern Ireland have evolved in the years between 1980 and 2005. It will look in particular at their aims, structures and methods, as well as the ways in which the churches have responded together to the crisis in which their doctrines and ideology play a part.

The lack of material prompted a number of questions centred on three themes: structure, motivation and outcome. The first explored the structure of inter-church dialogue in Northern Ireland and asked whether any contact had occurred beyond that described by Gallagher, Worrall and Ellis. Three main questions were posed in order to discover the form that these relationships took: how have the churches worked together? What form has this activity been taking in local areas of Northern Ireland? Were there any factors, such as organised opposition, preventing the development of this dialogue?

In response to the first question it became apparent that the churches in Northern Ireland had worked together on three main levels since 1980: national level dialogue, local relationship development and peace and reconciliation education initiatives. National-level ecumenical dialogue has been the most constant feature of inter-church relationships, with the four main churches[21] having sophisticated mechanisms in place to enable it to function successfully. Until the mid-1980s this centred upon theological discussion on issues such as mixed marriage and communion. This dialogue has failed to move further than the immediate circle of those involved and to disseminate its work beyond those already committed to inter-church relationships. This interaction is generally held to be of little consequence either for relationships between the churches or within the wider political sphere and its main value lies in its provision of a figurehead for the inter-church movement.

The most active form of inter-church relationships occurred within the local community, with the methods of contact employed ranging from community relations courses to the provision of centres for addiction treatment. This work has the greatest potential to impact upon the consciousness of the wider community as it offers participants a 'safe space in which to step out of [their] comfort zone'[22] and tackle the underlying causes of the conflict, an idea which was central to such inter-church work. Most of this has been based upon personal contact between the clergy and during the 1980s led to the establishment of two types of cross-denominational group: the first being the ecumenical community which lives and works within an area providing support for the local clergy and a neutral venue in which people can meet, such as the Cornerstone Community in Belfast. The second type of group is the clergy-led discussion group, which, as well as allowing local people a safe environment in which to get to know something of the beliefs and attitudes of the 'other side', affords them an opportunity to learn more about their own faith and culture. Such work enables them to replace an identity based largely upon a negative perception of the beliefs of the other community with a positive identity created by a firmer knowledge of their own and the other's belief system. In the 1990s these groups were joined by a new type of group: the Church Fora, which represented an amalgamation of this local relationship development with welfare provision projects. These organisations allowed the churches to work more closely with their local council's Community Relations Officer in a bid to tackle the problems of the area. This contact between local churches has seen its fruition in the establishment of a number of peace and reconciliation education initiatives, for example Youth Link: Northern Ireland, established in 1990. These organisations, with the help of bodies such as the Community Relations Council, aim to provide support and training for groups wishing to undertake community relations or reconciliation work.

The main aim of inter-church dialogue at each of these levels was to facilitate an improvement in relationships not only between the churches themselves but also between the wider Catholic and Protestant communities. However, one of the main problems facing those wishing to engage in such relationships centred upon the issue of church government and attitudes to ecumenical contact which slowed the progress of national level dialogue in particular throughout this period.

One of the main differences between the Protestant and Catholic faiths is the issue of church government. Differences in structure have the potential to prevent progress in national level dialogue as the representatives of the Protestant and Catholic Churches are unable to make unilateral decisions and consequently this dialogue is viewed as little more than a 'talking shop'. The Catholic Church is global and hierarchical with a chain of command from Rome to the parish priest. Although 'the Second Vatican Council sought to balance the chain of command by an awareness of "collegiality" – a process of discernment, co-responsibility and joint decision-making where all in the Church, clergy and laity, participate',[23] this has not yet been achieved with most decision-making on issues relating to the church, such as ecumenism, resting firmly with the clergy working through the Episcopal Commission on Ecumenism.

By contrast, the Protestant Churches operate nationally, throughout the island of Ireland, with some form of governing body in which the clergy and some laity are entitled to vote. The Presbyterian Church 'is shaped as a wheel, with congregations on the rim and the General Assembly at the hub'.[24] Its government structure centres on an 'egalitarian ideal'[25] with the church being divided up into congregations, which are represented at a presbytery, and are in turn represented at the General Assembly chaired by the Moderator. However, 'since the General Assembly meets for only one week in each year it cannot respond to situations that arise from day to day

or take time adequately to formulate policy in detail'.[26] This means that the
work of the Assembly is divided up into Boards and Committees, such as the
Inter-Church Relations Board, which reports on issues relating to ecu-
menism to the church's presbyteries. The government structure of the
Methodist Church runs along similar lines with its governing body being the
Conference to which members of the seventy-six circuits send representatives. The Conference then appoints a number of committees, including the
Inter-Church Relations Committee, which produces reports for discussion
and adoption. Although the government of the Church of Ireland is
Episcopal, its government structure allows for more active involvement by
its members. Ireland is divided into twelve dioceses, each of which holds its
own diocesan synod, attended by the laity of the diocese, with two lay members for each cleric. The laity are also represented at a national level, with
the General Synod consisting of 215 clergy and 432 laity, with a standing
committee in place to deal with the General Synod's functions whilst it is
not in session, and it is here that matters relating to inter-church relations
are dealt with. Thus each document produced or decision made by the Irish
Inter-Church Meeting, the main body dealing with national level dialogue
between the churches, has to go through a 'vetting process' by each of the
churches involved inevitably slowing the process of their implementation.

Despite the delays caused by structural procedures, it is the attitudes
of the churches to ecumenical contact which are most problematic, as
views on this issue are so divergent that it is often impossible to rectify
them. The Catholic Church became open to ecumenical dialogue after
Vatican II, an event which was crucial to the development of inter-church
relationships in Ireland. Its aims for such dialogue were based upon the
need for Christian unity under the umbrella of Catholicism: 'Concern for
achieving unity "involves the whole Church, faithful and clergy alike."
But we must realize "that this holy objective – the reconciliation of all
Christians in the unity of the one and only Church of Christ – transcends
human powers and gifts."'[27] The attitudes of the Protestant Churches to
inter-church relationships were diametrically opposed to this, with each
of the three Protestant denominations under discussion containing conservative elements who disagreed with any contact with the Catholic
Church due to its desire for reunification. This is especially problematic
for the Presbyterian Church, whose attitude to the matter also sum-
marises those of the Church of Ireland and Methodism:

> Fundamental to the Church's attitude to inter-church activity are
> two principles of the Reformation which are often in tension. The
> first is a conviction that the True Church ... is not encompassed

within any one earthly denomination; and the second, that the pursuit of the truth should never be compromised. For some Presbyterians these principles seem complementary and lead ... to inter-church activity, while for others they present barriers to such activity.[28]

When contact does occur between the Protestant and Catholic Churches, it is expected to centre more upon the development of trust and understanding than the need for reunification and acceptance of the beliefs of other churches. Consequently in recent years these three denominations have implemented 'peacemaking' measures nationally in an attempt to create such friendship and understanding.[29] This divergence of ideas concerning the role of ecumenical relationships makes relationships at a national level problematic as there is very little agreement concerning the nature of ecumenism. This lends itself not only to a failure to state clear aims and objectives, but also to the creation of opposition from conservative members of the Protestant Churches. However, as we shall see, this focus upon friendship and understanding has promoted relationships in local areas as a response to the perceived failure of the national-level churches, caused by their structures and conflicting ideas on the nature of inter-church relationships.

This divergence in understanding prompted the next set of questions, which examined the objectives and motivations of those involved, and each inter-church initiative was asked what its aims were and what these were founded upon. Thus, in addition to the need for friendship and understanding, it became evident that the core motivation behind inter-church relations in Northern Ireland was the need for Christian reconciliation based upon the teaching of the Bible. To those involved, Christian 'Reconciliation means change and transformation so that former conflicts can find resolution in new relationships and new frameworks. But it also means forgiveness, the healing of past wounds and the letting go of past hurts if we are to find the way to that new future.'[30] The inspiration for this came from the Bible and in particular the teachings of the Gospel, which were interpreted in the light of the situation in Northern Ireland. Biblical passages such as 'I now realise that it is true that God treats everyone on the same basis. Whoever worships him and does what is right is acceptable to him, no matter what race he belongs to'[31] were used as an indication that working towards reconciliation should be an imperative for Christians in Northern Ireland. Consequently, Protestants and Catholics should engage with each other as Christians first and members of their own communities second, talking with one another whilst respecting 'particular identities within wider commonalities'.[32] Such ideas resonated more within local inter-church initiatives as those involved were bound less by the constraints of church government and more by a desire to improve relationships and conditions within their own local communities. The dialogue and work that ensued resulted in a change in the definition of inter-church relationships in Northern Ireland.

The final set of questions centred upon the results of inter-church work and in particular the desire for Christian reconciliation and looking at the practical applications and outcomes of ecumenical dialogue in each of the three levels described above. Whilst the past twenty-five years have witnessed a steady growth in initiatives especially within local areas, a more significant result is the shift in the definition of inter-church relationships that has occurred. Inter-church relationships, even between the hierarchies of the churches, were not conceived as a purely theological matter and have come to be viewed in an increasingly pragmatic light, taking on board the challenges of ministering to a society as divided as Northern Ireland as well as addressing issues such as inter-communion and points of doctrine. These inter-church structures have not being working in an 'ecumenical vacuum' since 1980 and, as the political situation in Northern Ireland has progressed, so has the meaning of inter-church work. Pure theological ecumenism has taken a 'back seat' to the more pressing needs of improving community relations and reconciliation, which are of concern not only to church-goers but to the wider community as well. However, the way in which this change in the concept of inter-church work has occurred has been vastly different at each level of contact. Whilst at the national level the tone and nature of debate has changed, at the local level, this change in emphasis from ecumenism to community relations has prompted an evolution in the structures and methods used to promote contact between the Protestant and Catholic communities. Much of the innovation that has taken place in inter-church relations since 1980 has been at the local level and that debate between the church leaders reflects the tone and language of initiatives within the community.

The answers to these questions were collected through the use of oral history interviews which were combined with documentary evidence, such as the minutes of meetings, annual reviews and publications to ensure chronological accuracy. Interviews were carried out with approximately 70 participants, ranging from church leaders to members of ecumenical prayer groups. These were obtained by 'snowballing', whereby participants from the original interview list would provide introductions to others working in the field. The interview technique was employed for two reasons: first, most of the smaller inter-church groups in Northern Ireland had few records and therefore the interviews became a vital means of discovering their modes of operation and structures. Second, and most importantly, the interviews also revealed 'underlying philosophies and approaches [which] might have been so taken for granted by participants that no need was felt to elucidate them in the written record',[33] with each interview generally concentrating upon the ideologies and beliefs that lay behind the development of inter-church projects and the reasons for the implementation of schemes.

Due to the structure that inter-church relationships have taken in Northern Ireland, each of the three levels of inter-church work will be examined in turn. Chapter One will outline the establishment of inter-church dialogue between the hierarchies of the Catholic and Protestant Churches in the wake of Vatican II and the onset of the present troubles in the late 1960s. Chapter Two will examine the way in which this dialogue between the leaderships of the churches has evolved since 1980 looking in particular at their structure, the issues that they have chosen to address and the anti-ecumenical movement which has grown up in protest to such dialogue within the Protestant Churches. Chapter Three will study the form that local level inter-church relations have taken. It will examine the formation and work of each of the main forms of co-operation in turn and explore the way in which this has presented a challenge to the four main churches in Northern Ireland to become more directly involved in peacemaking and move away from a type of theological discussion that remains comparative in the abstract. Chapter Four will concentrate upon the seven ecumenical communities in Northern Ireland as they provide a microcosm of all of the modes of inter-church work occurring at a local level. Finally, Chapter Five will focus upon the peace and reconciliation education initiatives that have developed in the area since the late 1980s and their methodological evolution which, as we shall see, has radically affected the way in which inter-church relationships in local areas operate. The concluding chapter will consider the way in which each of these levels has affected the operation of the others and will look at the way in which external political events since 1980 have helped to shape the evolution of inter-church relationships in Northern Ireland.

## CHAPTER ONE

# The Ecumenical Movement
# in Ireland 1964–80

The Protestant and Catholic Churches in Northern Ireland have often been accused of failing to work together towards reconciliation, with charges such as 'reconciliation between the two communities is a recognised major objective [of the churches] and yet the church leaders had to be asked before they came together for a joint statement'[1] being levied against them. These statements illustrate a failure to understand the nature of the ecumenical dialogue which was flourishing during this period. Such statements were prompted by media coverage, which presented this dialogue as 'a magic formula' for solving all of Ireland's problems dismissing it as a failure when 'an utopian Ireland did not come into being the next day'.[2] In reality, early attempts at ecumenical dialogue were intended to create a deeper understanding on issues that represented major difficulties to the churches and were 'not primarily designed and should not be expected to "solve the Irish problem" or to end violence'.[3]

The years between 1964 and 1980 were ones of immense growth for inter-church relations in Ireland as they witnessed the foundation of each of the three levels contact with the first official meetings between the Catholic hierarchy and the Protestant leaders, the foundation of the Irish School of Ecumenics (ISE) and the establishment of the Greenhills and Glenstal Conferences.[4] Meanwhile, events at a more local level brought about the establishment of the Corrymeela Community and the Christian Renewal Centre in Rostrevor as well as numerous inter-church prayer and study groups. This chapter will discuss the development of ecumenical relationships between the leaderships of the Protestant and Catholic Churches, looking at the factors that allowed them to grow, and the establishment of the Ballymascanlon talks, which have become the main focus of national-level ecumenical dialogue since 1980.

The growth of national-level ecumenical dialogue during the 1970s was not an entirely new phenomenon. During the preceding 50 years such dialogue had been restricted to the three main Protestant churches,[5] with the

Presbyterian and Methodist Churches establishing a joint committee in 1905 'to confer from time to time on matters of common interest'.[6] This led to the formation of a similar body involving the Anglican and Presbyterian Churches in 1910 and culminating in the establishment of the United Council of Christian Churches and Religious Communions in Ireland in 1923 (changing its name to the Irish Council of Churches (ICC) in 1966). The membership of this organisation focused on the 'Christian Communions in Ireland willing to join in united efforts to promote the spiritual, physical, moral and social welfare of the people and the extension of the rule of Christ among all nations and over every region of life'.[7] Until 1968, the ICC was mainly involved in the discussion of religious or social issues that were closely related to the concerns of its member churches, such as temperance, with very little contact being made with the Catholic Church. In addition, other forms of inter-church co-operation were being developed, which included schemes for new housing in deprived areas and a committee on unemployment. Such projects laid solid foundations for future inter-church work by fostering personal relationships amongst the clergy and highlighted that in spite of their differences, common action was possible. However, it was becoming clear that there was a great need for some form of dialogue between Catholics and Protestants, for two reasons: first, the establishment of the Glenstal and Greenhills inter-denominational conferences and second, Vatican II and, in particular, its Decree on Ecumenism, which illustrated a shift in Catholic thinking on the issue of dialogue, moving towards a more open perspective, in sharp contrast to the isolationist stance of its past.

## THE GLENSTAL AND GREENHILLS CONFERENCES

'It should not be forgotten that, had it not been for Glenstal and the later conference modelled upon it at Greenhills, the establishment of the Ballymascanlon talks would have been much more difficult.'[8] These conferences were initiated by members of the Catholic clergy and, despite initial opposition,[9] were designed to be multi-lateral rather than bi-lateral, including Presbyterians and Methodists as well as members of the Church of Ireland. This was because 'although we Roman Catholics knew very little at that stage about how much we had in common with our fellow non-conformists, any exclusiveness seemed anathema to us in the first flush of our ecumenical enthusiasm and our slender resources seemed to offer little prospect of separate bilateral meetings with

Methodists and with Presbyterians'.[10] The adoption of such an approach was fully vindicated as 'the multilateral character of the conferences which beforehand may have seemed too bold for a beginning, too likely to be an obstacle for real dialogue, proved rather to be a help and an enrichment'.[11]

The Glenstal and Greenhills Conferences have been described by some as 'a meeting of minds between Irish Roman Catholics and Protestants'[12] as they discussed in an informal setting, and in the context of joint worship, a variety of theological issues such as the liturgy, baptism and marriage. It was this informality which was the key to their success as 'they ... provided a focus of wider ecumenical life in Ireland, as distinct from the work of officially structured bodies, and they have served as a constant and regular encouragement for committed ecumenists'.[13] Hence the Glenstal and Greenhills Conferences made a major contribution to the genesis of inter-church relations in Ireland, as they provided those involved with a platform to build the trusting, informal relationships with one another that would prove so crucial to the success of later ventures.

## VATICAN II AND THE *DECREE ON ECUMENISM*

However, if official links were to be established, the Catholic Church would have to change its position on the issue of dialogue with other Christian faiths. This change came in 1964 with Vatican II's *Decree on Ecumenism*, which 'signalled a more positive attitude towards ecumenism among Catholics worldwide'.[14] This change in attitude by the Catholic Church, and the Protestant Churches' reaction to it, was one of the most crucial factors in the development of contact between the hierarchies of the Protestant and Catholic Churches.

The *Decree on Ecumenism* was promulgated by the third session of Vatican II in September 1964. This was one of the central parts of Vatican II and demonstrated that ecumenism was pivotal to the work of the Council:

> It was, so to speak, a crucial and central point on which the Council's other three goals[15] converged, and which in turn presupposed and called for them. To speak of the restoration of unity you must first work for a more precise definition of the Church, one which will make due allowance for the ecclesial reality of other Christian communities. So too the hopes for unity were closely

linked to the renewal of the Church and with the needs of the modern world, and thus imposed the duty of a common witness to all Christians so that the Gospel could be more effectively proclaimed in a way that would meet the real and often tragic need of our day.[16]

The *Decree* signalled a turning point in the attitude of the Catholic Church towards ecumenical dialogue as 'it became clear to [them] that it wasn't really on to simply stand apart and expect others to convert back – they realised that it was important to participate in the ecumenical movement along with the other churches'.[17]

Before the 1960s the Catholic Church had adopted an isolationist stance[18] in its relationships with Protestant Churches, labelling the ecumenical movement, which was flourishing in the early twentieth century, as 'Pan Christian':

> It is clear why this Apostolic See has never allowed its subjects to take part in the assemblies of non-Catholics. There is but one way in which the unity of Christians may be fostered and that is by furthering the return to the one true Church they have in the past fallen away [from] … Furthermore, in this one Church of Christ no man can be or remain who does not accept, recognise, and obey the authority and supremacy of Peter and his legitimate successors.[19]

However, by the mid-twentieth century many Catholics were beginning to argue that this isolationist stance was damaging the Church and rendering it less effective. It became clear to many Catholic theologians that an enlargement and renewal of the Catholic Church's vision of itself was needed, and that it was necessary for it to seriously endeavour to forge relationships with those outside the Catholic faith, in order to fulfil its aim of bringing Christ's message to the world. By the early 1950s it was evident that the new insights provided by figures such as John Henry Newman and Yves Congar were beginning to have some effect upon the thinking of the Vatican, as the 1949 instruction *Ecclesia Catholica* (The Catholic Church and Ecumenical Contacts) illustrates '[The Catholic Church] has never ceased, nor ever will, from following with deepest interest and furthering with fervent prayer every attempt to attain that end which Christ our Lord had so much at heart, namely that all who believe in Him "may be perfectly one"'.[20] By the time of the Second Vatican Council, the groundwork had been laid within the Catholic Church for the adoption of a more open attitude towards ecumenism and a rejection of the solitude of the past. Despite such changes in Catholic thought and the relative openness of the Vatican to ecumenism, the

*Decree* itself was guarded on the matter; making steps forward in acceptance but still qualifying many of its statements on issues such as the validity of the other Christian Churches. The *Decree* was divided into three sections: Catholic Principles on Ecumenism, the Practice of Ecumenism and Churches and Ecclesial Communities Separated from the Roman Apostolic See.

The section concerning Catholic Principles on Ecumenism was the most doctrinally important as it outlined the Catholic understanding of ecumenism. It argued that ecumenism should be concerned with bringing about a visible reunion of the 'Church of Christ' by eliminating the schism of the reformation. Throughout this section it is clear that, even though the *Decree* sees all of those Christians baptised outside the Catholic faith as imperfect, it recognised the need for Catholics to acknowledge the mistakes that they themselves have made:

> For although the Catholic Church has been endowed with all divinely revealed truth and with all means of grace yet its members fail to live by them with all the fervour that they should, so that the radiance of the Church's image is less clear in the eyes of our separated brethren and of the world at large, and the growth of God's kingdom is delayed. All Catholics therefore must aim at Christian perfection.[21]

It goes on to state that Catholics must recognise the work of the Holy Spirit in the 'hearts of our separated brethren' but, once more, reiterates the fundamental desire for conversion of Protestants to the Catholic Church, which lies at the base of their ecumenical efforts stating that 'the divisions among Christians prevent the Church from attaining the fullness of catholicity proper to her, in those of her sons who, though attached to her by baptism, are yet separated from full communion with her'.[22]

The second part of the *Decree*, on the Practice of Ecumenism, argued that it was the task of all Catholics to work towards the goal of unity, as the key to the Church's approach to ecumenism lay in strengthening relationships between Christians. 'Hence, no one, neither an individual Christian nor a community, is exempted from the task of strenuously working to eliminate the barriers that are so often deeply rooted in human hearts, carried as baggage from the past.'[23] Once more, the pure representation of Catholic doctrine is paramount: 'Catholic theologians standing fast by the teaching of the Church and investigating the divine mysteries with the separated brethren must proceed with love for the truth, with Charity and with humility'[24] thus paving the way for the achievement of unity. This section also provides guidelines on the issue of joint worship, advising people that 'in certain special circumstances, such as the prescribed prayers "for unity" and during ecumenical gatherings, it is allowable, indeed desirable that Catholics should join in prayer with their separated brethren'.[25]

The final section consists of a discussion of the Churches and Ecclesial Communities Separated from the Roman Apostolic See, which is a reflection on the beliefs and practices of the other main Christian churches, and an analysis of the way in which they relate to the Catholic Church. The Orthodox Churches are seen to be closer to catholicism and are accordingly portrayed as 'the church breathing through its two lungs'.[26] However, it is the *Decree*'s attitude to the Protestant Churches that holds the most significance for relationships in Northern Ireland, as the language used has the potential to cause discomfort among those involved. Thus, 'the decree takes a more guarded approach when expressing the nature of the relationship with "the Churches and ecclesial communities which were separated from the Apostolic See of Rome ...". The words *church* and *ecclesial communities* are deliberately chosen in acknowledgement of the fact that some have greater identity in terms of structures with the Catholic Church.'[27] Hence, it becomes even more apparent that the Catholic Church believes that all churches must be measured against the standard of Rome, going on to illustrate the areas of difference between the Protestant and Catholic Churches, by looking, for example, at crucial issues such as baptism, the authority of scripture and the relationship of man to Christ.

Although a superficial glance at the *Decree on Ecumenism* would indicate that the Catholic Church had undergone an enormous sea change in its attitude towards this issue, it was not as far reaching as it could have been. The document still contained undercurrents of the language used by Pope Pius XI. Even though the Church was willing to engage in ecumenical dialogue, it was doing so in order to reunite the separated brethren under the umbrella of Rome, a nuance in understanding which Gallagher and Worrall believe many of those involved in the Irish Ecumenical scene in the 1970s failed to understand. They comment that 'to the discerning, the goal of Catholic ecumenism was clear. Many non-Catholics, however, who in the coming decade were to welcome increasing ecumenical involvement, did not fully appreciate the different shades of meaning attributed by Catholics and Protestants respectively to the word "ecumenism".'[28] Be that as it may, despite such problems with shades of definition, the *Decree* did represent a massive step forward in the attitude of the Catholic Church to ecumenical activity, as it officially sanctioned the actions of those Catholics involved in early attempts at dialogue such as Glenstal and Greenhills. Furthermore, it also provided the Catholic hierarchy in Ireland with an opportunity to reflect upon its own attitude to the issue. This resulted in the *Directory on Ecumenism* which, as well as providing an opportunity for a fully informed debate within the Protestant Churches, facilitated the earliest attempts at national level co-operation between the leaders of the Catholic and Protestant Churches in Ireland.

## THE *DIRECTORY ON ECUMENISM*

The *Directory on Ecumenism*, produced in 1969, with a second edition in 1976, was a response by the Irish Catholic hierarchy to the *Decree* and expressed the hope that the fledgling ecumenical movement in Ireland would grow. This document 'was destined to have a profound effect on Irish Catholic relationships with Protestantism'.[29] The first edition of the *Directory* 'was basically geared only to presenting those parts of the Roman Directory which had appeared up to date'[30] and dealt with the issue of baptism, the conditions under which Catholics may or may not engage in joint worship with 'separated brethren', and shared liturgy with the Eastern Orthodox Churches. However, whilst the *Directory* commended the ecumenical spirit of those involved in events such as Glenstal, it did contain a warning which served as a reminder to those involved of the fundamental aim of Catholic ecumenical endeavour: 'Catholics are reminded that they must remain fully loyal to the truth handed down by the Apostles and professed throughout the centuries by the Catholic Church, for it is through Christ's Catholic Church alone, which is the all-embracing means of salvation, that the fullness of the means of salvation can be obtained.'[31]

The second edition of the *Directory,* produced in 1976, was a much fuller document, and differed from its predecessor by dealing with issues that were of relevance to the Irish experience. In doing so, it was reflecting the discussions that had taken place at the Ballymascanlon meetings: containing sections on integrated education and mixed marriages as well as developing a diocesan structure for the promotion of ecumenical activity. For many the *Directory* was a disappointment as they felt that it did not go far enough in the promotion of ecumenism: 'many will be disappointed that the 1976 *Directory on Ecumenism* opens up so few new horizons and new possibilities for the ecumenical apostolate ... The sad fact is that the great majority have not yet become concerned for the unity and joint mission of the Churches.'[32]

Despite such accusations, the *Directory on Ecumenism* was a significant step forward for inter-church relations, as it indicated the Irish Catholic hierarchy's willingness to engage with the Protestant Churches. For example, the document states that 'There is in Ireland a new endeavour among Christians of different denominations to live in harmony and peace. It is to be devoutly hoped that this movement will grow and become even more permanently permeated by the truth and love of Christ.'[33] In spite of the underlying tone of the documents with their desire for reunification under Rome, they were read by the Protestant Churches as an alteration in the attitude of the Catholic Church in Ireland, which was now indicating its willingness to join Protestants in a form of dialogue that they had been engaging in since the turn of the twentieth century. This commitment was sorely needed as Northern Ireland descended into a period of violence and civil unrest, heightening the need for the churches to attempt to work together towards reconciliation. However this dichotomy in understanding between the Protestant and Catholic perspectives of ecumenical relations was going to be problematic as it prevented inter-church relations at a national level moving forward, as those setting the agenda were not at all clear about what they wanted to achieve.

## THE FOUR LEADERS AND THE JOINT GROUP ON SOCIAL QUESTIONS

As a direct result of the outbreak of violence and civil unrest in Northern Ireland, the Protestant Churches, under the auspices of the ICC, decided that the time had come for 'some form of continuing consultation regarding the developing unrest'[34] to take place between the Protestant and Catholic leaders. As they wrote to Cardinal Conway:

> We write as persons holding positions of major responsibility in our churches ... We have long been concerned for the establishment of justice and mutual respect in Northern Ireland (but) recent events have underlined the need for urgent action ... We believe that the achievement of (justice and respect) may be advanced by a better understanding of each other's position and concerns and, where possible, joint action ... there may be advantage from some type of joint consultative body ... We believe that in normal circumstances such a suggestion has much to commend it, but at this present time we are particularly anxious for bridges to be built and kept open.[35]

The resulting meeting of the Four Church Leaders' working group 'is generally regarded as the first sign of official Catholic–Protestant co-operation'.[36] The four church leaders aimed to present an example of reconciliation to the people of Northern Ireland, a desire summed up by their joint trip to Derry after rioting which 'The Press described ... as an "appeal for calm". It was much more. They, in the name of Christ, set the whole community an example of Christian brotherhood.'[37]

Spring 1969 saw the establishment of the semi-official Ad Hoc Committee,[38] which consisted of six clerics: two nominated by the Cardinal, one each by the leaders of the three main Protestant Churches and one by the executive of the ICC. The Ad Hoc Committee was designed to advise the church leaders on developments within Northern Ireland and counsel them on the best course of action, it 'had a short eventful, and occasionally tempestuous history. The committee was in almost continuous session during the traumatic weeks of August 1969. It discussed many issues, the setting up of a [previously unheard of] police authority ... However, it soon became redundant',[39] as 'the longer it continued the less relevant and helpful it became'.[40] Despite this, 'it undoubtedly performed a useful role and bore fruit as fears and grievances were shared'.[41]

By 1970, such communication had evolved into the establishment of the 'Irish Council of Churches/Roman Catholic Joint Group on Social Questions'[42] which was officially recognised by both the ICC and the Catholic hierarchy, and signified the growing normality of such contact. The Joint Group itself was an advisory body of 30 members, divided equally between the Protestant and Catholic Churches, consisting mainly of members of the Northern Irish clergy. The remit of this committee was to be wide-ranging, looking at 'the role of the churches in Irish society with special reference to matters such as alcoholism, drug abuse, unemployment, housing, world poverty etc.'[43] Many clergy initially expressed concern at the Joint Group's seemingly limited remit, which ignored issues such as the causes of the conflict. Hurley comments 'I distinctly remember Bishop John Armstrong of the Church of Ireland sharing with me his disappointment at these terms of reference but taking some hope from the *"etc."*.'[44] The Group offered the following defence of itself:

> In normal times the work of the Joint Group would have been acknowledged as important for the life of the nation as a whole and the Churches' place in that life. In the context of the present upheaval, however, it might appear to some that we have been concerning ourselves almost with trifles. It is nonetheless astonishing that we have met at all – in view of the disintegration going on

around us – and we have continued to do so not only in the group itself, but also in its working parties.[45]

Indeed, the 'etc.' was to prove fruitful for the Joint Group as its work included a report, *Violence in Ireland*, which on its publication attracted international attention.

## Violence in Ireland

The Working Party on Violence in Ireland led by Cahal Daly and Eric Gallagher was appointed in 1973. Once more the importance of friendship and mutual respect in developing inter-church relationships was highlighted through this group. As one member commented 'Possibly the friendship and good understanding which existed between the co-chairmen may have been a major factor in the group's ability finally to reach agreement.'[46] This view was confirmed by Cardinal Daly: 'You know how it is that that kind of chemistry exists between people who naturally feel an affinity and Eric for me was always one of these.'[47] The Working Party was constructed under the following terms of reference:

1. To enquire into the moral, physical and economic effects of violence or the threat of it on those who resort to it, on those against whom it is or has been used and on the community generally;
2. To indicate to the Churches how they may best educate their members in the social and political implications and application of the Christian Gospel so that they may promote the achievement of a society acceptable to the great majority of the people by means which rule out recourse to such violence.[48]

The report was divided into three parts: the first looked at the history and causes of the violence in Northern Ireland, followed by an examination of the ways in which the churches have reacted, both separately and ecumenically, to the problem of violence. The final section of the report looked at the way in which the churches could work together to combat the violent nature of Northern Irish society, providing them with a framework through which this could be done. For example, it suggested the establishment of a Christian Centre of Social Investigation 'which would conduct research into problems underlying social and communal unrest and would monitor continuously progress made in removing the basic grievances of discrimination and injustice within civil society that are related to the occurrence of violence'.[49]

The final report of the working party was published in 1976 to wide critical acclaim in both the British and Irish press, as well as from wider society. However, the recommendations of the report, which for the most part were extremely challenging, were never acted upon.[50] Nonetheless, the report did play an important role in the development of inter-church relations during the 1970s, as it recognised the part that the churches had inadvertently played in the conflict, through, for example, their tacit acceptance of paramilitary funerals, whilst providing a viable framework through which the churches could aid the resolution of the conflict in the future. Furthermore, through the publication of the report, the Joint Group were widening the terms of reference used by those involved in inter-church relations in Ireland, and in doing so were starting to move them towards a focus upon community relations rather than pure theological ecumenism.

## BALLYMASCANLON

The years leading up to 1973 were a time during which the church leaders and other clergy came to know one another better and develop friendships based on mutual respect, trust and understanding. It was from this base that the initial overtures were made towards the establishment of a more formal meeting between the churches. In 1972 discussions took place within the ICC concerning 'the possibilities of further dialogue on both practical and doctrinal issues',[51] the form of which was clarified by the organising secretary of the ICC:

> What is now envisaged is an extension of such co-operation [as already exists] to make possible joint study of the pastoral problems that arise from inter-church marriages and the moral issues raised by violence in all its forms and also an examination of subjects which may give rise to tensions and misunderstandings which are unworthy of the relationship between different Christian Churches.[52]

The Catholic hierarchy's reply to these overtures was positive, resulting in an invitation being issued by the Irish Episcopal Conference to the member churches of the ICC to attend 'a joint meeting at which the whole field of ecumenism in Ireland might be surveyed and in which all the members of the Episcopal conference would participate. What is contemplated is a general review of relations between the Christian Churches in Ireland and the possibilities of further dialogue on both practical and doctrinal issues … It is envisaged that working parties might subsequently be set up to further such dialogue.'[53] The Church of Ireland accepted this invitation almost immediately. However, the Presbyterian Church were more guarded, issuing an acceptance which stated that they were willing 'to discuss matters of church and community relationships, especially problem of mixed marriages and the proclamation of the Gospel in Ireland, but excluding the question of church union'.[54] With these provisos in place the first meeting of the Irish Inter-church Conference took place in Ballymascanlon on 26 September 1973, against the backdrop of intense media interest and a Paisley protest which, despite his initial bluster, was untypically muted:[55]

> Dr Paisley threatened to disrupt the conference, but when the day came he contented himself with a picket of about 100 people. These gathered at the hotel gates and sought entry. When the police came to say that the hotel management objected to a demonstration in the hotel grounds, Dr Paisley carried the letter of protest up the quarter-mile long drive and returned to his group outside. Within minutes the conference organisers made a public statement that the protest was based on a misunderstanding: the talks were not secret, the press being invited to attend; and they were not aimed at church union.[56]

On their foundation the Ballymascanlon meetings were greeted with great enthusiasm. As one participant put it:

> It was not without excitement and a sense of momentous departure that the delegates of the member churches of the ICC and the Irish Hierarchy convened on Ballymascanlon … It was also with a certain anxiety as to whether we had been too ambitious whether the meeting might fail to achieve the atmosphere conducive to ecumenical harmony.[57]

Much has been made of the establishment of these meetings both by contemporaries and later observers. For example, whilst some have declared 1973 to be 'epoch making',[58] the compiler of *Some notable events in the Catholic Life of Ireland 1973* proclaimed that 'a whole new era in Catholic–Protestant relations in Ireland has opened'.[59] The ICC wrote of 'an enormous step forward in inter-church relations in our country for which we would not have dared to hope over a decade ago'[60] and one journalist speaking twenty-five years later stated that 'The famous Ballymascanlon talks, first held in September 1973, paved the way for the flowering of ecumenism in Ireland and greater understanding between the various denominations.'[61] Others have spoken of the meetings in more muted terms by acknowledging that they 'have proved to be of historical importance'[62] but then questioning whether these early meetings represented the peak of inter-church relations in Ireland: 'Perhaps future historians will be able to show from the archives that this was a period of great openness between the churches on the island?'[63] Whilst the meeting may not have lived up to the initial expectations which 'felt that Ballymascanlon was going to be a decisive summit conference which would solve all the problems of Irish inter-church relations',[64] the meetings have facilitated 'a slow but steady improvement'[65] in relationships within Ireland.

During this period, 'the representatives of the churches [at the Ballymascanlon meetings] were preoccupied with what one can only describe as an exercise in predominantly comparative theology together with some discussion of community issues',[66] with their work laying the foundations for the development of national level inter-church relations in the 1980s. At the inaugural meeting, papers were read on the issues of Church, Scripture and Authority; Baptism, Eucharist and Marriage; Christianity and Secularism and Social and Community problems, issues which were chosen 'because they represented major difficulties to the other churches engaged in discussions'.[67] Working parties were then appointed to report on the matter to the meetings at a later date.[68] The findings of these working parties can be divided into two categories: those that dealt specifically with doctrinal differences between the churches and those that contained a community relations dimension.

The working party's reports on doctrinal issues contained no real surprises, and in many areas partial agreements were reached on crucial issues, such as baptism. 'The working party's report on baptism registered a wide agreement in baptismal theology, referring to baptism as the "foundation of Christian fellowship in the Church". The representatives of the churches in the working party recognised in one another's churches the "proper celebration" of baptism and recommended that this be established as a principle of ecumenical and pastoral practice.'[69] However, the dialogue dealing with 'community-related issues' proved to be much more contentious for those involved, with issues such as mixed marriage becoming increasingly controversial throughout the period. Some of those involved in the early stages of Ballymascanlon were concerned that the nature of their work would be misunderstood, arguing that 'there was, in the contemporary context, a risk of confusing the pursuit of ecumenism with the pursuit of peace in Northern Ireland'.[70] Despite such reservations and 'in spite of the prior existence of the joint group which

... had already produced two reports, it was felt that it would be unrealistic for the inter-church dialogue inaugurated at Ballymascanlon to ignore the social and community implications of the Gospel ... [It] was perhaps not surprising that the churches should reach the point at which they felt able to collaborate on social issues before they were ready for dialogue on the fundamental issues of belief.'[71] During the early years of the meetings, two reports on *Christianity and Secularism* and *Social and Community Problems* were produced, which contained discussions of issues concerning community relations.

The initial papers presented in 1973 on the issue of *Christianity and Secularism* examined the decline that was taking place in society in moral and Christian belief:

> It felt that the immediate need was for an analysis of the trends making for secularism in the modern world ... The working party addressed itself to questions such as the following: In God's world is there a line to be drawn between the sacred and the secular? ... Is the Church rightly concerned only with what is done in the name of Christ? If not, where does the Church stand when secular political issues have a moral significance and at the same time a party political aspect?[72]

Their final report produced the answers to these questions under the headings of: the meaning of secularism; the challenge of secularism to family life, from for example inflation, education, advertising and the law; the counter challenge and practical suggestions.[73] Their practical suggestions covered a wide range of issues, and many had direct implications for the maintenance of good relations between the churches, with, for example, suggestions being made concerning the areas of marriage guidance and adult education. The report also addressed the role that the churches play in the conflict in Northern Ireland:

> We suggest that early consideration needs to be given to the means and methods of communication between denominations, between church authorities and their members, and between the church and the world. Is our language meaningful? Does it get across? If not, why not? It is a sobering thought that in Northern Ireland where violent extremists are frequently condemned by churchmen, there are still people who support those extremists on the grounds of 'religion'.[74]

In direct contrast to the wide-ranging approach of the *Christianity and Secularism* report, the final report of the working committee on social and community problems was much narrower, choosing to focus solely upon the issues of internment and mixed marriage,[75] both of which were proving to be contentious throughout the 1970s. The report highlighted the need for the churches to work together on the issue of mixed marriages:

> Because of the deeply personal nature of the marriage relationship and of the way in which it impinges upon Church members in their daily lives it must be recognised that the Church teaching and attitudes in this field have a special importance for community relations. Should the tensions and problems of mixed marriages be compounded by any failure to act in the spirit of sympathetic understanding and pastoral care, those responsible for such a failure would be neglecting a fundamental Christian duty[76]

As a direct result of this report, the Ballymascanlon meeting decided to establish a Joint Standing Committee on Mixed Marriages to monitor the situation in a bid to resolve the differences between the denominations.

In the years between its establishment in 1973 and 1980, the Ballymascanlon meetings were engaged with numerous topics, looking at issues that were of deep and immediate concern to the wider Northern Irish community, as well as those that have perplexed ecumenists worldwide. As far as theological and doctrinal issues were concerned the meetings saw a vast improvement in relationships between the churches with the participants developing a greater comprehension of each other's positions. In this, the member churches of the IICM went some way towards fulfilling the aims of the initial invitation issued by the Irish Episcopal Conference in 1972, but stopped short of using this to work towards an open discussion on matters relating directly to the situation in Northern Ireland. As a consequence, in their attempts to address community relations issues, the churches were not as successful, choosing to ignore the root causes of the problems in Ireland as well as failing, to a large extent, to act upon the recommendations of their reports.

In 1977 these inadequacies prompted many members of the Church of Ireland to express discomfort and growing disenchantment at their Church's continued membership of the meetings:

> The Churches must engage in an open, honest and courageous examination of issues such as Church/State relations, law and morality, mixed marriages, experience in integrated education, freedom of conscience and basic human rights. We are bound to say that the reality of inter-church dialogue hitherto, e.g. the Ballymascanlon

meetings, are illustrated by an apparent inability to come to grips with these moral, social and practical issues which affect the lives of ordinary people and contribute to the maintenance of divisions based upon suspicion and fear.[77]

Despite, or perhaps because of, such criticisms, those directly involved in Ballymascanlon had identified these failures. They advocated the establishment of a committee (the report of which was produced in 1984):

1. To analyse and co-ordinate where desirable already existing inter-church activity.
2. To initiate before the end of the present calendar year a sustained and concerted Churches' programme for peace which inter alia will take note of the recommendations made in the report *Violence in Ireland*.
3. To ensure that adequate follow up and implementation of reports and recommendations emanating from working parties and other bodies appointed as a result of inter-church decisions.[78]

It could be argued that such criticisms on the part of the member churches were somewhat unfair: they were expecting too much of these talks too soon and were possibly overwhelmed by the weight of media expectation surrounding them. The Ballymascanlon talks were still in their infancy during the 1970s and as such their efforts should be treated as fledgling attempts at ecumenism inclusive of the Catholic Church rather than being judged as a well-developed and sophisticated ecumenical body. These meetings had, in essence, been established to facilitate discussion between the member churches on issues of theological difference, not to act as an unofficial peace process running in tandem with the political attempts at conflict resolution during this period. These meetings did, however, allow members of the clergy an arena through which to explore a number of contentious issues with one another, as well as to develop their ecumenical relationships even further, and in doing so laid the foundations for the developments in structure and scope which were to take place in the next twenty years.

CONCLUSION

The Protestant Churches in Northern Ireland, especially the Church of Ireland, the Presbyterian Church and Methodist Church, have displayed a commitment to ecumenical dialogue since the end of the twentieth century, proving themselves to be open to the overtures made by the Catholic Church in Ireland in the wake of the *Decree on Ecumenism*. However, once tentative relationships had been developed between the Catholic and Protestant Churches, through, for example, Glenstal and Greenhills and the more 'official'[79] avenue of the IICM, a reticence to become too deeply involved in any issues that may be considered controversial, such as those relating to community relations, can been seen. This could have been related to the nuances of the Catholic Church's change in attitude towards engagement with the Protestant Churches, as understandings of the term 'ecumenical dialogue' differed between the churches.[80] However, it is also related to a complete lack of clarity surrounding the role of inter-church relationships in Ireland: while the IICM had been established as a primarily theological body, other inter-church initiatives, such as, the Four Leaders and the Joint Group on Social Questions, had set an agenda for an engagement with the situation in Northern Ireland. This was never returned to once the Ballymascanlon meetings were established and may explain the criticisms that were levied at the IICM in the late 1970s. On one hand, *Violence in Ireland* had placed the issue of the conflict at the centre of inter-church relations but had been ignored by the IICM, whilst on the other it was failing to address issues relating to the welfare of the churches' congregations that defined Protestant involvement in such activity. Nevertheless, despite these inadequacies and problems, the inter-church initiatives developed at a national level throughout this period did lay the foundations of friendship and understanding between those involved, which should have led to stronger links between the leaderships of the Protestant and Catholic Churches and a clearer sense of purpose behind such engagement.

## CHAPTER TWO

# National-Level
# Ecumenical Dialogue

By 1980 ecumenical contact at a national level, under the auspices of Ballymascanlon, was beginning to move slowly out of its infancy and by this point there was 'more contact, more mutual respect and understanding ... than at any earlier period of Irish history'.[1] Nevertheless, despite these groundbreaking advances in friendship and increased understanding, the churches had failed to translate this general goodwill into a model of Christian reconciliation which, as well as further improving relationships between themselves, would be socially and politically effective. Indeed, it has been commented that the early years of the Ballymascanlon meetings represented a peak in ecumenical relationships in Ireland, with relationships between the churches having progressed as far as was possible. Such comments do contain some reflection of reality, as although relationships did continue to evolve throughout the 1980s and 1990s, the steep curve at which they were developing in the 1970s had begun to level out by the early 1980s, perhaps as the initial novelty of Protestant and Catholic dialogue wore off.

That is not to say that inter-church relations have stagnated. This dialogue was an activity more general and open-ended than that of more formal multi- or bi-lateral dialogues. On the contrary, since 1980 national-level dialogue has changed and evolvedconsiderably with such developments taking place in two areas: structure and remit. As a result, one of the most important developments within national level inter-church activity has been the way in which it has virtually reinvented itself, moving away from its original tentative base, and branching out towards two strongly linked but conceptually different areas, those of ecumenism and church-based community relations. This change has been reflected in the structural modifications that have taken place since 1980. However, these changes in structure and remit have not been embraced by all members of the churches involved, and since 1980 opposition to such ecumenical dialogue has become both more organised and vocal, eventually resulting in the quashing of plans to create one over-arching ecumenical body for the island in 1999, the plans for which remain at a standstill at the time of writing six years later.

But do such structural and topical changes blind us to the fact that dialogue between the leadership of the churches has not actually changed and consequently is not successful in its endeavours? When asked whether he thought that the purpose of national level dialogue had changed one respondent replied: 'I would say that it is not so much that the purpose has changed but that the way of fulfilling the purpose has developed and changed.'[2] Indicating that the answer to this question would be a qualified yes. Indeed, there seems to be little agreement on what the structures in place for dialogue between the churches are for. Are they ecumenical structures in the strictest sense of the word or should they be engaging with the conflict that surrounds them in Northern Ireland? As Christians, are they not answerable to the social and political implications of the Gospel? From the interviews conducted with those involved in national-level dialogue, it is clear that this confusion over definition, compounded by the fact that the IICM does not have a list of official aims, is one of the main problems preventing progress. A Catholic Priest involved in this work commented 'Ecumenism in Northern Ireland is probably one of the most misunderstood words and I think, in some respects, if you were to ask people in the road what they mean by it they would probably give you different definitions.'[3] Thus, whilst some put forward a classic definition of ecumenism, arguing that it should be concerned only with theological matters and ultimately church unity, others argue that it should be 'the same as that of the world ecumenical dialogues in general, namely as being partly theological and partly social – both of these being naturally, applied to the particular situation in Ireland'.[4] From this viewpoint the IICM is merely an arena in which the churches can 'give some expression to the matters [they] share in inter-church relations; to foster and improve those relationships; to engage in shared reflection about issues affecting Ireland and the Churches'.[5] Furthermore, the IICM is not particularly concerned with the restoration of church unity. In reality the IICM is a reactive group, there to improve relationships between the churches, and any work that they do, especially in the area of reconcilation, should be seen as a reaction to the events surrounding them, rather than an attempt to foster good community relations in the area.

Even so, there is an air of disappointment surrounding the progression of inter-church relations. Many of those closely involved believe that the IICM has not seized the opportunities presented by endless discussion and translated this either into positive action regarding the problems of Northern Ireland or even, as one would expect of such a body, the development of a local theology of reconciliation. Instead, it is perceived to be a body of some symbolic importance, as it provides a working example of Catholics and Protestants talking together, but little else. National-level ecumenical dialogue in Northern Ireland is an endeavour beset with problems, compounded by the fact that the structures of authority and decision-making within the churches involved differ so vastly from each other that it prevents any meaningful progress on issues, such as sectarianism or even points of doctrinal difference. This difference in structure has been put forward as a cause of the animosity that Protestants feel towards Catholics and in the sphere of ecumenical relationships these difficulties are still apparent. Thus, those representing the hierarchical structures of the Catholic Church, and to a lesser extent the Church of Ireland, have no tangible authority concerning inter-church decision-making and always have to refer back to their superiors. The more democratic churches, such as the Presbyterian Church in Ireland and the Methodist Church, are compelled to present the work of the IICM to their Assemblies for approval. Therefore, those representing their churches at these meetings have no power to make decisions autonomously, which results in substantial delays when trying to get any statement or change approved.

This chapter will show that these differences in approach to the issue of inter-church relations, and the tensions that they create, have caused significant problems for the participants especially when trying to deal with issues of reconciliation and community relations. Thus, although such issues are discussed, action is rarely ever taken on the recommendations of the working parties, and no attempt is ever made to create a synthesis of the work of the IICM, either at a theological or a communal level. Furthermore, although there is some evidence, mainly to be found in their publications, that national-level ecumenical dialogue has expanded its agenda in the past 20 years to encompass the obvious role that the churches have to play in the healing of Northern Irish society, they have failed unwittingly to translate this into the action needed.

## 1980–84

Between 1980 and 1984 the work of the IICM continued in the same vein as it had previously. During the fifth and sixth Meetings, held in March 1980 and March 1983, survey papers were presented on inter-church activities since 1968, as well as those on the issues of 'Christian Witness in a Secular World' and 'Mission to those in Prison',[6] whilst the working party on Marian devotion in Ireland also presented its final findings. In addition the Meeting held in March 1980 was designed to be one of reflection upon the achievements of the ecumenical movement since 1968. An aim indicating that its members were aware of the need for a transition in emphasis towards issues that were of importance to Northern Ireland, rather than those that were of ecumenical importance world-wide.

The participants of this meeting heard two papers on ecumenism in Ireland from Fr. Michael Ledwith of Maynooth and Rev. Eric Gallagher, a leading Methodist Churchman, who dealt with the situation in the South and North respectively. Both papers thus dealt with the development of ecumenical relationships since 1968, outlining the Meeting's successes and failures, as well as the initiatives taking place in local areas. By far the most significant part of this report lay in its analysis of the role of the Meeting, and in particular the way in which it should contribute to society, asking '[c]ould it be that our natural and commendable desire that the Church should not be involved in the party political field has made us in practice almost completely impotent?'[7] Opinion on this matter divided the two speakers, who took differing views on the role of the church in Ireland. Ledwith, whilst praising the advances made in the 1970s, advocated a measured approach to the churches' involvement in the political (and by definition the reconciliation) sphere. He argued that the maturation in approach, facilitated by the growth of ecumenical friendships should not pander to the desires of the media to be an unofficial peace process, but rather concentrate upon the real doctrinal difficulties and differences exposed by the earlier meetings:

> As we approach this mature stage it is important to realise that the ecumenical movement can actually be hindered severely by relating it too exclusively to the tragic problems of Northern Ireland. Whether the Churches have had their share of blame for the troubles or not is something that will be debated endlessly, but whatever way we may see the fact is we need to be careful in defining the limits of that responsibility, and to be honestly realistic in assessing the ability the Churches have to bring about a solution ... In addition ... the search for understanding among Christians is very inadequately understood if treated merely as a search for peace among the various communities.[8]

However, Gallagher, perhaps because of his direct experience in reconciliation, took a much more holistic view of the IICM's role. He argued that those involved were unwilling to compromise on their terms for peace, thereby preventing the Meeting from working towards reconciliation:

> Everybody or nearly everybody wants peace. But your idea of peace may not be mine and vice versa. The result is that people either want peace on their own terms or as they envisage it … There has been (and probably by consequence) little attempt made to involve people in the creation of the conditions that make for peace … The Churches have preached the Gospel but for the most part would seem not to have come to terms with the need to be agents of reconciliation.[9]

Gallagher went on to argue that the Meeting needed a new approach to its involvement in 'non-ecumenical' affairs,[10] especially those relating to community-relations issues. He asserted that it was their duty as churches to try and facilitate, even at the most basic level, some form of work towards reconciliation:

> It is … manifestly the obligation of the Churches to be concerned about anything or any combination of factors that makes abundant life impossible or difficult for either the individual or the community. And concern is not enough. Appropriate action is called from all of us. We cannot opt out of society or our obligations to it and at the same time claim to be disciples of the Lord in the fullest sense.[11]

Such an analysis of the meaning of inter-church relations highlights the direction in which many of the IICM's members were attempting to go, and illustrates a growing desire to incorporate more directly pastoral and leadership concerns into the everyday working of the Meeting, as well as aiding the growth of relationships at a local level.[12] Furthermore, this report highlights that the members of the IICM had developed sufficient understanding of one another to feel comfortable enough to move away from the comparative approach on theological and doctrinal matters, towards tentatively working to produce documents and statements on a broader range of topics and in the direction of tackling the problematic issues presented to them by the conflict. However, although some aspired to undertake such dialogue, the lack of definition concerning the remit of the Meeting was to prevent this new holistic interpretation, which would incorporate community relations as well as theological ecumenism from blossoming as vigorously as it could have done.

It is apparent that the Meeting had already been thinking about

adopting a new, more wide-ranging approach towards inter-church relationships, as a number of the reports produced in the late 1970s had
demonstrated a need for the work of the Meeting to move in a new direction. Consequently, between 1980 and 1984 a Steering Committee,
led by Fr. Michael Ledwith and Dr. David Poole, was established to discuss the future organisation of the IICM. This signalled a recognition of
the need to reconsider its scope in the light of recent criticism:

> Questions have been raised about its progress, its purpose and its
> intent. The criticisms have come from its member churches and also
> from the mass media. These criticisms can be divided into two
> groups: a) the assertion that the meeting has avoided adequate
> discussion on certain sensitive topics; b) failed to make spectacular
> ecumenical progress, or to make progressive decisions on behalf of
> its participating churches.[13]

The criticism from the media was based upon the failure of the Meeting
to act as an 'unofficial peace process', prompted, for example, by its
silence regarding the hunger strikes.[14] The member churches usually
argued that at the meetings there was 'much talk, perhaps educatively
helpful, but inadequate follow-up organisation leading to frustration, fear
that it is only a public relations exercise. There are those (on both sides)
who would be content to see the Conferences fold up, provided the
blame could be put clearly on the other side!'[15] In the case of the criticism
from within the Meeting, it is clear that its members had understood the
problems that were hindering its progress.

The authors of the report did much to respond to these two areas of
criticism, elaborating on their causes by arguing that the nature of the
Meeting represented an obstacle to any tangible progress being made
either ecumenically or pastorally. For example, they pointed out that the
intermittent and public nature of the gatherings made ecumenical discussion difficult. They went on to add that '[i]t should also be realised that
although practical and every-day issues may appear to have priority in
ecumenical discussion, for such discussions to have an adequate basis and
ultimate hope of reaching real solutions, the doctrinal and moral diver-
gences between the Churches must first be faced and resolved ... Those
who represented the Churches did not have the authority to make
decisions.'[16] Indeed, the structure of the Meeting at this point was its
main failing. By the late 1970s it was being convened infrequently, with
a three-year gap between 1977 and 1980 caused by the death of two
Popes, Paul VI and John Paul I, and the illness and death of Cardinal
Conway, the Catholic Primate. Such prolonged gaps, when combined

with the organising Committee's inability to make autonomous decisions,[17] and problems with the nature of authority and decision-making
structures of the member churches, meant that the Meeting was unable
to move as swiftly as some would have liked.

To those castigating the Meeting for its lack of progress on matters
relating to the political situation, they pointed out the need to resolve
theological concerns and build understanding. The meetings were primarily:

> An exercise in inter-church dialogue, and not designed to solve 'the
> Irish problem' or to end violence, not should it be expected to do so.
> The Irish problem is obviously very complex, with a wide diversity
> of causes, ranging far beyond the responsibilities or the competence
> of churchmen, and not capable of simple or ready solution by
> ecumenical dialogue. Obviously, however, the more Christian lead-
> ers can come together to think, pray and work in an attempt
> to grapple with the problems of a deeply divided and polarised
> society, the more effective will be their contribution to remedying
> these problems.[18]

Furthermore, before 1984 the Meeting was designed to focus upon theological issues and had been misunderstood by many as being the churches' attempt at peace talks. Despite this, Ledwith and Poole accepted that
a radical overhaul of the structure and organisation of the Meeting was
needed. This was based upon what Ledwith called a maturation in style,
as the foundation stones for the continuance and success of the Meeting
had been laid during the 1970s. Consequently, a high enough level of
friendship, understanding and trust had been established to allow for the
discussion and consideration of matters, both ecumenical and social,
which would aid the promotion of inter-church, and hopefully community relationships, in Ireland. In addition events, external to the workings
of the IICM, also helped to create an atmosphere in which such change
was possible.

Arguably, the most important of these was the shift in the culture of
Catholicism, which had begun with Vatican II, and had subsequently
been nurtured in Ireland in the post-Vatican II atmosphere of openness,
a process which was aided by increased secularisation. Thus, from a
Protestant point of view, it was felt that:

> Catholics are more formed by Vatican II as new people come in
> ... There are a number of things going on in the Catholic world,
> Vatican II is more absorbed and also this stable Catholic world is

starting to be questioned and to disintegrate so that there is less arrogance around on all sides, the sense of superiority and self-sufficiency [is also starting to wane].[19]

The papal visit of 1979 also provided encouragement to the Catholic clergy in their ecumenical activity as during this visit the Pope 'had discussed the problems of ecumenism, especially in the Irish context, with the bishops. He had urged them to renew their efforts in the field in the follow up to the visit.'[20] Whilst too high an emphasis should not be placed upon this, the Papal Visit did go some way towards demystifying the actions and beliefs of the Catholic hierarchy amongst those Protestant clergy and leaders who met him, as Cardinal Cahal Daly illustrates:

> The Pope's meeting with the church leaders in Dublin was ... an important ecumenical moment because of the historic stereotyped ideas that some Protestant people had, seeing him as a great enemy of Protestantism. The Pope pleaded that no Protestant should see him as an enemy but regard him as a friend and a brother in Christ ... That every Christian should be committed to reaching out to the other Christian communities ... in a desire to understand each other's position ... Whilst not necessarily agreeing but at the same time accepting the sincerity of our point of view and seeing an obligation to do what ever one could to get a better understanding of their position and convey a better understanding of one's own position to them in dialogue, with a strong emphasis on listening to one another instead of arguing with one another; to understand and respect the other rather than detest and oppose the other.[21]

As a result of these factors, Ledwith and Poole's report made a number of proposals aimed at rectifying the inadequacies of the IICM.

The key changes outlined in this document fall into three categories: membership, administrative organisation and structure. The first proposal suggested that the membership of the IICM be rearranged with clear guidelines on the nature of the gatherings. They advocated that the Meeting have a regular membership of fifty-five, split equally between the Protestant and Catholic Churches.[22] The format of each meeting was also clearly outlined, stating that the Meetings should consist of 'co-ordination of the responses from the Churches, and, where possible, organisation of positive follow-up action'.[23] Second, they recommended that the IICM should meet more regularly, at least every 18 months, as opposed to every two years as had previously been the case. Such meetings would be in conjunction with an inter-church committee, which would be more powerful than its predecessor and would facilitate the continued work and discussion of the IICM. This was central to the authors' plans to develop a wider remit for the IICM:

> It is absolutely clear that there are practical concerns and sensitive issues which need the united examination of the participating Churches. To promote this there should be an Inter-Church Committee representative of all the participating churches which would have the right to make representation and recommendations to the churches, to present a report to the Inter-Church Meeting and to set up Departments ('permanent') or Working Parties ('temporary'), or subcommittees as it saw fit. These would, in the first instance, report to the Inter-Church Committee. One of the responsibilities of the Inter-Church Committee would be the organisation of the Inter-Church Meeting.[24]

The creation of this committee was crucial to legitimising the work of the Meeting, as it allowed it to deal with matters more swiftly than before, thereby trying to eliminate the frustration that many Protestant Churches had felt with the work of the IICM:

> The establishment of the inter-church committee meant that it could do other things ... it wasn't just tied to running the meetings. It could make statements, although it didn't tend to do that much. It could become a sort of focal point for meetings between the ICC and the Catholic Church. The creation of an inter-church committee gave the [IICM] a more powerful impetus: before that there was basically a steering committee for the inter-church meeting and that had fairly restricted terms of reference. The creation of the committee, which had broader terms of reference ... pushed the thing a bit further forward. [As a result] I think that there was an increase in confidence ... and people saw that this was not a very threatening thing and that people's expectations of what was possible and [their] exaggerated fears lessened.[25]

The most significant suggestion in this report was that the work of the IICM should be divided into three departments: the Department of Theological Questions, the Department of Social Issues and the Department of Mission. This particular arrangement came into being because 'the working party process had run its course by the early 1980s',[26] which provided a further signal of the need to rethink the

Meeting's working arrangements. Each of these departments would have the power to set up working parties on issues of relevance which 'would produce situation papers or recommendations to be used at the discretion of the Committee'.[27] All of these proposals, apart from the foundation of the Department of Mission, were endorsed without controversy by the member churches, resulting in the establishment of the Department of Theological Questions and the Department of Social Issues.

These proposals, and their subsequent implementation, illustrate clearly the trust and understanding that was growing between the Protestant and Catholic Churches during the early 1980s, as they were in many ways representing a semi-formalisation of ecumenical relationships in Ireland: 'in the early 1980s it becomes more clear what is possible and what isn't. In a sense we get an embryo inter-church ecumenical body.'[28] Thus, in implementing these proposals the member churches were bringing the organisational structure of the IICM into a new era. Now their attention would be turned towards the creation of a broader ecumenical body, which in turn led to a distinction between doctrinal ecumenism and the churches' need to be involved in community relations. Consequently, they were playing a vital role in the maturation of the Meeting as an ecumenical body, eventually leading to attempts being made at the formal establishment of an Irish inter-church body in the 1990s. The work of this new-look Meeting began in the period after 1984, the results of which, whilst greatly improving relationships within the IICM itself, and illustrating the distance that the churches had come together since 1973, made very little impact upon those outside the immediate sphere of dialogue providing little more than a symbolic gesture of Catholic and Protestant friendship.

From 1984 onwards, then, the work of the IICM was divided into two parts, facilitated by the newly founded Department of Social Issues and the Department of Theological Questions. Within a year they had become stable bodies which could have the potential to sustain meaningful dialogue between the churches. The IICM of 1986 showed 'that the new structure was firmly established, and that there was a genuine desire for progress in dialogue, a readiness to examine real theological and social issues that [were] divisive, and an openness of mind and warmth of spirit that provides hope for the future'.[29] Despite this stability, both departments underwent modifications in their structure, as well as major shifts in focus which again serve to illustrate, not only the growing distinction between ecumenism and community relations, but also the increasing impact of secularisation on the work of the Meeting.

## THE DEPARTMENT OF SOCIAL ISSUES

The Department of Social Issues was intended to be an arena through which the member churches of the IICM could discuss matters of common social concern, as well as those directly related to community relations. Between 1984 and 1994 the Department produced five reports: *The Church and the Technological Age* (1986), *Marriage and Family in Ireland Today* (1987), *Young People and the Church* (1990), *The Challenge of the Urban Situation in Ireland Today* (1990) and *Sectarianism: A Discussion Document* (1993),[30] all of which were the result of two or three years research by a working party. However, from 1994, after a reassessment of its work, the working methods of the Department changed from being research and report based to being 'a meeting point for social responsibility people from the churches'.[31]

As with every other aspect of the Meeting's work, the Department of Social Issues has been heavily criticised, both by pro- and anti-ecumenical clergy, for its perceived failure to follow through on the recommendations made by its reports: 'The council [IICM] is only a talking shop, I personally think that if it closed tomorrow it wouldn't be any great loss to the Church because they are only ever really talking round in circles about things of no great interest.'[32] A close examination of the work of the Department and its consequences proves that these criticisms are not entirely unfounded, as the Department did not act upon the findings and recommendations of its reports, as one would traditionally expect of an inter-church body. However, its work did provide some of the inspiration necessary for the establishment of a number of inter-church initiatives, but these organisations were set up outside the Meeting's control by individuals and, therefore, cannot really be seen as a practical manifestation of their work, even though they have helped to provide a new dynamic in inter-church relationships in Northern Ireland from the early 1990s onwards. Three of the reports made some contribution to this new dynamic: *Young People and the Church*, *The Challenge of the Urban Situation in Ireland today* and *Sectarianism: A Discussion Document*. Although each looked at three diverse topics, they all went some way towards promoting the Meeting's more holistic approach to inter-church relations, first by helping to consolidate the Meeting's aspiration to separate ecumenism from community relations and second, in its contribution, albeit unwittingly, to the work and foundation of a number of peace and reconciliation education initiatives.

*Young People and the Church*

The working party on young people and the church was established in February 1987 and was co-chaired by Joe McDermott and Peter Moss. It was intended to look only at the churches' youth work and relationships with young people and was established as a direct result of concerns expressed within the churches about the direction of the churches' work and relations with young people in the context of a rapidly changing society. The terms of reference were 'In the context of the present position of young people in Irish society to look at (i) the work of the churches with young people; (ii) the involvement of young people in the life of the Churches; (iii) to make recommendations.'[33]

This report examined youth work in both the North and South of Ireland and the way in which it was being carried out in the churches, the alienation faced by young people and the issues facing the churches in their work. It concluded with a series of recommendations for the development of youth work in Ireland. It was these recommendations, along with the issues facing the churches, which held the greatest implications for the development of inter-church relationships, highlighting the key factors of secularisation and the message of reconciliation and social responsibility found in the Gospel, that were forcing the growth of alliances between the Protestant and Catholic Churches.

From the final report it is evident that the onset of secularisation was one of the Meeting's key motives for commissioning it:

> While other European countries have suffered large drops in Church membership, especially among young people, the churches in Ireland have until recently been relatively protected from this trend. However, significant changes are now clearly visible, particularly in large urban areas. Along with them is a more general trend away from the church and religious belief related to increased secularisation and materialism. All of this represents a serious challenge to our Churches even though many young people remain loyal members.[34]

The tone of the recommendations demonstrated the need for the reengagement of youth with the churches, hoping to find ways in which the image of the church held by young people could be addressed. 'Young people in particular see the clergy as remote and unapproachable, while the clergy find it difficult to find ways of communicating and building up trust with young people ... In addition, the church's image is often that of an introverted community, preoccupied with internal, institutional matters, especially its own survival.'[35] The report went on to recommend a series of measures that could be put in place by the churches, both at a national and local level, to help to prevent this disaffection with the church, and Christianity in general, occurring. They argued that the answer to the problem of the disaffection of Irish youth with the churches was one of empowerment. Thus, by involving younger, and in particular female, members of the congregation in the decision-making processes of the church, the leadership would make them feel more involved and less daunted by the hierarchical nature of the churches. Nevertheless, by far the most significant suggestion of the report regarding secularisation was that the churches should somehow work together to combat it: 'We share common problems, e.g. a decline in church attendance, especially in urban areas, and a lack of knowledge about our beliefs. Can we face them together even to a limited extent?'[36] Here we begin to see a new force in the continuance of relationships between the churches, as they were no longer meeting just out of a desire for meaningful dialogue on matters of theological concern but were also working together, through the medium of the IICM, to combat the problem of secularisation, as 'there is a sort of feeling that society is becoming more secular and the place that we [as churches] had in society is eroding which also encourages you to at least think that you are in the same boat'.[37]

Despite the influence of secularisation upon the report's findings and recommendations, it is through its suggestions on the non-spiritual engagement of young people,[38] and in particular on matters related to reconciliation, that we can see clear evidence of the IICM's adoption of a more holistic attitude to inter-church relations, especially in the context of the Northern Irish situation. This change in attitude was probably due to the realisation that the churches were perceived by young people to be failing, not only socially but also politically. Thus, 'young people often see a contradiction between the way Christ shared his message and how today's church approaches the needs of people'.[39] Furthermore, 'the majority of both Catholics and Protestants perceived their church to be a source of division in Northern Ireland and, to a lesser extent, in the Republic of Ireland. This view is all the more marked when one recalls that these young people are relatively committed church members.'[40] The recommendations of the report on these issues fell into three categories: training and fellowship, reconciliation projects and social action projects, each of which illustrates the Meeting's growing realisation of the need to address a wider range of issues than it had previously if it was going to be effective.

When addressing the issue of training and fellowship, the report argued that youth work should not be marginalised, as had previously been the case. Instead, they wanted to see a formalisation of training for youth work which should be the responsibility of members from almost every constituency of the congregation or parish: 'The need to train young people, clergy, parents and others for youth ministry ... should be given priority. Training for youth ministry should be an important element in preparation for ordained clergy. The Churches should provide more full-time staff to carry out youth ministry.'[41] In addition, they advocated the need for the IICM itself to take a proactive role in the promotion of youth work and participation within Irish Churches, suggesting that formal structures should be put in place to support youth workers and clergy. For example, 'the Irish Inter-Church Meeting should establish a regular Ecumenical Youth Gathering, the planning and organisation of which should be undertaken by a fully representative planning group, including young people and youth officers and leaders from the Churches'.[42] Such suggestions were particularly significant because, although they never actually came to fruition, they signalled the need for a new, more outward-looking approach on the part of the membership of the Meeting, which entailed an engagement with those outside the hierarchies of the churches. Furthermore, in their acceptance of this report, the members of the Meeting were demonstrating their realisation that inter-church relations meant more than just comparative theology or dialogue on matters, such as mixed marriage, and that it should include matters of wider social concern.

The recommendations on the issue of reconciliation serve to further illustrate this change in attitude. Once more, they argued for a more outward looking and holistic approach to the issue of church-based community relationships involving young people. They saw such activities as key to dispelling attitudes regarding the churches' involvement in the political arena:

> The time may now be right for the Churches and their Youth Departments to show formal or concrete commitment to a programme of cross-community activity. Realistic structures need to be found to enable Church Youth Departments to meet the hopes of young people. The primary motive for the Churches lies in the Gospel of reconciliation. The Churches ought also to be compelled by our history of sectarian division, conflict and violence, and the imperative of young people's hopes and dreams.[43]

The authors of the report went on to put forward practical suggestions for the implementation of such aims, including the development of 'common resource material',[44] such as social and political education material, designed 'to allow the sharing of traditions, hopes, perspectives and dreams in the journey towards a more Christ-centred community, united in faith and action'.[45] Finally, in their attitude towards social action and the churches' past failure to respond to the social elements in the Gospel, the authors of the report continued with their more holistic approach to the issue of engagement with society; again illustrating the need for the churches to work together on non-theological matters:

> The Churches should make a deeper commitment to urban ministry, recognising the large number of alienated young people in urban communities – this would include training for youth leaders and clergy and the development of fieldwork and appropriate support.
> The Churches should act together in organising and funding projects to combat problems such as unemployment and homelessness and should encourage young people to place a leading role in these programmes, more of which should be jointly organised by the Churches.[46]

Through this report can be seen the crystallisation of the IICM's attempts to adopt a more inclusive attitude to the issue of inter-church relations. Thus, its findings and, more crucially, its approval by the member churches of the Meeting indicate the inauguration of a redefinition of its purpose, and indeed the purpose of inter-church relationships generally, moving it towards an involvement in community relations, whilst remaining committed to purely theological ecumenism. This theme was to be continued in the next two reports of the Department of Social Issues. Furthermore, this report also contributed to the development of the 'Parachurch' sector in Northern Ireland, as Youth Link[47] was founded as a result of the experience of a number of the members of the working party, who wanted to put some of their findings into practice and '[i]t is interesting that Youth Link have taken reconciliation and peace building and tried to make it real in the young people of the church context'.[48]

## The challenge of the city

In addressing the issue of the challenge of urban living, the IICM were tackling one of the main causes of conflict within Northern Irish society: socioeconomic deprivation. The Working Party's terms of reference stated:

> We were asked to look at (i) the changes going on in urban society

today and (ii) their challenge to Church and Society. We have concentrated upon the problems of those who, in an urban situation
characterised by prosperity, opportunity and choice, are poor, lack-
ing in opportunity and deprived of choice.[49]

Their conclusions and proposals were based around two themes: first, the
obligation of churches to respond to the social implications of the Gospel.
Second, the need for the development of church-based Social Action
Projects, the implementation of which it was hoped would also combat the
challenge of secularisation in urban situations. Each set of ideas had implications for the development of inter-church relations at both a national and
local level.

Unlike their report on young people and the churches, the entire tone
of this report was scriptural, with its recommendations being based upon
biblical values and principles,[50] with a whole chapter devoted to an examination of Christian teaching on urban living. The authors argue that it is
essential that the churches respond to the social implications of the Gospel
adopting an integrated methodology in their work in urban areas: 'The
Christian community is a community of service. The Christian Gospel
cannot be divorced from its social implications and practical social action
can be a demonstration of Christian love. Therefore, the church will nor-
mally seek to be involved in some work of service in the neighbourhood,
no matter how small.'[51] Consequently their recommendations for church
action in deprived urban areas centred upon the need for a marriage of
the message of the Gospel to social outreach to those in need. It is in these
suggestions that we can see a move towards a more practical brand of
inter-church relationships within the IICM.

The most prominent theme within the report's recommendations was
the need for a radical re-assessment of what it actually means to be a
church in the context of the urban situation in Ireland, both North and
South. Thus, throughout the chapter devoted to the analysis of the
church's role in society, comments on the polarised notion of 'Church'
and the failure of its more affluent members to engage completely with
the social imperative of the Gospel are constantly repeated. For example:
'the challenge of the urban situation is to the whole Church, not just to
the Church in these areas … because whatever "answers" there are to their
problems cannot be found primarily within these areas'.[52] This theme
is reiterated with the suggestion that '[t]here is also the possibility of
partnership between suburban and urban congregations and parishes.'[53]
The authors argue, then, that the model of the church employed in urban
situations needs to be changed: moving it away from an over-concentration

upon the needs of just the congregation towards one which centres upon the needs of the whole area: 'The dominant model of the Church has been a pastoral one in which the major emphasis was on the care and nurture of Church members. The changes going on in urban society require a profound change to a more mission orientation.'[54]

The model of social action advocated by this report is one of reintegration, arguing for the need to reintegrate people in urban areas not only into the church but also into society. However, their suggestions are not entirely new but instead, appear to be picking up on projects and events that had been occurring at a local level throughout the past decade. For example, in the section on the need to rebuild community within the local churches before engaging with the situation in the local areas, we can see clearly the methodology being used by the ecumenical communities based upon the Belfast peacelines. The report states that:

> To make a contribution towards community building the Christian communities to which we belong need to exhibit those qualities [which allow them] 'to bear one another's burdens, suffer one another's pain, and participate in a common celebration' ... it is out of such living centres of community that we dare to go out into the neighbourhood to rebuild community there.[55]

This is reminiscent of the words of a member of a peaceline community speaking about its development in the 1980s and the need to get to know one another before engaging in community-relations work commented that 'you have to know what you are about yourself ... Communities have to do [that] first before going out to the rawness of the people to see what needs to be developed in that area.'[56] In addition, their suggestion that churches in urban areas should link with others in more affluent suburbs was already being implemented in areas of West Belfast.[57] There was a realisation of the value of local inter-church groups, as it was commented that the churches can only make a real difference in the local community 'through the work and witness of ordinary Church members'.[58] Furthermore, in common with the focus of the IICM's report on young people, it is evident that the use of Social Action Projects by the churches would have the added benefit of stemming the tide of secularisation that was just starting to take hold in urban areas in the late 1980s. This would be done by rebranding the church's image amongst those in working-class areas, moving it from the one of bourgeois irrelevance[59] to a vibrant body with 'an emphasis on a relevant faith formation for living in urban areas'.[60]

Thus, through this report the IICM were taking the concept of inter-church relationships a step further than they had previously. Although they state only once the need for Christians to work together on issues of social concern, there is an underlying concept of the need to reassess relationships between the churches in the light of a problem of common concern: that of the socio-economic deprivation which is causing the alienation of urban dwellers both from society and the church. Thus, in common with the report on *Young People and the Church*, *The Challenge of the City* highlights a growing realisation, on the part of the member churches of the IICM, that in order for inter-church relationships in Ireland to flourish, a new approach encompassing community relations as well as pure theological ecumenism had to be adopted.

*Sectarianism*

Nowhere can the IICM's new approach to inter-church relations be seen more clearly than in the discussion document on sectarianism,[61] which was published in 1993. In attempting to tackle an issue which lies at the core of the conflict in Northern Ireland, the Meeting was signalling its growing commitment to building meaningful relationships between the churches. The report on *Violence in Ireland* in 1976 had stated that:

> Lack of contact, lack of dialogue breed an environment of fear, suspicion, ignorance and prejudice, which can rightly be termed as sectarian. It is to the elimination of this whole frame of mind that the combined efforts of the Churches need to be directed. Ireland needs a programme to combat sectarianism wherever it is found.[62]

However, it was not until 1991 that the first meeting of the working party on sectarianism was held under the leadership of John Lampen and Mary McAleese.[63] A member of the working party argues 'the whole Drumcree thing has put sectarianism, at least in the Church of Ireland, as an issue. So, this is an issue which is receiving more attention which basically impacts on this issue of reconciliation.'[64] In setting up the working party, the churches, through the IICM, were signalling their commitment to an improvement in community relations by examining the role that their institutions had to play in creating sectarianism. They did so by asking how they as Christians could help to alleviate the problem, whilst at the same time illustrating the expansion of ecumenical boundaries that was taking place.

The working party was constructed under the following terms of reference:

(i) To look at how the different churches have regarded each other in their doctrinal statements and formularies, and in their public stances, and what is the present position.

(ii) To look at the role of different churches in Ireland in creating and maintaining separation, division and conflict– if any.

(iii) To look at how sectarianism may have operated in such areas as education, jobs, housing, ghettos, justice and criminal issues and the influence of Loyalist and Nationalist orders.

(iv) To look at what have been the effects, for the Churches and communities, of the substantial degree of identification of Protestantism with Unionism and Catholicism with Nationalism.

(v) To make proposals to the churches that might promote recon-ciliation and positive respect for difference.[65]

Sectarianism was defined as 'a complex of attitudes, beliefs, behaviours and structures in which religion is a significant component, and which (i) directly, or indirectly, infringes the rights of individuals or groups, and/or (ii) influences or causes situations of destructive conflict'.[66] The Report set out to examine the consequences of sectarianism,[67] rather than the causes, in order to 'separate religious differences from sectarianism'.[68] Asking the question 'Are varying understandings of where the fullness of Christian truth lies necessarily sectarian?'[69]

The result was a broad document that adopted a comprehensive approach to the issue of sectarianism within Northern Irish society. The document's recommendations clearly highlight the IICM's desire to develop a more community relations-based approach to reconciliation, as their recommendations encompass virtually every aspect of society, rang-ing from the Constitution and Government through socio-economic inequality to home, street and local community.[70] The main thrust of the suggestions and recommendations centred around the adoption of an equitable solution to the Northern Irish problem at every level, rather than just at the level of government, arguing that 'the two communities are entitled to equal respect and treatment … [and there should be] a willingness to treat other communities with the same fairness and con-cern for rights as one expects for one's own'.[71] A realisation that in order for reconciliation and peace to occur, every level of society must change and reassess its attitudes can be seen in these recommendations. However, in order for such a policy to be implemented, difficult issues needed to be addressed:

Clear policies, structures, arguments, procedures and rules are important when dealing with decisive issues, e.g. flags and emblems, sectarian incidents. These help to reduce and dissolve some of the fears which are around and give support to those who have to take responsibility to deal with difficult issues. They also, at the same time, put the responsibility on the organisation as a **whole**. It is the organisation's policies, structures, agreements, procedures and rules, not one individual's.[72]

Thus, in such recommendations and comments we can see the Meeting moving towards a more community relations-based approach to inter-church relations. This report guided the member churches away from theological matters towards an attitude of engagement with the whole of society, rather than just the realm of church.

Despite this, it is the recommendations specifically aimed at the churches which have the most salience for inter-church relationships, both at a national and a local level, in Northern Ireland. Unlike the other reports produced during this period, it is tacitly understood that the churches must work together on this issue, indicating that the idea of an all encompassing approach to the issue of inter-church relationships had now become part of the culture of the IICM. The members of the working party seem to have seen the opportunity to transcend the idea of working together on 'side issues' which could eventually lead to reconciliation, such as youth and urban regeneration, moving instead towards a fusion of politico-religious discussion amongst the churches which would strike at the heart of their involvement in the Northern Irish conflict in a way never seen before.[73] So, for example, in their list of fourteen 'Specific Actions' for the churches and individual Christians they suggest that they should:

- Avoid thinking in stereotypes but seek to understand the reality of the person from the other tradition. This will often involve becoming more accurately informed about their Church, its self-understandings, teachings, beliefs, worship and practices.
- Understand and evaluate the significance of the common ground as well as the differences between us. Not all differences of belief and practice are equally important or necessarily incompatible with a fuller unity of Christians. Particularly we do need to separate those differences which have to do with differences of Christian belief from those based upon Britishness or Irishness or political aspiration. Ultimate loyalty is owed to God alone who is beyond all our particular identities and divisions.

- Examine our own tradition to see what particular responsibility it bears for what has happened.
- Be prepared to repent for what our tradition has done wrong and seek forgiveness.[74]

Hence we see an articulation of the need to create understanding amongst the churches, combined with a blueprint of how this new understanding could be created. Of course, it could be argued that the entire *raison d'être* of the IICM was to create such understanding. However, with the publication of the *Sectarianism: A Discussion Document*, we see a desire to establish a new level of understanding, both amongst the churches and individual Christians, moving discussion away from points of theology to the issues which have prevented reconciliation taking place. In addition, these specific actions also consolidate the idea already entrenched in local relationships, that theological objections to ecumenical dialogue need not prevent people from working together on matters relating to community-relations issues, with the churches being asked to 'co-operate on projects for the common good, according to conscience'.[75]

The recommendations in this document also highlight the recognition of the need to encourage inter-church relationships at a local level: 'One of the most important tasks for the leadership is to help church members see that to live with God is to take risks and that the improvement of community relations is an urgent task.'[76] Consequently, the document recommends that the churches encourage reconciliation projects at a parish level and support 'those who take a stand for positive change'.[77] However, in making these recommendations for local level relationships, the working party were for the most part taking their cue from the numerous projects that had already been established throughout the province. Indeed, groups such as Corrymeela and other parish-based clergy and lay discussion groups had been using and developing the methods of relationship building outlined above for around 20 years.

Unlike the other documents produced by the Department of Social Issues in the years between 1984 and 1993, *Sectarianism* was entitled a *Discussion Document* rather than labelled as a report. 'The Inter-Church Committee when it received the text had to consider how to deal with it and what status to give it. The Committee felt that this was a potentially controversial issue and it wanted to emphasise the provisional nature of the conclusions and it therefore called it a "discussion document".'[78] Such an action was particularly significant for the development of inter-church relations, as it made clear the reluctance on the part of the member churches to openly associate themselves with a set of recommendations which so blatantly called for the churches to work together. However, the very fact that the document was published at all under the auspices of the IICM, did highlight that the member churches had gone some way towards an acceptance of the need for a more community relations-based approach to inter-church relations. Be that as it may, although the actual impact of the discussion document itself is hard to determine, as one clergyman put it: 'the report was used a lot but it is difficult to gauge the impact or affect of these documents – it is a general permeation of consciousness, things change gradually',[79] the report did have an important impact upon inter-church relations outside the remit of the IICM. It fed into the ISE sponsored research project, *Moving Beyond Sectarianism*, which focused 'upon the role of Christian religion in sectarianism in Northern Ireland ... [offering] a new definition of the phenomenon, a detailed analysis of sectarian dynamics, and a series of models for helping people to transform such dynamics.'[80]

The discussion document on sectarianism was the last document produced by the Department of Social Issues, as it underwent a profound change in the mid-1990s. Since 1995, 'it has become more of a meeting place for people from within the social responsibility groups within the church',[81] and in the summer of 2005, the Department of Social Issues changed its name to the Inter-Church Committee on Social Issues, as it was felt that this name more clearly reflected the group's work.[82] This was part of an ongoing series of changes to the Committee's methodology, which had begun shortly after the publication of *Sectarianism* and were implemented because it would 'enable it [the IICM] better to respond to social issues on an inter-church basis'.[83] Instead of producing a constant stream of reports, the Department of Social Issues has become a more reactive body, determining its agenda in the light of the current concerns of the members. 'Sometimes the parent body would say "will you have a look at this?" For example, Sean Brady [the Archbishop of Armagh] brought out a paper about eighteen months ago on dealing with the past and that got pushed down to us to look at. We are open to that, otherwise it is a matter of the issues that people feel collectively are important and also issues which our members are interested in.'[84] Such project work makes up the majority of the committee's agenda and involves taking 'particular issues and running with it for a period'.[85] Instead of focusing solely on one particular issue, since around 2003, the Inter-Church Committee on Social Issues has become more engaged with the society in which it operates. These issues have included poverty, asylum seekers, the environment and racism, all of which have been the subject of social debate both North and South of the Irish border. The Committee has also signalled its intent to speak ecumenically for the

Protestant and Catholic Churches by making representations to various government organisations regarding issues such as community relations and human rights.[86] However, despite making initial plans and employing a project officer to carry out the work on racism, the Committee has not produced any material which would fulfil its ambition to 'communicate to the ordinary person in the pew',[87] once more bringing into question their impact beyond their immediate membership.

The IICM's Department of Social Issues has radically altered the focus of national level inter-church relationships since its inception in 1984, bringing about realignment in the way in which ecumenical relations in Northern Ireland operate by providing a reassessment of what inter-church relationships should actually be. Through the three main documents produced between 1984 and 1993 we see that the emphasis of the IICM had moved towards understanding and community relations, with initial moves being made post-1993 to help the members to engage more closely with matters of common concern. Nevertheless, some critics of the Department of Social Issues would argue that the production of such documents was a 'time-wasting' exercise, making no contribution to either ecumenism or community relations. Whilst they have made the position of the churches on certain matters clearer, through the IICM's failure to ensure the widespread dissemination of these documents this has indeed been the case. Despite this, they have unwittingly been instrumental in creating an entirely new dynamic in inter-church relationships in Northern Ireland by providing the ideas and research necessary for the foundation of a number of peace and reconciliation education initiatives, all of which have been continually contributing to an improvement in community relations since their inception.

## THE DEPARTMENT OF THEOLOGICAL QUESTIONS

Through the work of the Department of Social Issues, the IICM was indicating a desire to work towards the creation of a more inclusive and holistic form of ecumenical dialogue. Although this dialogue did not have much impact beyond the Meeting itself, it could reasonably be expected that this move towards a discourse on reconciliation would be extended to the Department of Theological Questions. As its name suggests, the Department of Theological Questions was established to facilitate discussion between the member churches on theological issues and points of doctrine. However, not only was the Department of Theological Questions not as prolific as its Social counterpart, after 1984 it remained wedded to the comparative model of theology created in the early Ballymascanlon meetings. Thus, 'the theological model that is still dominant is in some senses the historical and confessional model, it is about the documents and the theologians from back wherever'.[88]

The early publications of the Department of Theological Questions bear such an observation out and between 1984 and 1993 two publications were produced on *Ecumenical Principles*[89] and *Salvation and Grace*,[90] both of which were exercises in comparative theology. Their aims state that 'the chapters attempt to express what we hold in common and where we diverge'.[91] Each of these pamphlets were doctrinal studies designed to be used by local groups as discussion guides. Consequently, the members of the working parties discussed two major doctrinal issues which were problematic for Catholic–Protestant relations: church unity and salvation and grace, in the hope that an understanding of each other's perspectives concerning these would deepen relationships further whilst underpinning the work of the Meeting. In their study on Christian unity they aimed to demonstrate that:

> Unity is not a peripheral concern for the life and witness of the Church, but a fundamental expression of being reconciled in Christ. Having explored the parameters of the Gospel vision, an outline of the ways in which this vision has been frustrated and of some ways to overcome the divisions which characterise the contemporary life of our churches will be offered as a contribution to the search for Christian unity in Ireland.[92]

The language used in the documents suggests that such a growth in understanding did occur within the Committee, as through the discussions they discovered 'the depth of unity in faith among our churches'.[93] Although differences did exist between the Protestant and Catholic Churches in their emphasis upon certain aspects of doctrine, such as the sacraments, they noted crucially that 'even as we perceived these differences, we learned how a new language enables us to articulate our respective doctrine in such a way that we can understand one another better'.[94] The creation of such an understanding between the churches on these matters was undoubtedly crucial for the internal strengthening of the IICM itself. However, the discussion of such matters in a manner entirely identical to that used before the structural changes in 1984 indicates that whilst the Department of Theological Questions was doing much to improve theological and doctrinal relationships between the churches it was doing so in a vacuum.

As the later efforts of the Department of Social Issues suggest, it could be expected that the churches would work together through the medium of the IICM to create at the very least a theological understanding of social and political reconciliation, and at the most a theology of reconciliation for Northern Ireland which would try to redress the balance of politicised theology that is so prevalent amongst the churches. Such an exercise would be mirroring and enhancing the Department of Social Issue's attempts to expand the agenda of the Meeting into more community-relations based concerns. However, in its refusal to do so the Department of Theological Questions was in effect failing as an ecumenical body because:

> Ecumenism is a process of dialogue that has to go right across the board and it has to involve theological issues, worship issues, church order and organisation issues and also social and political justice issues and the interaction between all of these. Ecumenism is about Christians engaging with each other and being self-critical and critical of others in a good relationship to try and develop it.[95]

Such a failure on the part of the IICM to grasp this imperative in Northern Ireland has been remarked upon by three theologians,[96] who believe that at a national level the church leadership has failed to work together towards reconciliation. They argue that: 'we are still trying to find the reflective model of theology that is prepared to do social analysis, that is prepared to do political analysis in this community in some depth and connect it up with theological reflection. In other words we need a shift in the theological paradigm.'[97] In a society as divided as Northern Ireland, working together on issues such as reconciliation and related ideas of social inclusion and community relations 'is not an optional extra'.[98] Instead

> it is something that we must get involved in and if we have contributed to the division of mindsets ... and bitter memories by our stand offs as well as by our doctrinal divisions then we have to be in there trying to see what we can contribute both generatively in terms of making a new theology together [and] creating a new model of church together.[99]

However, a process of creating a new theological paradigm would be extremely demanding, requiring a great deal of trust and understanding to have been previously developed between the Protestant and Catholic participants, and those arguing for its development fail to address the issue of whether contextual theology would improve relationships between the churches in Northern Ireland. Indeed, whilst there is division on what form this contextual theology should take and the pace at which it should be developed, with theologians such as Smyth *et al* arguing for its immediate implementation and members of the IICM advocating a slower, more measured approach, it is assumed by all involved that some form of contextual theology for Northern Ireland is needed and would be beneficial. As a result of this tacit agreement, there has been no consideration of the opposing argument, which asks whether a specifically Northern Irish contextual theology would actually have any positive benefits for relationships between the churches, and indeed for wider society. It could be argued that an attempt to develop a Northern Irish theology, along the lines of that produced in South Africa and Latin America, would be artificial as the conflicts there are based upon opposing political blocs rather than the fusion of economic, historical, cultural and religious factors seen in Northern Ireland. In addition to this and on a more basic level, from the Meeting's past use of its publications, it is evident that little use would be made of the material produced, and that, once more, the initial push for a consideration of the theological issues surrounding the conflict in Northern Ireland would have to come from local groups, although how this would manifest itself is as yet unclear.

There is a strong argument to be made for such discussions to take place within the IICM. It is obvious that the members of the IICM pride themselves on the quality of relationships, trust and understanding that has been developed since 1973. Indeed, it has been noted that this is one of the main ways in which the Meeting has changed: 'the way of doing business has changed because relationships between the individuals involved have grown, there is a greater understanding of our respective constituencies'[100] and, as their exercises in comparative theology illustrate, relationships between the members of the IICM are good. Thus, whilst the creation of such an understanding is in itself an extremely important element in the development of national level inter-church dialogue, such strong relationships should allow for an attempt to ecumenically address the theological implications of the situation in Northern Ireland, even if this would serve no wider purpose than further improving relationships within the IICM.

An attempt to address the Irish situation was made in 1997 with the publication of *Freedom, Justice and Responsibility in Ireland Today*,[101] but this effort stands as a lone, and not very effective, monument to the creation of an ecumenical and contextual theology for Northern Ireland at a hierarchical level. This report seems to have been linked to the *Sectarianism: A Discussion Document* in that it attempted to assess the role that the churches have played in the perpetuation of the conflict in Northern Ireland, hoping to translate this into a blueprint for church-based reconciliation.

> Our aim is to present a critique or audit of the effectiveness of the Churches in Ireland today in relation to key trends and issues on which freedom, justice and responsibility have a bearing ... Our audit does not claim to be exhaustive, but it does aim to help the Churches identify areas in which their own contribution to society on the island of Ireland might be more in line with Gospel values.[102]

Whilst the authors take the ideas of liberation theology and South African contextual theology as a starting point,[103] they are not willing to go as far as their Latin American and South African counterparts in the production of a theology for Northern Ireland. They prefer, instead, to concentrate upon the themes of forgiveness and healing in society, believing that attempts to develop a specifically Northern Irish contextual theology could be detrimental to relationships arguing that 'fired up by the Gospel vision and by a "politically correct" theological response, one might be tempted to propose some radical action that would simply not work'.[104] Furthermore, the development of a contextual theology is not possible because they argue, quite correctly, that 'the Churches are not in a strong position as institutions to be agents of change and blanket proposals will not automatically work'.[105] They thus begin by looking at the churches' role in the conflict concluding that 'the Churches ... have become not "places of meeting with differences" but "protective fortresses for threatened people rather than places of open and profound discussion"'.[106] Consequently, any Christian theology for the area needs to centre on the two key issues of reconciliation and solidarity. These twin processes are presented as long-term strategies and are likened to the political process of negotiation that was being carried out in Northern Ireland.

Through this document the IICM are indicating their desire that the churches should be a part of the possible solution by working together rather than continue as a divisive influence:

> The role of the Churches is not to insist on one particular political solution to the exclusion of all others, still less to claim that any such solution is absolute or imperative on religious grounds, but to create the conditions in which political compromise becomes possible by giving an example of reconciliation based upon forgiveness. Far from watering down the Christian faith, this would vindicate it as a force for peace.[107]

However, this is as far as the document goes and most of the language used was in the future tense indicating that as churches they were not prepared or ready to work together on this theology until some future point.

However, as part of their conclusion the members of the working party did offer three suggestions for reconciliation within Ireland. First that the member churches each undertake a review of their pastoral strategy, second that the churches 'come together in a common confession of guilt'[108] by naming their failures as churches and finally that they all take up the suggestion of 'ecumenical tithing'[109] put forward by Michael Hurley in the 1980s. Each of these suggestions were practical rather than theological and have not been implemented fully by any of the member churches. Thus, although, they were taking into account the societal element of reconciliation, instead of the personal,[110] *Freedom, Justice and Responsibility* could not even be seen as an attempt to create a new theological paradigm; rather it is an articulation of the initial thoughts of the Meeting on a theology for Northern Ireland.

As McMaster, Smyth and Lennon have pointed out, the dialogue that is needed for the churches to take their ecumenical role in Northern Ireland seriously has still not occurred, and the Department of Theological Questions has subsequently returned to its comparative model of theology. Immediately after *Freedom, Justice and Responsibility* was published, the IICM established a working party entitled 'Being Church in the New Millennium', which reported in 2000, 'the aim [of which was] to encourage people to reflect on what being Church means and what it might mean'.[111] Shortly afterwards, in 2001, a working party on spirituality was founded which explored the various definitions of spirituality held by the churches in Ireland, the results of which were published in 2005.[112]

Both of these documents focus on similar themes and without actually explicitly stating it, it is apparent that the IICM are exploring the ways in which the churches can deal with the challenge of Ireland's rapid secularisation. So for example, *Being Church in the New Millennium* states that 'there has been much discussion – both within the Department of Theological Questions and outside it – about the ways in which church and society are changing rapidly, and about the ways in which the Church can hope most effectively to continue to speak to that changed society'.[113] Similarly, in the introduction to *The Dearest Freshness Deep Down Things*, David Stevens asserts that

Exploring what is meant by the word 'spirituality' in Ireland today raises profound questions as to how Christian faith and the Church relates to contemporary Irish society ... The search for meaning and for transcendence beyond contemporary consumerism comes in many guises. The fundamental challenge for the Church ... is the need to undergo changes that will make it more fit to engage missionally with the new spiritualities.[114]

As a result of this common theme of secularisation, these two reports build upon one another, whilst doing little to develop an agreement between the member churches of the IICM on the issues discussed. Both reports, or discussion documents as they were called by the IICM, were entirely comparative in their approach, failing even to create a synthesis of the working party's findings, as had previously been the practice, and instead producing a series of essays on the topic under discussion.

*Being Church in the New Millennium* is essentially a position paper. It aims to determine the place that the churches, both Protestant and Catholic, hold within society by examining issues such as public perception of the churches and the influence that the increasing pluralism within Irish society is having upon them. Some of the conclusions reached in the discussion document are challenging. For example, 'The Church's task is always to open up, stretch and expand horizons and to challenge all local and denominational parochialism. Indeed, denominational or confessional traditions are becoming less and less meaningful in today's global experience. We may well be in a post-denominational, post-confessional age.'[115] However, the discussion document does little to build upon these ideas, offering them merely as starting points for debates between unspecified groups of people. Similarly, *The Dearest Freshness Deep Down Things* focuses upon the changes in Irish society, its attitudes towards spirituality and the means by which the churches can harness new ideas. It asks questions such as how are people nourished by the faith of your church? What is going on in Ireland today that makes the word 'spirituality' so prominent? And finally, what is the way forward for us as churches?

These documents represent a new departure for the Department of Theological Questions, signalling a wish to engage with Irish society regarding issues that the Meeting obviously feels to be of theological concern. However, both documents do this in what can only be called a superficial manner, the results of which indicate that the members of the working party are not engaging with one another, but merely providing an account of their thoughts and ideas on the topic at hand without discussing what these actually mean for ecumenical relationships. As a result, since 1997 the Department of Theological Questions has not been producing material that demonstrates an advancement in relationships between the member churches of the IICM. Instead, they appear to have gone backwards, no longer producing the statements which demonstrate the common ground and differences between the churches, seen for example in *Salvation and Grace*, preferring instead to present eclectic material in the form of discussion documents, which does little other than exhibit the opinions of those writing.

## THE RECORD OF THE IICM 1980–2005

Whether by accident or deliberate design, when restructuring the IICM in the mid-1980s those involved put structures in place which were to take national- level ecumenical dialogue in a whole new direction. Thus, through the work of the Department of Social Issues and the Department of Theological Questions, we can see firstly, a growing realisation that the churches needed to be involved in social issues and secondly, the idea that ecumenism and community relations were two separate areas through which the churches could work together. In their desire to redefine their role, the churches seem to have gone too far trying to redress the balance in favour of social issues and in particular community relations, placing more of an emphasis upon social than doctrinal issues, a point acknowledged by the Executive Secretary when he stated that 'the social issues have dominated over the theological issues for quite a long time. DTQ has been put onto the back burner',[116] when in the 1970s the converse had been true. In essence the purpose of the IICM did not really change after 1984, although the balance of emphasis did. However, if the *raison d'être* of the IICM was merely to foster relationships and understanding between its member churches, then by 2005 through their publications they had done just that, even if the exact means of doing so had changed. Nevertheless, the subjects tackled, especially by the Department of Social Issues, indicate that they aspired to be something more than merely a talking shop attempting instead to create models whereby the churches could work together to promote good community relations and reconciliation, both between Protestants and Catholics and more recently the new migrant communities living in Ireland, and in this they have failed. Although their work could be credited with inspiring the establishment of a number of peace and reconciliation education initiatives, it was left to a number of committed mavericks who brought the vision of these reports and discussion documents to fruition rather than a concerted effort by the institutionalised churches. Furthermore, in doctrinal and theological discussion they appear to have gone backwards, living in splendid isolation from world-wide theological trends and producing one feeble attempt at a theology of reconciliation for Northern Ireland, preferring instead to concentrate upon the comparative theology that had characterised their pre-1984 encounters.

Much of this failure on the part of the IICM to build upon the foundations laid by their working parties is due to their lack of definition and purpose. During this period, despite the organisational restructuring, they were still very much an *ad hoc* body with no aims or objectives, moving from one project to the next in reaction to suggestions by individual members. Furthermore, their failure to tackle the Northern Irish situation theologically may have been a result of attitudes towards terrorism amongst the churches. Thus, the employment of the models of critical theology used in Latin America and South Africa would be seen as an endorsement of terrorism:

> No Irish Protestant church ever made a statement about South Africa against Apartheid because there was a reading of the rest of the world through the narrow lens of Northern Ireland, if you were to come out against apartheid you would be seen to be pro ANC and viewing them through Northern Ireland lens they were terrorists and that would get the whole thing messed up and cloudy in relation to the Provisional IRA ... The other thing that you would perhaps find is that there would be a prejudice still on the part of a lot of people to Liberation theology about something to do with again upsetting the status quo, revolution, terrorism, communism and the shutters go up.[117]

However, by the mid-1990s, despite or maybe because of the continued drift of the work of the Meeting's two departments, attempts were being made to address the haphazard nature of the IICM and to redefine its purpose as an inter-church body. The plans for this new council of churches for Ireland and the reactions to them tell us much about how far inter-church relations had progressed at a national level and indeed how much impact it had made beyond those directly involved in its work.

## THE NEW COUNCIL OF CHURCHES FOR IRELAND 1996–99.

By the early 1990s the members of the IICM were beginning to realise that the Meeting's work was ineffective. A discussion document, written in 1992, noted that '[t]here is an air of drift about our work, we go through the motions, we don't expect to be taken too seriously, and generally we need a renewal of purpose and a sense that what we are doing is worthwhile.'[118] Consequently, they realised that the structure and organisation of the IICM's work needed a radical overhaul if they were going to have any affect upon Northern Irish society, especially in relation to supporting the political process that was occurring during the mid 1990s, as they had argued was their role in *Freedom, Justice and Responsibility*. The proposed restructuring of relationships would, for the first time, see a formalisation of relationships and more importantly dialogue, between Catholics and Protestants in Ireland (as the IICM had previously been an unofficial body). Accordingly, both the proposals and the reaction to them, within the Presbyterian Church in particular, demonstrate the progress that had been made in inter-church relations since the early 1970s.

In 1996 a review group was established to assess the structures of inter-church relations in Ireland mainly because 'the agenda of the [ICC] had decreased and that of the [IICM] had increased but the [ICC] was still the body with the staff and was having to pay them'.[119] The report argued that changes were needed because:

> Beyond and more important than issues of appropriate structures, all churches are now operating in the context of increasing secularism and indifference. Added to this there is in Northern Ireland a context of conflict, division and sectarianism which puts an onus on the churches being seen to work together as much as possible. This suggests the particular importance today of co-operating together, where faith, church discipline and conscience make this possible, as a witness to Irish society, North and South, 'so that the world may believe' (Jn 17:21).[120]

It was suggested that changes take place in two areas: structure and role. As the new Council of Churches in Ireland (CCI) was to become the main focus for inter-church relations on the island, a more formal set of arrangements was put forward in the report. Thus, in addition to the previously established inter-church meeting and inter-church committee, forum meetings were proposed which would:

- Provide an opportunity for deepening the relationships between the churches;
- Discuss and deliberate on issues of importance to the member churches;
- Help to establish the direction and agenda of the IICM;

- Perform necessary legal and constitutional functions, receive accounts, elect office bearers, etc.;
- Receive reports from the IICC, Departments, sub-committees etc.[121]

The work of the forum would be to support the Committee in establishing 'the direction and agenda'[122] of the IICM itself. The report also suggested that steps be taken to try and stabilise the membership as:

> Those who attend the Meetings have no responsibility for the IICM structure, nor is the working of the structure responsible or accountable to them. Those who attend the meetings may only have a limited knowledge of what the IICM does, as they are often only appointed for a particular meeting. All of this made sense at the beginning, but there are now issues around the purpose of the meeting that need to be looked at.[123]

This, the report argued, would be crucial to the success of the new arrangements as by requiring 'the churches to appoint people to be their representatives on the IICM rather than attend "one-off" meetings ... significant continuity of membership'[124] would ensue. It was also recommended that the Meeting increase its membership from 56 to 74 and that the members continue to be divided equally between the Protestant and Catholic Church, with the Catholics having 37 members, the PCI and COI 10 each, the Methodists 5 and the other churches 12 between them.[125] Such changes would have seen the formalisation of inter-church relations, with the Meeting becoming the main focus for relationships between the Protestant and Catholic Churches and 'would for the first time, become a proper legal entity with its own constitution, which could then obtain charitable status'.[126]

However, despite the changes in structure, the authors of the report were content with the direction that the IICM had been taking previously, as the aims and functions of the new body demonstrate. They recommended that it should be:

- A forum where the member churches meet, discuss and consult together;
- To assist the member churches to grow in their understanding of each other, in accordance with the will of Christ;
- To assist the member churches to co-operate and act together as appropriate;
- To foster and support inter-church initiatives at local level;

- To make known to the churches and community what is happening at all levels in the area of inter-church activity.

The IICM will continue not to be a forum for church union negotiations.[127]

Each of these represent a continuation of the IICM's work since 1973, high-lighting that the changes were not 'going to change the agenda or what the inter-church meeting [was] about [but rather were] a tidying up process'.[128] Consequently, little is said in the report regarding the issue of dialogue on either theological or social issues and this lack of clarity was to prove to be one of the most problematic elements for those opposing the new structures. This was because many feared that the confessional basis of the Meeting encapsulated in their guidelines for membership which stated that 'The Irish Inter-Church Meeting is a fellowship of Churches in Ireland which confess the Lord Jesus Christ as God and Saviour according to the Scriptures and therefore seek to fulfil their common calling to the glory of the one God, Father, Son and Holy Spirit',[129] would allow dialogue on church unity to creep into the Meeting's agenda, despite reassurances to the contrary written into the constitution. Indeed, it was viewed by some members to be a failure in the restructuring that some kind of doctrinal basis[130] had not been established, as this would have indicated the progress that had been made in relationships, and consequently the plans were seen by such people as 'the best that could be achieved at this stage'.[131]

In these proposed changes to the IICM there were plans which, if implemented, could have radically altered the form of inter-church relations in Ireland, whilst doing very little to address the drift that was occurring in its purpose and intent throughout the 1980s and 1990s that had caused the review group to be established in 1996. Nevertheless, these proposals were sent to the member churches for their comments. Most welcomed the implementation of such plans believing them to reflect the needs of the society that they would be serving, presumably because they formalised relationships and reflected the spirit of the Good Friday Agreement as 'there is an analogy between the role of the churches in the future and the role of the participants in the new executive ... if you get ... different ... groups working together tackling common problems then you will overcome the hostilities gradually by getting people to focus on things other than differences'.[132] Thus, the Methodist inter-church committee stated that 'the need for a more formal structuring has been emerging for some time ... There is life and vitality as churches seek relationships of understanding and co-operation. The context also changes as inter-church relationships in Ireland now develop within a peace process moving towards a political settlement and change.'[133] However, despite such endorsements from the other churches, the General Assembly of the Presbyterian Church in Ireland voted against the measure 244 votes to 144 in its meeting in June 1999.[134] Three main reasons have been put forward for the failure of these proposals in the Presbyterian Church: first, dissatisfaction with the structure of the proposed body, second, anti-Catholicism and, third, the political uncertainty faced by the Protestant community.

Many of those opposing the new body were uncomfortable with its composition as it 'was to be fifty per cent RC and fifty per cent Protestant we had a major problem with that needless to say. They [the Catholic Church] had a veto on absolutely everything.'[135] However, this explanation has been totally dismissed by David Stevens, who argues that 'we had sought to remove all the issues that people could fight about ... there was no [doctrinal] base to the body, we had created a situation where there had to be a very high level of consensus: there had to be a 90% agreement before decisions were taken which meant that Presbyterians had a veto. So a lot of safeguards were built into the structure.'[136]

It is generally agreed, amongst those who witnessed the debate on the changes in the General Assembly of the Presbyterian Church that the primary motivation for those who fought against the new body was anti-Catholicism: 'those who were against it would say that it wasn't just anti-Catholic stuff, but I would see it as that, it sounded like that'.[137] However, the basis for the opposition to the body was not sectarian but rather was theological in nature, motivated by a fear that closer links with the Catholic Church would facilitate a dilution of reformed theology. Those who voted against the measures were situated on the more conservative, evangelical wing of the Presbyterian Church and were strongly opposed to any resolution being passed that would see stronger, more formal links being created with catholicism. They feared that it could lead to more concessions being made to Rome in the future arguing that 'folk might infer that it was anti-Catholicism but if it was, it was anti-Catholicism on theological grounds'.[138] Furthermore, they were concerned that involvement in a formal body with the Catholic Church would lead to key doctrinal issues being compromised:

> We wish to maintain and promote good relationships with all the people of Ireland of all religious persuasions, but this is not done at the cost of doctrinal compromise. That doctrinal compromise is reflected in the ICRB [inter-church relations board of the PCI] by the vague confessional basis proposed, by woolly phrases such as

'journey in faith together' and by the tacit acceptance throughout that the Roman Catholic Church is a true church ... We cannot participate in spiritual business with those who detract from the centrality of Christ and the glory of the Gospel of His grace.[139]

Thus, according to both members of the pro and anti-groups it was theological differences that caused the failure of this motion. However, this was not just caused by the innate conservatism of the members of the General Assembly themselves but also by the attitudes of their congregations. Thus, this fear of the conservative forces within the PCI both clergy and lay, contributed to the result as many of those who were entitled to vote found urgent reasons to be elsewhere resulting in only 400 out of a possible 1200 ballots being cast.[140] This was because:

> Evangelicals are intent on preserving what they call doctrinal purity, fearing that compromising Calvin on one issue will lead to more com-promises. Moderates are hesitant to cast a ballot for more ecumenism because they would have to go back home and face more conserva-tive folks who sit in their pews many of whom don't consider Catholicism to be Christian faith, and who use the Roman Church's doctrines about justification, transubstantiation and the role of Christ as evidence.[141]

Or, as one Presbyterian minister put it, 'they are scared of the mayhem that it [would] create in the congregations that they [would] not want to do that'.[142] Furthermore, the anti-ecumenical group within the Presbyterian Church was highly organised and many of those in favour of the motion felt that the campaign established by this group was cru-cial to the failure of the vote. This was because 'they went out and made very considerable efforts to make sure that their supporters who would all be voting no turned up to vote no',[143] whereas those in favour of the idea were reluctant to turn their church into a political party by cam-paigning in such a manner. John Dunlop summed up the feelings of the pro-ecumenical group thus:

> My general policy is that the boards of the church like the inter-church relations board does its work, keeps the church informed over what it's doing as it has done over the years and brings its reports to the General Assembly and it ought not to be the case that people are campaigning out round the churches, producing leaflets and running meetings and all kinds of stuff. That's not the way I personally want to see the church run because it's to turn the ethos of the church into a kind of political party and I'm not much in

favour of that. I think what happens from time to time is people like me lose votes which are key votes because we are not prepared to engage in that kind of lobbying activity.[144]

The anti-ecumenical group within the Presbyterian Church is a highly organised machine and this factor contributed greatly to the failure of the vote. They were initially established about 1979 as the Campaign for Complete Withdrawal by a group of Presbyterian evangelical clergy who were determined to see the withdrawal of the Presbyterian Church from the World Council of Churches. The basis of their argument was 'that this kind of ecumenism was not really in line with biblical ecumenism,[145] that it didn't define matters clearly enough in respect of the doctrine of scripture, of salvation and the church'.[146] They thus organised rallies and public debates with those in favour of the work of the World Council of Churches in a bid to force the General Assembly to vote for the withdrawal of the Presbyterian Church in Ireland from the Council. Once this was achieved they changed their name to the Campaign for Concerted Witness to Reformed Truth, stressing that they wanted to see the growth of biblical ecumenism rather than dialogue with the unreformed tradition of catholicism culminating in the withdrawal of the Presbyterian Church from the Council of Churches in Britain and Ireland. They then changed their name to the current Movement for Presbyterian Reform, which has:

> local groups drawn from Presbyterian areas, its magazine deals with general issues trying to encourage this positive education. I think that it would be fair to say that there has been quite a change in evangelicalism within our church, over the years it has grown from a low ebb to a position of respect and authority within the church and what we are trying to do now is to foster an attitude of biblical reform which has a biblical basis for what it does.[147]

It is evident from the vote in the General Assembly in 1999 that consistency, despite the numerous name changes, has been the motif of the anti-ecumenical movement within Presbyterianism. Thus, the ideology of this group has been constant in the years since its foundation with its discomfort with formal dialogue which involves the Catholic Church. Indeed, even the most cursory of glances at the language used in their promotional literature would bear such an assertion out. So, for example, whilst a pamphlet written in 1979 to support their campaign to withdraw from the World Council of Churches states:

> We are opposed to the [World Council of Churches] for we see it as a corruption of or a counterfeit Christianity, but our ardour and

intensity of feeling is towards what we believe in, not an attack upon those whose views differ from our own ... We can extend the hand of **friendship** but **not of fellowship** to those who do not hold the essential doctrines of the faith. Yet membership of the [World Council of Churches] commits Presbyterians to a fellowship with those who, by our standards, are apostate.[148]

The same themes regarding the potential pollution of reformed theology through contact with Catholics are repeated in 1989 during the campaign to prevent association with the new council of churches in Britain and Ireland, as they 'are uncompromisingly committed to the Biblical and Reformed Faith of our Church and its Doctrinal Standards' and that they monitor any form of ecumenical relationship which involves Presbyterians 'as part of our concern that the Biblical and Reformed witness of our Church should be unhindered or undiminished by association with error and compromise'.[149] Finally, as we have already seen, similar language was used by the Movement for Presbyterian Reform in their 1999 campaign, with sole concentration being upon the unreformed nature of Catholicism and the need to guard against Rome:

> That the Roman Catholic Church has a fifty per cent membership in all aspects of this proposed body indicates a desire on their part to control proceedings ... It is often emphasised that the various churches hold many doctrines in common, but side by side with this should be remembered that additional teachings can radically alter the overall message ... The decision of the [PCI] in June to reject proposals to constitute the Conference of Churches in Ireland was in line with examples of biblical concern to guard and preserve the integrity of the Gospel of grace.[150]

Thus, their anti-catholicism is an ideology based upon theological and doctrinal factors and, as they see it, is their main motivation in campaigning against formal links with the Catholic Church. Furthermore, such arguments indicate that theological discomfort was the key factor in the failure of the motion in the General Assembly in June and that any other factors can only be seen to be relevant in so far as they would compromise the anti-ecumenists' desire to protect the reformed faith from Roman influences.

However, it has also been suggested that the political climate of the time contributed greatly to the outcome of the vote. The General Assembly took place during a period of political flux, with the Peace Process facing an uncertain future. Thus, it has been argued that many of those who voted no did so because they felt that as a community the Protestant population had already conceded too much to the Nationalist/Republican/Catholic community and they therefore refused to concede any further: 'You can't avoid the fact that the divisions within the political systems are not (purely) over political issues. There's a deep-seated religious feeling in there. That's all a part of it.'[151] Despite the timing of the vote those standing against the establishment of the new conference of churches in Ireland totally dismiss this idea, arguing that:

> We are committed at our ordination to teach doctrine ... and defend it, I think the phrase is, to our utmost power. And I'm not too happy to become deeply involved with a denomination that does not (have) the same doctrinal standards ... Obviously the Roman Catholic Church has many doctrines that are unscriptural. This has nothing to do with politics.[152]

Whilst another leading member of the campaign has pointed out that the political problems of the time could have prompted people to vote either way:

> I think it could have influenced people in both directions because I think that some people had a siege mentality and thought that they were going to be sold down the river and therefore we really need to take this opportunity to back off from the RC church. But I think others probably felt that if we opt into this body it may well in someway endorse the peace process and they were saying that we are not in the business of cutting ourselves off from people we are willing to draw nearer to them and I think that I heard those arguments probably mentioned at the General Assembly.[153]

It would seem that a number of factors, most notably the strength of anti-Catholic feeling within the Presbyterian Church, contrived to bring about the failure of this motion and as a result, plans for the new body have been suspended after the other member churches of the inter-church bodies were asked if they wished to continue with the scheme. All agreed, with the exception of the Non-Subscribing Presbyterian Church and the Catholic Church.[154] The Catholic hierarchy explain their stance thus:

> in theory eleven of the twelve accepted it. The fact is that the largest (Protestant) grouping in the North was saying no and there was no way that I could have got it past our conference that we should go on putting resources into a new body that would have been excluding the contact we have with the largest Protestant church in the North.[155]

In reality, it is unlikely that the subject of a merger between the ICC and the IICM will be broached again for a number of years. As one Church of Ireland clergyman put it:

> As things stand at the moment there's no indication whatsoever that there would be a change ... I did actually try to get the matter onto the agenda [of the IICM] again but there was very strong resistance from the Presbyterians not to have the matter considered again ... The General Assembly [of the Presbyterian Church] doesn't like to reconsider a matter that it's dealt with, and certainly [not] within a short period of time.[156]

Nevertheless, the period after the failed vote saw a 'considerable [financial] restructuring of the ICC/IICM relationship and since the failed CCI initiative the Roman Catholic Church has significantly increased its financial contribution'.[157] However, this financial restructuring made little difference as between 1999 and 2005 relationships between the Catholic and Protestant Churches continued in much the same vein as they had before the attempts to amalgamate the IICM and ICC, as the work of the Departments of Theological Questions and Social Issues so clearly demonstrates.

Perhaps the most interesting feature of the failure to establish a Council of Churches for Ireland has been the reactions of the various churches involved since the Presbyterian rejection in 1999. Events since this demonstrate a great deal about the nature of inter-church relationships at a national level and the difficulties faced by those wishing to engage in dialogue. The strongest reaction came from the Church of Ireland, which had been the main instigator of the proposed changes. Indeed, it has been observed that 'the most pessimistic ... would have been the Church of Ireland ... because in [a] sense the whole movement towards [the changes] were to some extent Church of Ireland driven'.[158] A general sense of frustration at the progression of national-level relationships pervades the discourse within the Church of Ireland on the matter, with the Annual Reports of the Church Unity Committee to the General Synod making this clear.[159] Indeed, as recently as 2004 an editorial in the *Church of Ireland Gazette* demonstrated the Church's feelings on the matter quite clearly:

> The 'twin track' ecumenism of the Irish Council of Churches (without the Roman Catholic Church in membership) and the Irish Inter-Church Meeting (including the ICC churches and the Roman Catholic Church) is a cumbersome arrangement that cannot be as

efficient as a single structure would be. While attempts have been made in the past to bring a single organization into being, they have not proved fruitful, in particular because of the unwillingness of the Presbyterian Church to agree to proposals. Our national ecumenical structures are not good ecumenical practice and we must never become resigned to these circumstances. Indeed, when the new General Secretary of the Irish Council of Churches, Michael Earle, arrives next month (he has been General Secretary of the Conferences of Churches in Aotearoa New Zealand), it is to be hoped that the Church of Ireland will appoint a senior delegation to meet with him and outline current reservations about the ecumenical structures.[160]

In short, the Church of Ireland seems to believe that 'relations are always as they were'[161] and that a willingness for them to remain so is preventing progression at a national level.

However, it would appear from the reactions of the Presbyterian Church, and to a lesser extent the Catholic Church since the events of June 1999, that many of those involved in national level inter-church dialogue in Northern Ireland simply are not ready for the formalisation of relationships that the establishment of the Council of Churches in Ireland would have entailed. As the events of June 1999 so clearly demonstrated, matters pertaining to ecumenical relations in Ireland have always been highly contentious within the Presbyterian Church, as one Presbyterian pointed out 'there's always been a tension over that issue'[162] and it is unlikely to be resolved. This tension manifested itself once more at the Presbyterian Church's General Assembly in 2004 when the Moderator Elect, Rev. Ken Newell, invited the Catholic Archbishop, Sean Brady, to attend as a personal guest. This angered many conservative members of the Church, especially the Movement for Presbyterian Reform, and led three of the 21 presbyteries in Ireland, Foyle, Tyrone and Ballymena, to write to Ken Newell to express 'concern and hurt at the invitation'.[163] However, during the Assembly itself the matter was not raised because of a protest by Ian Paisley. 'Rev Paisley did Dr Newell a very great favour. By the extremity of his language[164] and behaviour outside Church House in Belfast on Monday, he silenced those would be critics-within of Newell, for inviting Archbishop Brady ... No matter how deeply some delegates felt, none wanted to be associated with Dr Paisley's protest.'[165] Be that as it may, such events highlight the problematic nature of any form of inter-church contact for the Presbyterian Church, which is 'divided theo-culturally'[166] between the Conservatives and Liberals. At present, this division is managed, more by accident than design, by the election 'in alternate years [of] a moderate ecumenically minded Moderator, followed by a more conservative evangelical non-ecumenical Moderator'.[167]

As a result, since 1999 relations between the Presbyterian Church and the Catholic Church have been proceeding quietly and it is evident that this status quo is one that most Presbyterians are happy with. As one observer put it, 'I think the Presbyterian Church is much more open than sometimes supposed. Well, a larger number of its people are more open to dialogue and contact than they are given credit for, provided you don't scream to the General Assembly of the Presbyterian Church, that this is what is happening!'[168] Indeed, it is evident that the Presbyterian Church would like to maintain an informal relationship with the Catholic Church, arguing that 'We have an informal link through the IICM and the anti-people are happy with that informal link.'[169] Furthermore, even many of the anti-ecumenical group are not opposed to contact with their Catholic counterparts:

> You can go into all sorts of places where you have ministers who have the greatest difficulty in terms of worshipping with Catholics but are more than happy to be involved in typical church projects on the ground because our aims in terms of the well being and welfare of the people are very similar.[170]

This indicates that in their adoption of a two-pronged approach to relationships between Protestants and Catholics, separating community relations out from ecumenism, the IICM have been picking up on a trend which is increasingly occurring at a local level in Northern Ireland. However, they have not been able to harness such advancements into a formal structure.

Consequently, the events of 1999 and the subsequent reaction to them tell us a great deal about the nature of relationships between the Protestant and Catholic Churches at a national level. The first, and arguably most important, concerns the speed at which such relationships develop and the need for those involved to be sensitive to the problems that their co-ecumenists face within their own denominations. However, despite this need, frustrations concerning the 'messy' structure of national level dialogue are so high in some quarters that the Secretary of the Irish Council of Churches felt compelled to offer his counsel regarding this issue. In the 2005 *Annual Report*, he said that: 'I am very aware of the ongoing frustrations in maintaining these dual structures (ICC and IICM) but maintain this is a matter of waiting for God's Kairos/timing to include everyone and that the member churches' commitment to each other is more important than finding perfect structures.'[171] This lack of synchronicity on the part of the member churches of the ICC/IICM regarding structure indicates two further issues resulting from 1999, denominational commitment and definition, which both raise questions regarding the work of the IICM.

Whilst relationships between individuals had undoubtedly matured, this work has not been translated into a commitment on the part of denominations to the work of the IICM. Contact at a national level between the Protestant and Catholic Churches is still fundamentally based upon relationships between individuals which 'require a certain amount of history'[172] as well continuity and commitment over time because 'if you bring in a lot of new blood, you end up starting back where everybody started'.[173] However, the individual denominations do not view this need for continuity as important to the work of the Meeting with the membership changing from year to year. The ICC 'is not aware of any member church giving priority to appoint/employ a person with the sole focus of advancing the ecumenical mandate in their church; ecumenism is more likely to be reduced to being an extra voluntary role to be added to many other tasks of ministry'.[174] Consequently, the IICM is reduced to 'hobby' of a few committed individuals rather than something that the whole denomination could feel ownership of – a problem which undoubtedly led to some of the reactions and misunderstandings seen in the debates surrounding the creation of the new Council of Churches.

This problem is exacerbated by the 'drift' in inter-church relations noted by O'Hanlon.[175] This issue was still very much in evidence throughout the proposals put forward by the review group and even in 2004 there were serious debates being carried out regarding the definition of ecumenism in Ireland.[176] Thus, whilst the Meeting would have been formalised had these ideas been implemented, there was no clear plan detailing the direction that the Meeting would take especially in relation to theological matters. Furthermore, in that matter the Council of Churches in Ireland would still have been an improvised body committed to pursuing the two roads of ecumenism and community relations and improving relationships between the individuals who came into contact with it but would do little to move relationships between the Protestant and Catholic Churches themselves beyond a polite comparison of points of doctrine.

CONCLUSION

When asked what he thought of national-level ecumenical dialogue, a minister, who had been closely involved with the IICM, replied that it is 'of some symbolic importance but not much else'.[177] This assessment of the relationships occurring between the leaderships of the churches during this period is accurate. Indeed, despite the cosmetic changes in structure and attempts to broaden its remit, national-level inter-church relations were not any further developed by 2005 than they had been in 1980. This was because, at the most fundamental level, the participants were unable to move forward, prevented from capitalising upon the structural improvements of 1984, and acting upon the recommendations of their documents by the constraints of the member churches authority structures on the one hand, and a vocal conservative, evangelical element on the other. The record of the IICM and its contribution to inter-church relations in Northern Ireland, then, can be considered in two separate respects: its structural development and its work, represented by the various documents produced during this period.

At the end of the 1970s, ecumenical relationships involving the Catholic Church in Ireland were just moving out of their infancy, and one would have expected that in the years between 1980 and 2005 they would have improved to a point where formal structures, with a clear vision of their aims and objectives, would be in place. Whilst the structures of the IICM have improved to a certain extent, the organisational growth of inter-church relationships between Protestants and Catholics at a national level has been completely inadequate. The ease with which the structural improvements were implemented in 1984 indicated that the member churches of the IICM were willing to move relationships beyond the development of friendship and understanding witnessed in the 1970s, into ones which would allow for the measures recommended in the reports to be realised. However, as we have seen, this has not been the case, and the 1984 changes were, in fact, merely cosmetic, reorganising the way in which the IICM worked, instead of helping it to change its methods and therefore move forward. This lack of progress in national level dialogue was blatantly highlighted by the events of 1999, which cast doubt upon the strength of relationships in which the IICM take so much pride. The opposition showed that, despite all the dialogue, the IICM had done little to address people's objections to inter-church contact and was, in effect, merely talking to a converted and committed few, consequently, failing to try to reach beyond their immediate inner circle.

The changes that have taken place in the remit of the IICM tell a similar story. It cannot be denied that the ideology of the IICM has changed, and that they have radically altered their outlook on what inter-church relationships should mean in the context of Northern Irish socie-ty. Consequently, they have implemented a dual strategy of dialogue on ecumenism and community relations and through this separation have allowed some progress to be made on topics, such as sectarianism, where previously there would have been none. However, in the area where it could be argued that most was expected of them, theological dialogue, they have been comprehensively unsuccessful, ignoring world-wide trends in theological dialogue and clinging to their comparative method-ology. As a result, they have failed to address the situation in Northern Ireland from a theological perspective as one would expect of the churches or indeed, consider their own role in the conflict from a theo-logical perspective. Their only attempt to do so has been an ineffectual document which did not gain the wider currency needed to have an impact.

Much of this ineptitude may have been to do with the cyclical nature of inter-church relations, as the personnel of the Meeting is prone to change and time is needed to build up understanding and trust. However, this factor cannot be seen to account for twenty years of work. Furthermore, even when they tried to address matters of wider social concern, through the auspices of the DSI, they were unable to implement any of the necessary steps recommended in each of the three reports dis-cussed and, although they were to prove the inspiration for the founda-tion of a number of peace and reconciliation education initiatives, this was more due to good luck than good judgement. That said, however, the structural changes brought about as a result of the Ledwith–Poole report in 1984 have laid the foundation for an improvement in dialogue between the Catholic and Protestant Churches, and it is clear that the quality of work being produced after 1984 was an improvement on that of the 1970s even if it was not used. Thus, like their counterparts in the 1970s, the participants in the Meeting were afforded an opportunity to increase understanding of, and friendship with, other clergy, chances which they used to produce reports on matters of common concern but were unable to translate these possibilities into action. They failed to move further than their immediate circle and disseminate their work beyond those already committed to inter-church relationships. Consequently, from 1980 to 2005, the IICM was little more than a 'talk-ing shop', providing a figurehead for the inter-church movement, whilst the real work occurred within local churches and their communities.

## CHAPTER THREE

# Local Churches
# and Community Relations

In contrast to the slow progress being made in ecumenical relations at a national level, since 1980 the dynamics of inter-church relationships between Protestants and Catholics within local communities have radically altered. Indeed, 'one of the profoundest changes in the political climate in the North in recent years has come from the concerted effort by the Churches, among their members as well as between themselves, to further the cause of reconciliation'.[1] The years since 1980 have seen a blossoming of the relationships between members of the Protestant and Catholic Churches in many areas, as people began to express a desire to build meaningful relationships with one another. These relationships, although founded upon the Christian faith, were of a totally different nature to those seen at a national level. Instead of being based upon endless discussions concerning church unity and points of theology, it consisted of a desire to strive for reconciliation and unity through practical action based upon the faith of the participants and the values of peace[2] and reconciliation[3] found in the Gospel.[4]

Such interaction within local communities has occurred in five ways. the Ecumenical Community, discussed in the next chapter, lived and worked within an area providing support for the clergy and a 'safe,' neutral venue in which people could meet. The Clergy Fellowship is a clergy-only cross-denominational group hat allowed local clergy to meet and discuss matters of common concern and develop a much-needed support network. The third type of group is the clergy-led prayer and discussion group, which serves as an opportunity for people from the two communities to meet and pray together. Practical Ecumenism or Social Action Projects (SAPs) make up the fourth type of inter-church work in Northern Ireland through which the churches aimed to act together on the problems of the area, through, for example, the provision of unemployment advice centres or after-school play groups. In the 1990s, these were joined by a new type of group, the Church Fora, which represented an amalgamation of local discussion groups, both clergy and lay, and SAPs as the churches began to work more closely with their local councils' Community Relations Officer (CRO) in a bid to tackle the problems of the area. In the 1980s such groups were developed mainly through the personal contacts of the clergy. From about 1990 onwards the foundation of such projects has been aided, and indeed accelerated, by the increasing significance of the peace and reconciliation education initiative within Northern Ireland, which, with the assistance of the government, voluntary organisations and the hierarchies of the churches, aimed to provide support, training, resources and contacts for those who wished to develop any form of inter-church project.

The landscape of inter-church relations in 1980 was, to say the least, bleak and sparsely populated. In the early 1980s, there was an over-concentration of projects in urban areas in the eastern part of the province, with such relationships being mostly the preserve of the clergy and a few committed middle-class churchgoers.[5] However, the 1980s and early 1990s witnessed a massive growth in local inter-church relations, with new ways of encouraging contact between the two communities being introduced. During this period, the number of ecumenical communities and clergy groups in existence doubled, whilst discussion groups and SAPs increased their numbers more than four-fold. The social stratification of those involved in inter-church work was starting to change dramatically and by 1993 groups had been established in both rural, urban, inner-city and suburban areas with their form changing to take these new demographics into account. The paramilitary ceasefires and the accompanying political peace process of 1994 represented a turning point in local inter-church relations in Northern Ireland. For example, in the five-year period after 1994 nearly as many projects were formed within Northern Ireland as had been in the previous fourteen years. This trend was particularly noticeable in areas that had until that time been under-represented, such as Co. Tyrone, and highlighted the growing sophistication of the inter-church groups as they began to mould a number of different methods together to form a new one, the Church Fora, which took into account the changing situation.

This chapter will examine the evolution of local inter-church relationships looking at how Clergy and Lay Inter-Church Fellowships, Social Action Projects and Church Fora have redefined inter-church relations within Northern Ireland. It will first consider the early motivations and methods of these groups in the 1980s, then going on to examine their reactions to the changes in the nature of the Northern Irish political landscape which came in the mid-1990s and the fresh attempts at new methods of inter-church contact in the shape of the Church Fora, which these developments fuelled, whilst also looking at the apparent reasons for the vast increase that occurred since 1980.

## CLERGY AND LAY INTER-CHURCH FELLOWSHIPS

Although the initiatives taken by the Corrymeela Community and other organisations are more widely known, the earliest local inter-church contact took place through inter-church fellowships. These were the most common form of inter-church contact until 1994, when the paramilitary ceasefires enabled participants to develop more formal relationships through the Church Fora. Such fellowships were small parish-based prayer and discussion groups, consisting both of clergy and lay people, and were one of the most crucial and consistent elements in the development of community-based inter-church relations since the first group was founded in Co. Down in 1965.[6] They operated on a small scale and, although originally intended to be forums for shared prayer and Bible study, eventually developed into arenas in which matters of common concern, such as sectarianism and the political situation, could be discussed in a supportive and trusting environment. This occurred because 'so many of our problems, pastoral and spiritual, as well as social and economic problems, such as poverty, unemployment, youth alienation, marriage breakdown, are common to the members of all our Churches that the exchange of ideas regarding them could not but be mutually beneficial'.[7] The evolution from purely ecumenical prayer into the discussion of other non-theological matters did not occur within a specific time scale or even within every group. Instead, the move into more secular discussion occurred within some of the groups, based upon the growth of trust and understanding within that particular fellowship and not because of external events. The relationships formed through such groups have proved to be the springboard necessary for the development of numerous types of inter-church groups in Northern Ireland, including most of the ecumenical communities, a number of social action projects, and by 2005 most of the inter-church fellowships had transformed into Church Fora.

### Clergy Fraternals and Fellowships

The story of Clergy Fraternals and Fellowships in Northern Ireland is a varied one, their development and success almost entirely dependent upon the commitment of the clergy involved and, in the case of Protestant ministers, the attitudes of their congregations to contact with the Catholic Church. The Clergy Fraternal has been defined as a purely ecumenical body, centring upon prayer and theological issues, with the Community Relations Council Directory stating that 'the activities of these groups mostly include shared prayer and fellowship. Some of these groups organise specific events for the community in these areas.'[8] The experience of many members of Clergy Fraternals would concur with such a definition. Their activities centred upon prayer and reflection upon biblical passages with, for example, the members of one group meeting 'in each other's houses on a rotation basis ... one of the members delivers a short paper on the designated text. (This year we are studying St Luke's Gospel.) We finish with a prayer.'[9] The importance of the meetings lay not in their theological content, although this proved to be invaluable in understanding the differing theological perspectives of the Protestant and Catholic Churches, but instead was to be found, as their name suggests, in the fellowship developed. As the friendship and unity of the group grew, the members, like their counterparts at a national level, felt increasingly able to discuss issues unrelated to theological matters, which was of benefit to the community as a whole:

> It was a good meeting point in the sense that we did eventually move on from talking about the psalms and start talking about marching. Obviously there was no agreement there but at least there was an understanding of each other's position and I think that that understanding to some extent was fed back by the clergy there to their respective sides.[10]

The development of such friendships and understanding gave them the confidence to display their support for their fellow clergy, both Catholic and Protestant, in times of trauma and stress. For example, during the peak of sectarian assassinations in Belfast 'quite frequently several of the local ministers would come along to the funeral [of a victim of sectarian violence] to show their solidarity with the local priest and also to the local community. The example and strength that they gave to the people in mourning'[11] should not be underestimated. By their very existence these fellowships served to provide support and understanding for local clergy especially in areas where each of their congregations were faced with similar problems of, for example, sectarian violence.

Once a high level of trust and understanding had been developed within the group, the members often tried to strengthen and aid local community relations, with the Clergy Fraternal frequently serving as the voice of the area: 'Our Fraternal serves us well when it comes to liaison with either the press or the Borough Council. They want a united churches voice and we try to provide it.'[12] Thus, their greatest contribution to the local area is the example and support that they provide for the community. This can constantly be seen in the 'spiritual example' that they set:

> I think the fact that these meetings take place is a sort of sign to the wider community of an alternative way of doing things, so it's a sort of sign of the Kingdom, which is set up in the middle of a society which is suspicious, is polarised and has come through some very difficult times in the past.[13]

As well as providing a sign of acceptance of the 'other sort' to the local residents, the Clergy Fraternals and Fellowships were also frequently able to offer practical support to their communities. This has taken many forms, depending entirely upon the needs of the people in the area, and can be divided into three categories: negotiation, social activities and prayer.

The role of negotiator tended to be undertaken by Clergy Fraternals working in areas with contested marching routes or during times of civil strife. The members would approach the leaders of other groups in the area and discuss the issues with them as well as representing the views of the local residents to the police and political parties. A member of a North Belfast clergy group describes their role as talking

> to various people concerned with the parades issue because there is a big parade due to take place this year [2000] called the Tour of the North and it has given trouble in past years and we've been trying to encourage people to see if they can reach some kind of an agreement with one another, so we've met people from the parades commission, from the Orange Order and from Sinn Fein.[14]

Such activities were also of benefit to the growth of inter-church relations in the area because 'as well as that the meeting is providing us with the opportunity to interact with one another in that kind of way and address some of the issues in the area'.[15] This demonstrates exactly how the initial methods of these Clergy Fraternals can precipitate a move into community-relations work as enough trust and understanding had already developed to allow them to tackle a sensitive matter that was of concern to both communities in an equitable manner. Some Clergy Fraternals took a more active role in their local community than others, and this variation in activity and scope is due to the commitment of local clergy to the expansion of inter-church relations in their area, the amount of time actually available to them and to the length of time that the fraternal itself has been in existence.

As they become more established, many Clergy Fraternals become involved in organising cross-community events, which included both social activities and prayer. Many of these Fraternals, especially in Belfast, have been the motivating force behind the establishment of inter-church discussion and prayer groups involving members of their congregations, whilst others organise social events, such as quiz evenings, as a means of encouraging cross-community contact. Indeed, many local people look to their Clergy Fraternal to organise acts of joint witness, in the aftermath of an atrocity such as Omagh or during flash points during the year, such as the marching season. For example, in a mixed working-class area of Belfast the Clergy Fraternal organised an act of witness in the local park which is attended by 500 people who wish to counter the negative image projected by the Loyalist parades:

> On Easter Monday, the first loyalist parade of the year is always blocked at the bridge at the end of our area. So, on Good Friday we have organised an act of witness in the Ormeau Park here and we would have people from all Christian traditions here. We invite people from the churches from the other side of the bridge to come to us so that we show that despite the division that will appear on the TV in fact there are far more people coming together in unity. We have a march of witnesses up the road and we have a service, there would be five or six hundred people at it, whereas the Monday thing will have about 30 Apprentice Boys. The mass of the people we show are people who don't want to be polarised.[16]

Despite their differences in pace, attitude and approach to the issue of ecumenism and inter-church relationships, the Clergy Fraternal or Fellowship has proved to be one of the most important factors in the evolution of local inter-church contact in Northern Ireland since 1980. It has enabled friendships, which would otherwise have been unthinkable, to grow and has provided an example, both practical and spiritual, for the local community, in addition to creating an understanding of the viewpoints of the 'other side' which the clergy often relayed to their congregations. Such contact has benefited the local area by providing an alternative to sectarianism and has also helped to encourage lay people to establish and become involved in inter-church prayer and discussion groups themselves.

### Inter-church discussion and prayer groups involving lay people

In 1999 Johnston McMaster, co-ordinator of the Education for Reconciliation Programme at the Irish School of Ecumenics described the meetings between Protestant and Catholic lay people as 'integrated groups, some long standing, others more recent, and all initiated by a variety of experiences and responses to needs. Their aims and activities also reflect rich diversity, they also reflect rural, provincial and urban situations and highlight what is possible in many parts of Northern Ireland.'[17] From such a definition, it is clear that a great deal is expected of this form of inter-church contact. In their own way, each of these groups have been fundamental to the evolution of local inter-church relations and have taken on board the imperative for reconciliation found in the Gospel and applied it to their own specific situation. They do so by trying 'to get to know people from the other side of the community ... hopefully this will lead to a better understanding of each other. On our own we can accomplish little and through conferences and discussion groups we encourage others to do whatever is possible in their own situations.'[18]

Until the mid-1990s, the establishment of such groups was constant, and although this would suggest that their motivation was mainly spiritual and based upon a desire to pray together, this was not the case. Instead, the discussion and prayer groups founded during this period were established for myriad reasons. These ranged from those founded in West Belfast by clergy who were interested in cross-community relations to those, like the Enniskillen inter-church project, established in response to acts of terrorism, or the Fitzroy/Clonard Fellowship which was founded 'in response to the [ongoing] situation of violence from a conviction that Christians should be a reconciling force'.[19] However, despite the range of reasons for their foundations, each of these groups, be they based in interface areas, affluent suburbs or rural market towns, were established with a similar idea in mind: the promotion of friendship and understanding between Protestants and Catholics, as the stated aims of a cross-section of groups suggest. They want 'to increase the impact of the Christian Churches by doing together what cannot be effectively done separately. To work closely together as Churches promoting friendship and understanding.'[20] 'To foster understanding and fellowship.'[21] 'To promote the understanding of each other's Christian beliefs and views. To build friendships and organise joint Christian activities.'[22]

Clergy and lay inter-church groups in Northern Ireland have taken a number of forms. During any given period, there have been women's prayer and discussion groups, biblical study groups, groups convened in the area for reflection and prayer for Lent and Advent, permanent inter-church councils, youth groups and inter-church partnerships between segregated areas, such as the Falls and the Shankhill. Like their clergy counterparts, the establishment and growth of these groups has been entirely dependent upon the situation in which they operate and has not been subject to trends. Nevertheless, the methods of discussion that they employ have been affected by the advent of the peace and reconciliation education initiative bringing with it the availability of outside help in running the group as opposed to the methods employed prior to 1990, described as:

> informal contacts with our friends who are working in other parts of Belfast and we find out what is happening in other areas. There is always some rotation of clergy especially in the Roman Catholic and Methodist churches and people come with experiences from other areas and sometimes we are able to apply them here.[23]

As with almost everything else in Northern Ireland, a person's experience of inter-church contact is entirely dependent upon the type of area in which they live and there is no clear definition of who the committed member of a local inter-church group might be:

> there is a broad range of people prepared to do it ... sometimes people think that it is only being done by professionally well-educated people in the community but this is not true, sometimes you can find the most bigoted people are wealthy middle-class well-educated people and some of the least bigoted people are people who come from poor areas of this society. On the other hand some of the people who are most heavily into this are affluent well-educated people and some of the people who are against it are in working-class areas so it splits right across the whole of society. There is no single stereotype in a sociological term of the type of person who is liable to be involved in this.[24]

Consequently, 'most parishes are at some level trying to do something on it,'[25] although the initial establishment of cross-community relationships is dictated by the demographic profile of the area in which the scheme is being established:

> We have a problem in this area which is shared by a lot of people [which] is that although I would have a very strong ecumenical dimension, in my wider ministry it is very difficult to apply it at street level as there are very few Catholics around here! There are only two Catholic parishes in the wider area, which are quite frankly drowned out by well-meaning ecumenical Protestants. We've a problem of building up a personal relationship between parishes.[26]

Once this issue had been overcome, socio-economic factors and the area's experience of violence play a much more crucial role in the development and form of cross-denominational groups.[27]

The experiences of a Protestant minister and a Catholic priest, both working ecumenically in West Belfast during the 1980s and early 1990s, illustrate the problems as well as the methods of inter-church contact. They testify that the development of inter-church links in such an area was an extremely slow and painstaking business, as 'a lot of the success of trying to encourage ecumenism at a grass roots level depends upon going at the right pace, listening to where people are and what questions they have instead of trying to push your own agenda'.[28] Both adopted such an approach, gaining the trust of their congregations before trying to establish links with other churches. They were able to tentatively establish inter-church discussion groups aimed at developing friendship and understanding between Protestants and Catholics in the area. However, due to the local paramilitary presence[29] even this was fraught with difficulty: 'Now we publicly announced the whole thing here and we would willingly have had them here but they couldn't come here and they could not announce it publicly because of the fear of the paramilitary elements in Sandy Row. We met in a neutral venue, which turned out to be a Dominican convent.'[30] Those that did respond to the idea of inter-church contact were enthusiastic and committed to the idea, with other groups, such as a youth group, being formed from the initial core group. Once the group was running successfully, the more reticent members of their congregation had warmed to the idea: 'In my parish in West Belfast I found that those who would have left the parish in the beginning when I first invited Catholic clergy to come and talk were becoming involved by the time that I left',[31] illustrating further the need for the development of trust in such encounters.

The clergy involved in these inter-church groups in West Belfast employed a number of methods, all of which are universally used by inter-church groups in Northern Ireland, highlighting the need to adopt a lowest common denominator approach[32] in building relationships between Protestants and Catholics. They began by inviting members of the clergy of other churches, with some success, to come and preach to their congregations. As trust and friendships grew and facilitators[33] became available, they started to introduce courses designed to foster understanding of the other side's identity within a controlled and safe environment. The experience of the group in West Belfast demonstrates this process:

> Cathy [Higgins of the ISE] took us through a whole process of getting to know one another. It was fascinating the way in which she did it

because here were people from very similar areas: working class, deprived, unemployment, the whole lot and living close to each other. She took us through one very interesting exercise where she put us into a Catholic and Church of Ireland group and said 'I want you to reflect on your own church, your own social condition and your own politics' ... and after we had done that she said 'I want you to reflect on their church, their social condition and their politics.' Then she said 'I want you to reflect upon what they said about you.' The result was *so* accurate – apart from one thing, we thought that they were bound to say that we are republican and we hadn't said that but they did not say that we were Republican. The other one was that they thought that because they were Church Of Ireland that they would support Drumcree and that never crossed our minds.[34]

Despite the success of such initiatives and others, where for example such groups have been to the Republic of Ireland and met its President, Mary McAleese, the clergy quickly discovered that those involved 'would dialogue together but not worship'[35] together, highlighting that whilst community relationships may have been vastly improved and enhanced by their ventures, ecumenical relations had not.

Whilst the groups founded in interface areas were to inspire the foundation of most of the ecumenical communities, there were a number of groups formed in Belfast's suburbs and market towns that served as the forerunner to the Church Fora established after the 1994 paramilitary ceasefires. One such group was the Belmont and District Council of Churches, formed in 1971 in an affluent Belfast suburb. This council was a more structured body than its counterparts. Instead of the *ad hoc* arrangements employed in the discussion groups, it was run in a formal manner with each church in the area appointing members of its congregation to sit on its committee which generally met five or six times a year. The local churches were asked to make a number of commitments, which included providing members for the Council and organising joint services.[36] The Council took on the role of ecumenical organiser for the area rather than solely concentrating upon relationships within the group. For example, they ran social events for the local area:

We went to Dublin. We went to the Benedictine Monks in Rostrevor. We had a weekend in Corrymeela. Somebody comes up with an idea or something happens. Somebody will have been somewhere and they will say 'oh maybe we should go there!' We do walks for L'Arche and then we donate the money to them. This year we went with the Philippinos to Armagh to get them out into the countryside and we thought that it would be nice for them to see Northern Ireland. The Catholic Church suggested it but we ran it.[37]

Over the thirty years of their existence, the members of this council themselves had developed strong enough relationships with one another to be able to discuss emotive issues. These ranged from sectarianism, policing and the Good Friday Agreement with the Council offering responses to a number of government consultations, such as *A Shared Future* in 2004.[38] Their methods have taken on a different form to those of the inner-city inter-church groups, consisting of lectures or 'talks' on key issues. Since 1994, they have opened such meetings to the public, a decision that they believe to have been a successful one.

> **Muriel:** We did have politicians into speak. PUP and the Women's Coalition.

> **Jean:** The night we had the politicians, we had to bring in extra chairs because the hall was absolutely packed. It was the best event we'd ever had.

> **Muriel:** That was because it was what it was. The female was Roman Catholic and the man was the Protestant. It was brilliant, afterwards not everybody went home; they were all hanging around and talked and talked!

> **Jean:** There would be a lot of cross-community mixing. This is the idea; it's the whole point of the thing.[39]

This format was successful for two reasons: first by the length of time that the group had been in existence and secondly the demographic profile of the area. Most of those involved in this discussion had come from middle-class backgrounds and because of their university education were more likely to have been in close contact with people from the other community. Prior to attending an event, they had probably developed a tacit understanding of cross-community contact and a willingness to listen to their opinions on matters. The atmosphere of the meetings was 'patient, listening and diplomatic. I do not remember any rows or huffs or ill-feeling and this shows what can be done when God's call is listened to, even by people like us.'[40] The Council of Churches therefore did not have to engage in the intense bridge-building work that other groups may have had to conduct.

The Clergy Fraternal and the clergy and lay inter-church groups were the most organic and accessible form of local level inter-church contact in the years between 1980 and 1994. They allowed clergy and their parishioners to build friendships and relationships with people that they would not have encountered previously, dispelling the myths about the 'other sort' caused by ignorance of their beliefs both religious and political. The members are

> people who have begun to realise that there is a world outside their own church door, who have begun one way or another through personal contacts, through engagement of one kind or another ... begun to realise that their denomination has not got all the truth and the whole truth but that they can learn so much from other Christians. Those are the lay people who believe in reconciliation – often they are very highly motivated in terms of bringing the community together.[41]

Furthermore, with the advent of the peace and reconciliation education initiative these groups became a vehicle for the implementation of their courses on community relations and reconciliation, and whilst their impact upon inter-church relationships may not have been highly visible or spectacular, they were each making a contribution by responding to the reconciling message of the Gospel. However, their most important contribution to the development of cross-denominational relationships lies not in their very existence but in the trust and understanding that they had established between themselves and within the local community. They enabled the creation of conditions in which every form of local inter-church work (the Ecumenical Community, the Social Action Project and the Church Fora) could be founded.


## SOCIAL ACTION PROJECTS

Whilst the Clergy and Lay Inter-Church Fellowships provided a space through which their members could get to know one another, the Social Action Project provided a means through which the local churches could practically help to improve the environment in which they were living and working. Although the Inter-Church Fellowships and the Ecumenical Communities[42] both contained some elements of Social Action work within their remit, there were a small number of groups who concentrated solely upon a practical form of Christian reconciliation, thus, avoiding the potential objections and difficulties associated with common worship. These projects were highly individualistic but were all based upon the premise that the 'Churches [involved] have come together on social action in response to the diverse social needs of the local community.

These projects provide ways for Protestants and Catholics to work together and in partnership to seek to enhance the well being of local community life.'[43]

This form of inter-church co-operation tended to operate outside Belfast in towns such as Newtownabbey, Co. Antrim, Strabane, Co. Londonderry and Irvinestown, Co. Fermanagh with the majority of projects being founded in the late 1980s and early 1990s prior to the paramilitary ceasefires.[44] They generally concentrated upon specific types of local need, such as the elderly, poverty or unemployment and were designed 'to promote the well-being of the inhabitants of the [area] without distinction of sex or of political, religious or other opinions, by associating the four main churches, local authorities, voluntary organisations and inhabitants in a common effort to be caring'.[45] These Social Action Projects were a form of church-based social welfare provision for the areas in which they operated, working by utilising the resources available to them to produce a practical manifestation of the desire for Christian reconciliation between the Protestant and Catholic communities which forms the core of all inter-church work in Northern Ireland. Two types of Social Action Project have emerged in the area: the Parish-based Community Project and the Social Welfare Provider.

*The Parish-based community project: The Forthspring Inter-Community Project, Belfast, 1997–2005 and Parents and Kids Together, Lurgan, 1993–2005*

The community centre has been one of the most prevalent forms of Social Action Project, adding a fresh dimension to the churches' involvement in the lives of their congregations by contributing a neutral venue where Protestants and Catholics can meet in an attempt to improve community relationships through the achievement of shared goals. Most of these centres concentrated upon one group within their community, most commonly the unemployed or elderly and in doing so have been 'providing a service to those in need and those disadvantaged in the area'.[46] However, two of these community centres, the Forthspring Inter-Community Group in Belfast and the Parents and Kids Together (PAKT) project based in the Shankhill Parish Church in Lurgan, have adopted a more extensive approach to their contact with the community, with their work ranging from parent-and-toddlers groups to cross-community educational programmes and counselling services. Throughout their existence their methods have radically evolved. As the groups gained the trust of the community, local people began to feel confident enough to become involved in their work, thereby taking ownership of the organisations' methods and developing schemes that directly reflected the needs of the area.

Although Forthspring is unique, being the only Social Action Project founded after the paramilitary ceasefires with the support of two local ecumenical communities, it is, like the project in Lurgan, a product of local circumstance rather than a final retrospective glance to an outdated form of inter-church co-operation and a rejection of the Church Fora Model. The evolution of both Forthspring and PAKT can be seen to provide a clear demonstration of the development of this form of Social Action Project having adopted the most holistic approach to the idea seen in the province. Thus, whilst not typical of individual Social Action Projects of this type, they do represent an amalgamation of their style and aims. Forthspring and PAKT were founded in segregated locales and in both areas 'the effect of the troubles [had] been to emphasise a tendency ... for the two communities to live in separate areas. By the 1990s the segregation of the communities was almost complete and the opportunities for social interaction between Catholic and Protestant were few'.[47]

Forthspring was founded in 1997 in a renovated Methodist church on the Springfield Road, Belfast, next to the peaceline dividing the communities of the Falls and the Shankhill. The building in which the project is based straddles the peaceline and according to the project's founder '[t]he interface at Springfield Road has long been a symbolism of community conflict and represents quite graphically the deep community divisions that the North of Ireland has become synonymous with.'[48] Although this project was not inaugurated until 1997, the area had a strong history of inter-church work with the Cornerstone and Currach ecumenical communities both operating locally. Initially, the idea for the project came from the Methodist minister, Rev. Sydney Callaghan, who during the early 1990s realised the potential that the building had for the whole community and asked how the Gospel's message of Christian reconciliation could be translated into their situation. Tentative enquiries were made within the congregation to see how they would react to the conversion of part of their church into a community centre which were met with a negative response due to the atmosphere created by the paramilitary violence in the area.

With the arrival of Rev. Gary Mason in 1992, the idea was mooted again as he felt that because the church was 'in the midst of a conflict situation [it] needed to get its hands dirty'.[49] He argued that the congregation should open the premises to the whole community throughout the week for a variety of activities, seeking funding to upgrade the buildings.

Although these plans faced opposition from the surrounding area they were eventually pushed through as no alternatives had been offered. Furthermore, Gary Mason argues that the Forthspring project was established through the foresight of those involved stating that 'while leadership theory says you need to bring people with you, sometimes visionaries need to take risks and believe what you are doing is right'.[50]

Once the Methodist congregation had consented to the conversion of their building they were joined by three other cross-community groups in the area who already had close links with the church having worked on cross-community projects together, the two Ecumenical Communities, Cornerstone and Currach and a secular group the Mid-Springfield Community Association (MISCA) which had been 'started by two women who lived on the road who were committed to the idea of the children [living there] being together'.[51] The result of this was the division of the church building into a cross-community complex and church: thus the front of the building was converted into halls, kitchens and office space with the church forming the centre of the building which was formally opened on 17 October 1997. It is evident then that the Forthspring project was founded due to local circumstance, being the result of relationships that had already been established between the church and secular community groups involved.

PAKT was founded in 1993 in a large segregated town in Co. Armagh as an initiative of the local COI parish church. The idea was developed by the church's parish administrator, Cyril McElheny, who realised that there would be funding available for a project which attempted to provide a means through which young Catholics and Protestants could meet one another. In order to gain the acceptance of the local community the project was forced to start slowly and 'the initial reaction with some people was not positive: they thought it was a bit of a threat, they weren't sure about where it would all lead, we started it gently and gradually confidence has been built so now they do see it as respectable and worthwhile'.[52] Thus, both projects were founded in order to meet a need within the local community attempting to improve community relationships by gaining the trust of those living in the area.

Although these community groups were developed with an ethos of Christian reconciliation in mind, their aims and vision contained few references to their Christian background, concentrating instead upon the community-relations aspect of their work. Initially Forthspring's aims were based entirely upon addressing local needs as they strived to 'offer a programme of activities open to all people in the local Catholic and Protestant Communities. To address community division and social disadvantage along the Springfield Road interface.'[53] These were under-pinned by the project's core values:

1. It is important to be involved in building peace and promoting harmony within our community.
2. It is better to make friends than enemies. We should follow the teaching of accepting all people, not just those we call our 'brother' or 'sister'.
3. Peace is preferable to conflict. This group believes that co-operation, lending support and reconciliation are preferable to competition, conflict and criticism.
4. That we provide positive role models, leading by example showing patience, kindness, gentleness and trust to those that we encounter.
5. The concept of creating a 'Shalom Zone' has been another crucial dynamic for shaping our ethos.[54]

These aims demonstrated the desire of the Methodist Church to create a space which was owned by the whole community, rather than just the church's congregation, that could contribute to the area's social regeneration.

As the project grew, the management committee at Forthspring felt that they needed to think more strategically about their role within the local community. This was a result, not only of a desire to provide the services that were required, but also sprang from a need to attract more external funding. In 2001, PMG consultancy were commissioned to carry out a Needs and Perceptions survey and one of their main recommendations was that Forthspring redefine their aims and vision to allow the users of the project a sense of ownership over it. From 2001 onwards Forthspring had a vision, mission statement and strategic aims which stated:

> **Vision:** Our vision is of diverse and peaceful community, where all people are free to live with dignity, hope, respect and understanding.
> **Mission Statement:** Forthspring works alongside people in creating an environment that builds trust and relationships within and between our communities.
> **Strategic Aims**
>
> 1. To enable and encourage local community participation, belonging and leadership in Forthspring.
> 2. To participate in and promote local networks.

3. To increase personal and community development.
4. To support individuals and groups in finding alternative ways of dealing with difference, continuous issues and divisions.
5. To provide an appropriate voice, space, services, information and training.[55]

These new statements reflected the methodological development of the group in the years since their establishment and clearly demonstrated their growth as an organisation. Thus, the initial aims and values highlight the tentative nature of their early programmes and their need to discover the requirements of the local community before outlining the formal strategy produced in 2001.

The evolution of PAKT's aims and vision followed a similar formula with the strategy developing as the organisation became more sophisticated in its methods. Once more, their aims demonstrate a desire above all else to improve community relations through practical action. Initially, they wanted to:

> Provide a welcome to members in a meeting place which is there to share, where friendships can be made and council sought. Develop activities which stimulate and challenge its members in an environment which enables them to take responsibility and find a sense of achievement. Involve all members in care and work for others – particularly the disadvantaged. Create opportunities for exchanging views, so that its members can improve their understanding of the wider community, of themselves and of one another.[56]

However, in the articulation of their vision or values they differed slightly from other community centres by using language based upon their origins as a Christian organisation stating that: 'PAKT (Lurgan) is a Christian organisation [which stands for] a fellowship based upon an equal value of all persons, respect and freedom for all, tolerance and understanding between people of different opinions. Active concern for the needs of the community united efforts by Christians of different traditions.'[57] This was possibly the result of the direct involvement of the clergy in the establishment of the organisation.

The new millennium saw a change in the management of PAKT and with this came a change in the strategic aims of the group. They now wanted:

1. To facilitate community relations skill building to enable local communities to contribute to the peace building process by exploration and management of religious and political differences.
2. To establish and develop effective partnerships with statutory, community and voluntary organisations to develop strategic

community relations approaches and share best practice.

3. To assist people to examine the complexities of the past and promote healing and reconciliation.
4. To provide opportunities to meet and develop relationships with people of different religious and cultural backgrounds/beliefs to enable meaningful and sustainable co-operation.[58]

These changes demonstrate the development of PAKT as an organisation, as like Forthspring, the years leading up to 2000 saw the local community take ownership of the group and shape its methods, resulting in the strategy outlined above. Furthermore, the removal of the religious language used in the earlier vision statement highlights a move towards a community relations-focused approach to inter-church work that was occurring within most forms of inter-church contact during this period.

Through their avoidance of 'religious' or 'ecumenical' language, both Forthspring and PAKT were maintaining the precedent which had been set by the other inter-church community projects who had also decided to take a more secular route in their formal ethos. For example, another community centre concentrating upon working with the elderly aimed 'to improve the social conditions of the elderly and less able inhabitants',[59] whilst another saw itself as 'serving the community and providing encouragement to other social groups'.[60] In this, such groups were concentrating upon the need for an improvement in community relations, focusing upon a more all-encompassing approach to inter-church relationships based upon the fact that 'there is general recognition of the benefits of a developmental strategy which is holistic (i.e. focusing on the spiritual, physical, intellectual and social development of participants), integrated (i.e. providing a range of inter-connected and complementary interventions) and inclusive (i.e. inclusive of ... people from different religious traditions)'[61] rather than just a need to promote religious understanding. These aims and vision are a manifestation of the idea that community relations and reconciliation needed to be separated from the theologically-associated ecumenism that dominated the inter-church scene throughout the 1980s. In their separation of these two elements such groups have carried this idea much further than any others in the province, including the other form of Social Action Project, the Social Welfare Provider, by completely removing the biblically based ideas of reconciliation that would be expected in their aims and objectives, instead focusing upon listening to the needs of the local community and responding appropriately.

As their aims and visions indicate, this form of Social Action Project set out to be a collaborative venture between the local churches and the community, rather than just amongst the churches themselves. From the outset, their management structures were highly organised, being 'based on the concept of power-sharing and the groups have committed themselves to an equal partnership in the management of the project'.[62] Both projects were run as businesses having being incorporated as limited companies and attaining charitable status once the initial pilot stage had been completed. Forthspring was run by a management board which met every three months delegating everyday issues to a management executive which met monthly.[63] PAKT was run along the same lines, centering its management policy upon the idea that local parents should play a role in the management of the project.[64]

Neither project was exclusively church-based being run instead by all sectors of the community. Such an approach to their organisation has influenced their programme work, taking it in directions which would not have been possible if it had not been for the influence of non-church groups. Those running these projects ultimately wanted the local community to gain ownership of them, with Forthspring stating, for example, that it 'works with all local people to help build a community free from sectarianism, violence and fear and encourages their participation in all areas of its work, from planning, implementation and management through to project activities'.[65] Initially the founding groups involved did much more than manage the centre and it was their contributions which dictated the programme work of the projects on their foundations. The involvement of the founding groups in the strategic management was to have a larger impact upon the work of Forthspring. As a consequence the range of their work reflected the interests of those involved as 'Cornerstone's family worker and youth worker were offered to Forthspring to develop the work as was MISCA's play worker',[66] whilst the Currach Community's Women's Group became part of Forthspring. PAKT was founded with a much clearer plan for the delivery of their aims and concentrated solely upon family and youth work. However, by 2000 both groups were delivering programmes which centred upon the personal development of those involved whilst continuing to address the communal issues that were their focus at the outset.

The work of these community projects primarily centred upon the improvement of relationships within the local area. They 'delivered programmes for parents and toddlers, young people, women and senior citizens so that Catholics and Protestants can build relationships and create trust primarily through getting to know each other',[67] eventually moving into '[supporting] groups of people to engage in more focused and specific programmes of dialogue and discussion around contentious issues'.[68] Their work fell into two categories: practical programmes which eventually blended into community relations courses using the friendships and trust developed through the practical programmes as a starting point. Whilst Forthspring worked with all groups within the community, such as women and senior citizens, work with families and consequently young people was one of the main focuses of both projects. This factor reflected PAKT's foundation as 'a family and community project for children and their parents from all areas of Lurgan'[69] and in Forthspring's case was less deliberate, being due to the presence of MISCA's play worker as well as Cornerstone's family worker. It is through this work that the progress of both organisations can most clearly be seen.

Both projects started by working with young people using methods which were 'gentle ways in which people would meet across the divide'.[70] Forthspring ran a pre-school carers and toddlers group, an after-school club and facilitated an active youth outreach programme which 'from the beginning has been primarily aimed at providing a safe place for children to play in an area which has very few such places'.[71] PAKT's work followed a similar pattern with the provision of a children's programme, PAKT plus (for the 10–13 age group), a parent's programme and a family programme.[72] The premise of this work was simple, providing 'an alternative to the almost total polarisation of children'[73] in both these areas by organising events such as arts and crafts, soccer and outdoor activity weekends as well as more structured programmes 'which educate the children about different world issues such as the environment, health and poverty'.[74] Through such work the projects were laying the foundations for an improvement in community relations based upon encouraging the children and young people 'in various ways to think beyond the boundaries of their experience and their communities'[75] with activities such as fundraising for charity being employed to help them do this. A similar ideal was also employed in relation to the children's parents with the idea of safety, friendship and personal development taking precedence over the immediate implementation of formal community relationship development courses. Thus, courses on parenting skills were run by both projects through which it was hoped that parents would be able to engage with each other 'across the religious divide in a non-threatening and open environment'.[76]

For the first few years of their existence both groups were adopting a strictly lowest common denominator approach to relationships based upon the premise that:

a fairly gentle approach needs to be adopted in the area of community relations with opportunities initially being created for Catholics and Protestants to meet together in relatively safe, secure, non threatening environments – following this period of contact and getting to know each other, it might be possible to directly address issues relating to politics, diversity and cultural identity.[77]

This approach, known as 'the politics of avoidance ... is an inadequate response to the community relations challenges which affect individual communities throughout Northern Ireland'.[78] Consequently, in their engagement of such methods both Forthspring and PAKT were failing to fulfil their aim of improving community relationships by promoting an understanding of the different traditions within the community.

The groups themselves were aware of this issue but balanced this problem against the need to establish themselves within the local community and gain its trust and acceptance before trying any work that would be considered sensitive, especially that relating to identity. In the late 1990s, both organisations felt sufficiently secure of their status within the area to begin to strategically develop their programme work, providing some form of community relations courses for their participants. These courses were designed using established guidelines to meet the specific needs of the participants. As a result, both youth programmes contained distinctive aspects, whilst retaining the key elements of communal and personal development that remains at the core of the work of community projects. Their evolution highlights the importance of knowledge of the local area and its needs as well as the value of communal support.

The youth programme at Forthspring has developed rapidly since 1999. Initially, the youth workers only felt able to engage in single identity work, using this to establish a strong sense of identity amongst the young people concerned as well as protecting them.[79] According to their programme worker, 'Youth is the only programme that operates at times on a single identity basis and this is due to external factors. As young people are often the instruments of inter-community violence, if there are times of high tensions or actual violence we have resorted to single identity work for safety purposes.'[80] In 2002, the participants requested that some cross-community programmes be developed as a result of their interaction with each other in the practical programmes, such as dance, creative writing and drama. These activities have 'deepened their friendships and developed understanding and good levels of trust',[81] all of which are pre-requisites for any kind of cross-community contact involving an exploration of identity. The programmes offered by Forthspring in response to this request used a number of methods to promote the personal development of the participants whilst increasing their understanding of the 'other' community. However, in contrast with the cross-community work being done with adults by the other forms of inter-church groups, the approach adopted by Forthspring centred upon a series of activities rather than discussion. The most notable of these was the establishment of the Youth Enterprise Group which aimed to help 'a group of young people learn new skills in enterprise and marketing'.[82] This resulted in the publication of a photo journal by the young people demonstrating their experience of living on an interface.[83]

Such projects established Forthspring's place within the community and provided the participants with a sense of ownership which encouraged their continued attendance, thereby strengthening relationships. Forthspring have found a formula which works for their local community and have sustained their momentum by employing new staff to cope with the demand for their services. Their approach has been a reactive one, which as we shall see, has resulted in the success of many inter-church groups working in interface areas and clearly demonstrates the need for trust and understanding in cross-community contact.

In contrast to the reactive strategy used by Forthspring, PAKT's programme was driven by a need to secure its future so that it could continue to serve the community and target social need.[84] The development of its work demonstrates the organisation's strategy of establishing a professional and sustainable approach to the delivery of their programme which facilitated a growth in the number of children that they were able to involve.[85] The programme offered centred upon personal development as a means of encouraging cross-community contact, friendship and understanding. This was based upon the notion that 'Young people may not be able to vote before they are 18, but they can make a positive contribution to their communities. Young people should be actively involved in decision-making both in schools and in the wider community. They should be encouraged to thing critically about their role in society and their potential as agents for change.'[86] PAKT wanted to create a sense of ownership and participation towards society amongst the young people it worked with, creating a programme called 'Agents for Change' that acted in partnership with local organisations to teach young people that they could have a positive impact upon society. The organisers took the participants through a programme which introduced them to concepts surrounding active citizenship and participation such as 'rules and laws, leadership and group work, barriers to active participation, degrees of participation and rights and responsibilities'.[87] This course was more formal in its approach to building better community relations. Instead of adopting the *ad hoc* approach favoured by Forthspring in which community relations were not the focus of the project but instead a by-product, the methods favoured by PAKT were generally more educational. Such an approach again highlights the need for a knowledge of the local area and the nature of inter-church work. Thus, whilst the underlying desire of improving relationships between the Protestant and Catholic communities was the same, these two community groups had to adopt different tactics when putting their aims into practice.

These community projects demonstrate just how far inter-church relationships have changed since the early attempts at contact in the late 1960s. In their work with the surrounding area, they have engaged a wide range of methods and activities that are far removed from the prayer or discussion groups that by and large characterise this work. It is generally agreed by those in the locality that their presence has a stabilising influence. A report on Forthspring concluded that:

> In spite of the difficulties, it is generally felt that Forthspring's presence in such a difficult area brings hope to those who use its facilities as well as providing an opportunity for interaction between the communities. In addition, the project has helped the local community to understand, and deal with, community differences and provided an impetus for reconciliation and peace building.[88]

Furthermore, PAKT was equally successful in its integration into the local community and is 'considered to be performing an important role in relation to the work which it is carrying out with children and with parents'[89] with its model of relationship development being syndicated all over Ireland with the help of the YMCA. However, despite its roots as an inter-church project, they have both developed into an almost secular community group[90] fulfilling their aims through the provision of practical schemes such as carer-and-toddler groups and citizenship education rather than concentrating upon creating an understanding of the different Christian traditions which has been the norm in inter-church work since 1980. Nevertheless, through their programme work both Forthspring and PAKT provide a clear demonstration of the way in which inter-church community centres work in Northern Ireland, as they operate by adopting a lowest-common-denominator approach, hoping that Protestants and Catholics will build relationships by engaging in activities together, such as mountain climbing, which they anticipate can remove the barriers of difference. In this the community project represents an amalgamation of cross-community work and social action, being neither one nor the other in their strictest definitions. However, the purest form of inter-church

Social Action Project can be seen in the Social Welfare Provider, the most successful of which has been operating in Derry since 1983.
*The Social Welfare Provider: The Churches Trust and the Churches Voluntary Work Bureau, Derry 1982–2005*

> Basically, [our social action work] was an attempt to reach out to the local community wherever there was a social need and to meet that social need … These things are quite peculiar to Derry and it says a lot about how the churches and people get along together … In a place like Derry we are able to take initiatives together that other people might find a greater difficulty with … there is a more relaxed approach to ecumenism here.[91]

Derry has one of most highly developed and sophisticated mechanisms for inter-church social action work in Northern Ireland and in this, it provides a large-scale example of the type of social welfare provision seen in other parts of the area.[92] The social action work undertaken in Derry takes the most practical form possible and has only come to include any form of formal cross-community relationship building since the late 1980s.[93] It has manifested itself in the establishment of three projects which are interlinked and have evolved out of one another. The first was founded in 1983 in the Protestant part of the city and was initially called the Waterside Churches Committee for Community Needs, changing its name in 1992 to the Churches Trust;[94] this was followed in the same year by the Churches Voluntary Work Bureau. In 1996, a Church Forum, Churches in Co-operation, was founded as a result of the work of these two projects.[95]

These organisations saw themselves as 'a very practical way of doing ecumenism, it wasn't just sitting down and talking about how our churches approach faith and theology – it was trying to put into practice our joint co-operation for the good of the inner city and a tremendous lot has been achieved'.[96] Once more it is apparent that the Social Action Project is a model of inter-church activity which initially tried to move beyond difference by adopting a purely practical approach to relationships between the denominations. It did so by ignoring the concept adopted by other inter-church groups of promoting an understanding of difference in favour of working towards the tangible results that can be seen through job clubs and community visiting schemes.

During the early 1980s, unemployment was becoming a major problem for both communities in Derry and whilst it had always been prevalent within the Catholic community, for the first time 'Protestants found themselves with an unemployment problem and … didn't know how to cope with it. Men in their late forties and early fifties suddenly [found themselves] without a job. Catholics had their own advice office which kept them updated with all their welfare rights entitlements and so on.'[97] Due to the almost complete segregation of the area, the leaders of the Protestant Churches felt that an unemployment advice centre was needed for their community which would be designed to mirror the Catholic one.[98] The Church Leaders were persuaded by George Glenn to include the Catholic Church in their plans and with the help of funding from the government-based ACE scheme,[99] the Waterside Churches Committee for Community Needs (later the Churches Trust) was established in 1983, initially operating from a room over a pub rented to them by the landlord for a penny a year. The work of the Churches Trust was addressing a community need and this led to the foundation of the Churches Voluntary Work Bureau as a satellite organisation later the same year. This project was

> opened to help engage the unemployed in voluntary work ... Other needs began to be identified in the Waterside such as a gardening service and a home decorating scheme, and a Community Visiting Scheme was established which employed 19 workers through the ACE programme, 12 in the urban area of the Waterside and 7 in the rural areas.[100]

The Social Action Projects established in Derry were entirely functional, concentrating upon the practicalities of everyday living, and the problems facing both communities within the area and their management structures provided a reflection of this. From the outset, these two projects were run as businesses with their structure providing a precursor of the organisational and techniques that would be seen in the post-ceasefire funding boom. The management of the two projects has changed little since 1983, with both being run by a board of directors with 'the leadership of the Churches Trust [being] indirectly in the hands of the four [Church] leaders because we nominate the people who sit on the Committee and run it'.[101] In addition, the leaders of the four main churches in Derry are all members of the board alongside 'members of both sections of the community, including clergy from the larger denominations',[102] with volunteers and staff overseeing the day-to-day running of the projects. These projects were therefore not purposefully established or managed to aid the reconstruction of community relations through education and social interaction as other types of Social Action Project had been. Instead, they were aimed at fulfilling the Christian duty of those involved to help those in need thereby improving living conditions and, as a consequence, began eventually to promote recon-ciliation within the area.

In common with the ideas which inspired their foundation, the aims and objectives of both the Churches Trust and the Churches Voluntary Work Bureau emphasised the practical, choosing not to accentuate their role as an inter-church group. Rather they used their stated aims and objectives to provide a literal definition of their work rather than the ethos behind it as has been the case with the aims and objectives of other forms of inter-church group. On their foundation, the Churches Trust aimed to:

> Promote the benefit of the inhabitants of Waterside and neighbour-hood in the City without distinction of sex or political, religious or other opinions. By associating the local authorities, churches, voluntary organisations and inhabitants in common effort to relieve poverty, sickness and distress and to advance education so as to improve the conditions of life for the said inhabitants.[103]

On their part, the Churches Voluntary Work Bureau, who have retained the same aims since their foundation, wanted 'to promote volunteering activities in the North West of the Island for the benefit of individuals and the community'.[104] Thus, through these statements, both groups highlighted the way in which they aimed to work in partnership with a number of forms of group, both church and secular, within the area, plac-ing an emphasis upon their availability to both communities. The Churches Trust retained this aim until 1992, when the organisation was restructured to reflect a more corporate image, producing the following aims: 'to identify the practical and social needs of the local community; to help satisfy, in a Christian way, those needs which we can physically and financially undertake and refer to other Agencies those other needs which we cannot tackle'.[105] In these can be seen a development of the Churches Trust as they have become more plainly defined as an organi-sation and no longer feel the need to identify their unbiased nature or their partnerships with other organisations. Instead their aims manifest themselves much more concisely than previously, offering a definition of the Trust as a social welfare provider founded upon a Christian ethos. These aims were fully employed in the development of the work of both organisations. As the Churches Voluntary Work Bureau was established as a satellite organisation of the Churches Trust, their work has a ten-dency to blend into each other, with the main focus of both groups ini-tially centring upon methods of alleviating the massive unemployment problem blighting Derry in the early 1980s.

The Churches Trust rapidly realised that the community in the Waterside needed much more than an unemployment advice centre, which led them 'to try to identify other community needs and we came up with the other programmes: a visitation service, for example, to the elderly living alone to complement the existing home help services, the government were giving us finance to do this. We [also] built up a large gardening task force.'[106] Such programmes were facilitated using workers from the government's ACE scheme and highlighted the practical nature of inter-church relationships in Derry and the surrounding area. It was this expansion in the remit of the Churches Trust which brought about the foundation of the Churches Voluntary Work Bureau in October 1983 when they

> were asked to develop and promote the community-volunteering programme, over counties Londonderry, Tyrone and Fermanagh, the whole west of the province. The Community Volunteering programme was to encourage unemployed people, bearing in mind that the ACE programme would only last for a year, to keep their skills going. We were given money to run the programme for a fairly wide area.[107]

Although the Bureau no longer facilitates voluntary work in such a wide geographical area, this aspect of its work has played a central role in its development, with nearly all the other areas of its work being variations upon this theme, thus 'volunteering remains at the very core of [their] commitment to the community'.[108] By 2005 some fifty groups were using the Bureau's voluntary service with around 300 volunteers being deployed to work in projects as varied as Age Concern, Well Women drop-in centres, play resource centres and environmental projects with an estimated 40 per cent of volunteers gaining full-time employment.[109] The work of the Bureau has been central to the successful continuance of the voluntary sector in Derry as many of their clients have made comments such as 'the project couldn't exist without the volunteers'.[110] In addition, it is also apparent that the demographic profile of those involved in the Bureau's work has changed somewhat since its inception in 1983.

> The majority of our volunteers joined us because they were unemployed, but new trends are emerging. We are now also working with a significant number of part-time students, with retired people and with people recovering from mental health problems. We are also, for the first time, placing people with learning difficulties as volunteers.[111]

As a result of the growth of its volunteering work, by the end of the

1980s the Bureau had started to become involved in facilitating the establishment of cross-community voluntary organisations in other parts of Northern Ireland and providing them with help and advice:

> Over the years of the 1980s we acted as a catalyst in setting up things – looking at community work and what its needs were. We set up Victim Support here for example and we serviced it here for a few months and then the committee was up and running and we pushed the boat out. We did this in many cases, for example with an environmental programme and Marriage Guidance. We could have taken it on ourselves but there was a national scheme so all we did was recruit the volunteers and let them use this office as their initial base. We do this all the time. All these projects up until now have been meeting the needs of the community because of our successes we were responsible for setting up similar organisations in Coleraine and we've got the Churches involved there.[112]

Although outside agencies such as Victim Support and Marriage Guidance were involved, most of the work carried out by the Bureau's Management Agency centred once more upon the provision of opportunities for unemployed people to expand their skills base, cultivating contacts with groups and 'providing advice and training for each of the groups and funding for out of pocket expenses'.[113] They also concentrated upon offering vocational training to their volunteers in work-related areas such as first aid, health and safety issues and computer skills.

It would seem, then, that an improvement in community relationships in the area was low on the agenda of the Social Action Projects operating in Derry who instead preferred to take a practical approach by helping to alleviate unemployment and support the local voluntary sector. However, the Churches Trust and the Churches Voluntary Work Bureau were also responsible for the facilitation of a scheme designed to improve relationships between young Catholics and Protestants, by providing them with an opportunity to work together in the US for three months. The Wider Horizons scheme, founded in Derry during the mid-1980s, was based upon the experiences of those who had taken part in the Ulster Project.[114] In common with the Ulster Project, 'the [Wider Horizons scheme] … has been a transforming experience. [The participants] have often spoken about broadening their horizons, their increased self-confidence and their commitment to work for reconciliation and boundaries has been one of the outstanding results.'[115] However, the Wider Horizons scheme has been greatly influenced by the ethos of both the companies running it and therefore differs in the form of encounter that it offers, being based upon a combination of the provision of work experience for unemployed young people with a desire to facilitate an improvement in community relations. They operated by taking a mixed group to a host city in America to work on a project such as renovating housing for those with special needs thus providing participants them with training and experience in areas which would help them find employment on their return.[116] In addition this experience made a small contribution to improved community relations: 'I am totally convinced that when you take people out of Ireland and get them away they are never the same again; you don't change their beliefs or their attitudes but they are more tolerant.'[117] Such a view is supported by some of the comments from the participants themselves; for example one stated that 'I had to cross an ocean to meet friends who live just over half a mile away.'[118]

Both the Churches Trust and Churches Voluntary Work Bureau have remained committed to their founding aims and objectives and have achieved the creation of an unemployment and voluntary centre for the Protestant and Catholic communities in Derry and the surrounding area. They have identified their target group, the unemployed, and have devised a number of ways in which to help them find work according to their age and educational status eventually moving into the area of cross-community relationship development but moulding their methodology to fulfil their criteria of the provision of work experience. Their longevity would indicate that both these schemes have been successful and it is evident that they are targeted at a specific market rather than designed to be all encompassing as some other Social Action Projects and indeed inter-church projects are. However, although they were founded with a Christian ethos in mind by an inter-church group of leaders they do not fit neatly into the mould of inter-church work in Northern Ireland providing instead an anomaly which serves to illustrate the diversity of ways in which churches are working together. Thus, they are overcoming their differences by working together on practical schemes for the economic betterment of the area and the people in it but it is arguable whether such a scheme has made any substantial contribution to Christian reconciliation in promoting an understanding of difference between Protestants and Catholics.


CHURCH FORA

The cessation of violence declared by the IRA on 31 August 1994 followed by the statement of the Combined Loyalist Military Command announcing that they would 'universally cease all operational hostilities as from 12 midnight on the 13 October 1994'[119] was greeted with optimism, with the then Taoiseach, Albert Reynolds, commenting that 'this decision effectively signifies the end of twenty-five years of violence, and the closure of a tragic chapter in our history'.[120] Despite events since 1994, these actions on the part of the paramilitaries, when combined with the subsequent Peace Talks and Good Friday Agreement, did lead to a more relaxed attitude to cross-community contact within Northern Ireland. This change was to have a great impact upon the way the Protestant and Catholic Churches worked together at a local level. Consequently, a new form of interaction between the churches in local areas began to occur because of political events rather than inspite of them. The result was the establishment of the inter-church Forum in Northern Ireland, fourteen of which were established between 1994 and 2005 in both urban and rural areas.

This phenomenon has been hailed as a new era in inter-church relationships:

> As we enter a new millennium local inter-church co-operation in Northern Ireland has never been better. The increase in confidence level can be traced from the 1994 ceasefires which led to a new atmosphere and the building of new relationships. One of the recognised signs of the new atmosphere was the development of inter-Church Fora ... Relationships, trust and better understanding are growing and people are discovering, not only other traditions, but new insights into their own. There is also a healthy focus on wider community issues and hard questions are no longer being avoided.[121]

Furthermore, they are constantly cited as examples in inter-church work by practitioners with four of the five examples used in a practical resource being Church Fora.[122] However, such an assessment of the importance the Church Fora overestimates their significance in the landscape of inter-church relations in Northern Ireland as many of the elements described in the *CRC News* were occurring in the area prior to 1994, under the auspices of the Ecumenical Communities or the Inter-Church Fellowships, but were not widely known or were not part of a closely monitored inter-church network as the Church Fora are.[123] Instead, these Church Fora signify a natural progression in relationships prompted by external political events.

Church Fora are defined by the Community Relations Council as being 'primarily focused on ways in which the churches can co-operate on addressing social and community needs, reconciliation issues and community life'.[124] In this, instead of presenting a groundbreaking new model of inter-church co-operation, they represent a continuation of the other inter-church work being carried out in Northern Ireland since 1980, and more importantly a formalisation of the separation of church-based community relations from the popular interpretation of ecumenical activity. This factor has been crucial in the establishment of the Church Fora as they are:

> more inclusive than an ecumenical group because it is seen as a communication of information and issues type place – it is not necessarily seen as a council of churches or as an ecumenical group – those labels wouldn't be used and so some folk, who would run a mile from those, would be willing to participate in the church forum. [The clergy] are able to take on a facilitating role to get it up and going [acting] as a point of contact and exchange. Some of the [Fora] have moved on to do some very interesting seminars and group work and others are tackling areas of common concern that may be drug education [for example] ... They don't have to agree theologically ... They are finding common cause around local issues and are willing to address this or ways of reducing community tension. I think one of the things which has been helpful in recent years here has been... the distinction at times between ecumenism and peacemaking and [the recognition] that it is important to build relationships with your neighbours which may not include affirming them as fellow believers.[125]

Thus, the contribution of the Church Fora to inter-church and community relationships in Northern Ireland is somewhat wider than the definition provided by the Community Relations Council would imply. In addition to the idea of the churches working together to address the needs of their local community, the picture painted of these Fora by those involved presents them as something more than just a Social Action Project that aims to improve community relations by providing practical solutions to the community's problems. Rather the early 'meetings were less about direct politics than about channels of relationships which might allow other decisions to be taken in the light of greater mutual respect and cycles of violence and revenge to be ended more quickly'.[126]

The Church Fora are a formal expression of inter-church relationships within an area or an attempt to develop them – an idea that is borne out by the aims, objectives and work of those involved. However, it has been argued that:

> Every local church forum has developed its own identity and activity. There is no blueprint, no prescribed model, and no traditional inter-church or community relations agenda. The local context is all important and a group is formed in a way appropriate to local needs, challenges and sensitivities. What works in Clogher Valley does not work in Cookstown.[127]

Whilst the nuanced experiences of the members of the Church Fora may be slightly different, it is somewhat inaccurate to argue that there is 'no prescribed model' for Church Fora in Northern Ireland. Instead, by their very nature the Church Fora, like other forms of local inter-church co-operation, are indeed a model of inter-church activity, with a management and methodological structure which can be imported into areas to be filled with activities suitable to the needs and talents of those involved.

*Origins and aims*

Between 1994 and 2005, fourteen Church Fora were established in Northern Ireland.[128] The Church Fora represent a collaboration between the local Churches, the Community Relations Council and the District Council's Community Relations Officer[129] who worked together to establish these groups in local areas. The establishment of the Fora was aided greatly by the formation of the Churches Advisory Group (CAG) by the Community Relations Council[130] in 1996 along with the appointment of a Churches Officer in the same year – a post which was 'aimed at trying to increase inter-community contact within and between the Churches'.[131] The support of the Community Relations Council of these initiatives was crucial, a factor which came to light during the organisation of three regional conferences in 1998 which were intended to act as a spring board for the foundation of more groups. Thus, 'it was important for the CROs (Community Relations Officers) that [the conferences were] organised in partnership because some of them would find the churches issue a wee bit contentious to get involved with so that they weren't the fall guys'.[132] Representatives from all the churches in the area were invited to these conferences held in Omagh, Coleraine and Newtownabbey which were designed essentially as a networking and facilitational event at which clergy were given 'the opportunity to meet other clergy in their own local areas [and] to share information, and help to build friendships and relationships'.[133] These conferences succeeded in opening up dialogue within a number of areas but only led directly to the foundation of two Fora

(Limavady and Coleraine).

There were a number of catalysts for the establishment of the Church Fora and most centred around the identification of a local need for some form of visible interaction between the Protestant and Catholic Churches. This generally took one of two forms: either the production of a research report by the local council or more informally the desire of a member of the clergy to see such a group established. So for example a research report produced in 2003 for the Ards Borough Council Community Relations Unit recommended that 'consideration be given to establishing a new Churches Forum on Social/Community/Civic Issues',[134] with the Ards Churches Forum being established the following year. By contrast, the Lisburn Inter-Church Project was created after a local Presbyterian minister, Gordon Grey, approached the Community Relations Council, the administrators of the Peace I funding pro-gramme[135] with his idea for a larger cross-community project after the success of his work with the local Catholic church became apparent.[136]

Once this potential function for the churches had been established, the creation of the Church Fora was not a *fait accompli* as their existence in only fourteen out of twenty-six local district councils would suggest. Three factors were significant in enabling plans for the Fora to progress beyond the initial suggestion: a sympathetic or apathetic council, pre-existing inter-church groups and an external event, such as Drumcree. Whilst the first two of these were crucial to the success of these ventures, many of the members of the Fora saw the third as a backdrop, creating prevailing conditions that gave their work its impetus. The leadership of a local council could, if it chooses, prevent a Church Forum from being established, either by withholding funding or refusing to allow the report suggesting the creation of such a body to go to council. Since 1994, there have been a number of instances of this occurring within DUP-controlled boroughs. Many of their objections relate to the doctrinal issues of contact between the Catholic and Protestant Churches as they view the Catholic Church to be in error, a viewpoint tacitly supported by their voters. In the areas where this has occurred, plans for the Church Forum have had to be put on hold and as one Community Relations Officer commented 'maybe we should look at re-wording [the report] a little bit ... I don't know how far we're going to get with it ... now that we have a much stronger DUP influence'.[137]

The existence of local, more informal, inter-church organisations has also been central to the creation of the Church Fora. All of them grew out of existing inter-church groups, demonstrating that, even with the most formal structures in place, the development of inter-church relations within a local community is organic. The experience of the Dungannon Area Churches Forum is typical of this:

> One of my predecessors developed a programme with the Irish School of Ecumenics amongst local women, and that became [the] Women in Faith project and all the churches work has snowballed from that. When those women then had been meeting for maybe two years, they decided to expand and bring in men so it became Friends in Faith, and then from that it developed into the Churches Forum. And then from the Churches Forum, the clergy forum developed as well.[138]

Indeed, the importance of pre-existing structures is so important that one research report felt the need to demand their inclusion: 'The participation of the churches that are members of the Inter-Church Group would be essential for this to be a success.'[139] Finally, external events or ideas that went against the nature of Christianity often provided the momentum for the formation of the Church Fora – most commonly, these centred around events like Drumcree or terrorist atrocities. Ploughshare, a group working in Bangor in Co. Down, has its origins in the events surrounding Drumcree: 'Drumcree was the thing that inspired us. Even our local Catholic church had its windows broken and the people were absolutely appalled that this was happening. They wanted to express the fact that even if they had totally different views they wanted nothing to do with this desecration of churches.'[140] The Armagh Churches Forum was founded in response to the bombing of Canary Wharf in 1996: 'The Clergy Fellowship had a public rally which I was speaking at and after that someone from the Council suggested that we set something up that was more formal.'[141] By contrast some of the other Churches Fora were established from a desire to challenge sectarianism as well as a wish to apply 'a more prophetic and critical faith to the healing of relationships and the reconstruction of the community in Northern Ireland'.[142]

The story of each of the fourteen Church Fora's origins demonstrates a remarkable similarity indicating that they can be seen as a model of inter-church contact rather than as something unique to the area in which they were working. Indeed, their origins tell us something of post-ceasefire inter-church relations as it became apparent to local councils that they should lend their support to the churches working together and that the political climate was now such that it allowed them to do so. That is not to say that this contact has been simple and the aims and methods of the Fora reflect this. As one member put it:

> It is very low key and that would be a tension within the Forum: if

you try to do anything too grand you are being hypocritical saying everything is rosy and it is not, and you are also spoiling the long-term aim which is to get people to understand one another. People don't feel secure yet they feel exposed, it is a long-term thing.[143]

Despite the slow pace at which the Church Fora found themselves working at the outset, they demonstrate the formalisation of inter-church work especially when compared to the type of work that had occurred within local communities before. However, they do not represent a new beginning, rather in the aims and objectives of these Church Fora we can see the fruition of the holistic approach to inter-church relationships that was developed at a local level in Northern Ireland throughout the 1980s and early 1990s and latterly embraced by the churches' leaderships. The Church Fora's aims and objectives represent a move away from an over-concentration upon prayer as a means of transcending sectarianism and difference witnessed in the work of inter-church fellowships, towards an acknowledgement of the need to engage meaningfully with tensions in the community and find creative ways to overcome difference. The aims and objectives of the Church Fora fall into two categories: ideological and practical with the aims representing the ideological purpose of each of the groups whilst the objectives provide a representation of how they envisage these being implemented in the local community.

The overwhelming tone of the aims of *all* of these groups centred upon the need for a church-based project to facilitate reconciliation and an improvement in local community relations. In short, each of these groups shares a set of aims which they then translate into their localised objectives. Such commonalities can be seen in the stated aims of a number of the Church Fora. The Armagh Churches Forum wants 'to promote and further the work of the Forum within its area to increase mutual understanding and respect and establish cross-denominational friendships'.[144] Ploughshare aims to 'get to know, understand and appreciate each other's beliefs, traditions, cultures and aspirations'.[145] The Lisburn Inter-Church Project is also committed to community relationship improvement stating that: 'Our vision is of supported and encouraged Churches working together in the name of Christ, healing division and enriching the life of our community ... Lisburn Inter-Church Project promotes contact between churches and the community, through dialogue and working together, to build a fair and peaceful society, encourage community development, work towards the eradication of sectarianism and address social needs.'[146]

The aims of all of these groups are more complex than a simple wish to be yet another church group or community relations organisation. It is in the aims of the Cookstown Forum that we see an articulation of one of the key elements of the work of these Fora which indicates their attempt to move away from the form adopted by Clergy and Lay Inter-Church Fellowships towards a more formal place in the community. Thus, they seek to be 'an open space to respond to local community issues'.[147] It is this desire to be a 'neutral venue' combined with their practical objectives which lies at the heart of their community relations work providing the bridge between their stated aims and their practical outcomes witnessed in their objectives by offering a direct response to the needs of the local area. Thus, in the objectives of these groups we see a practical response to the issue of community relations, based upon training and education rather than prayer. So, for example, in Derry they want to 'address key social and economic needs of the community'[148] and in Lisburn they hope to develop 'opportunities for working in partnership to address poverty [and] social exclusion ... within Lisburn'.[149] In order to do this each group aims to try and provide some form of community relations training within its local area thereby promoting 'reconciliation initiatives by providing discussion and training opportunities'.[150]

In the development of the aims and objectives of these Church Fora, we can see the construction of a framework for local level inter-church relationships based upon formal strategic planning rather than the reactive approach previously employed by other local groups, such as the ecumenical communities. Nevertheless there is a clear continuance in the aims and objectives of the Church Fora from those of the other inter-church groups as they are integrating and building upon the work of ecumenical communities in trying to provide a neutral venue and discussion on reconciliation and relationship issues, for example, and fusing it with a form of facilitational work, which by 2005 was only just beginning to emerge within some groups.

## Management and membership

The Church Fora are a highly structured organisation with long-term strategies in place for their development. The involvement of the Community Relations Council and the CROs has lead to the implementation of a formal management structure in all of the Church Fora. The management and recruitment methods of each of these bodies are strikingly similar and indeed provide one of the key foundation stones for the creation of identifiable models of Church Fora for Northern Ireland. Prior to their foundation, each of the Fora commissioned studies and formed steering groups to identify the key areas of concern for the local

community. The findings were then translated into a clearly defined set
of aims and objectives outlined above along which they could develop
their programme work.

Their membership is also highly structured, with clear guidelines in
place for denominational participation. So, for example, the Cookstown
Forum was 'open to members of all the Christian Churches in the
Cookstown District Area, with the proviso that a balance [was] maintained between the two main traditions'.[151] At the outset, membership
of the Church Fora consisted of twelve members, clergy and lay, who
represented their denominations and served on the Forum's committee,
undertaking roles such as Chair and Treasurer in strict rotation. Members
of the committee were usually recruited through direct appeals from the
clergy:

> **Committee member one:** I was on the Catholic Parish council and
> at a particular meeting, the Priest said that he was looking for three
> or four members to represent the Catholic Church on the Church
> Forum so that was how I became involved.
> **Committee member two:** My wife and I were both leaders in the
> Methodist Church and we were asked if we would like to go along
> and represent the Methodist Church.[152]

However, the membership of the Church Fora, although designed to be
equitable and encouraging to potential members, has proved to be highly
problematic for two reasons. First, 'the members of the Forum are nominated by their churches and they tend to be people who are committed
and interested'.[153] In practice, this has meant that the membership of
the group consists of retired, middle-class church elders who are already
ecumenically committed and are therefore not part of the 'target group'
at whom such community relations work is aimed. As one Community
Relations Officer suggested, 'if you wanted to really have an aggressive
critique of it, you could say it's very, very middle-class. You're speaking
to the converted in many ways. But I suppose that's being over critical.'[154]
Second, apathy and a lack of time has also proved to be a major problem
for the Church Fora in their recruitment of members, as many churches
felt uncomfortable asking members of its congregation to commit to yet
another church-based activity. 'The churches are caught up in internal
issues, lack of leadership, people don't seem to have the same amount of
time that they had in the past, those who are volunteers have to spend
more time in training, there's more accountability.'[155]

In spite of the problems with recruiting a mixed base of active participants, the management of the Church Fora is formulaic, consisting

in each case of a combination of long-term strategic planning and the principle of inclusive membership. As we shall see, this has allowed for the development of a proactive approach to the issue of community relations with each Fora having a more clearly defined set of aims and objectives in place at their foundation than any other form of inter-church group in the area, which translated into an organised programme of work with the community.

## Programme work

The Church Fora were designed to respond to the needs of their local communities. As they evolved as an organisation, the Fora's methods gradually began to reflect the spirit of their aims and objectives, although they discovered that their aspirations and the results did not always match. Three identifiable phases have evolved in the work of all the Church Fora within Northern Ireland, which indicates that it is indeed a model of inter-church co-operation, rather than just a label that can be used to describe any inter-church group founded after the ceasefires. The first phase involves the internal strengthening of relationships within the Church Fora itself; this is quickly followed by the provision of community relations events within the local area. It is during this stage that the local environment radically affects the way in which they operate, completely determining the form that their work can take, although even here the similarities between the work of different groups is striking. By 2005 almost all of the Fora had experienced these two phases in the development of their programme work. However, only one had been able to move into the third phase of their expansion by training their members to become community relations trainers, thus indicating that almost all of the Fora failed to achieve their aims in the initial years of their existence.

Each of the fourteen Church Fora in Northern Ireland began their work in the same way, structuring their initial meetings around the idea that 'we needed to get to know one another as we explored our role in the wider community, and tried to fulfil our aims there'.[156] This work initially centred upon forming an understanding of the different denominations involved in the initiative and took a number of forms. In Lisburn, for example, they 'had a different minister or priest come down each evening for six weeks and that was good in terms of getting the clergy involved. The brief we gave the Clergy was [to] justify the differences in your denomination – what makes you unique?'[157] The Bangor group, Ploughshare, adopted a different approach to achieve the same end:

> We used to have house groups ... they would take some topic and it
> would be common across all the groups and one person would lead.
> It might be how we celebrate Christmas or communion, it ... was a
> discussion, everyone chipped in. It allowed different perspectives,
> we were able to ask why do you do it that way for example, now the
> protestants felt that we had far too much pomp and ceremony. Now
> one lovely lady said to me 'I see that its lovely and I see that you
> enjoy it, but to me that's more like theatre than church.' This was
> because I'd been talking about *Lumen Christi*. Fair enough, she came
> from a Quaker background and I didn't realise that the Quakers sat
> in a quiet room and let the Lord talk to them until she told me that!
> This was all letting us see the different perspectives.[158]

Once this understanding had been developed, these programmes moved
on to other issues such as the problems that the Forum members would
have to deal with, for instance the political situation, sectarianism and
unemployment, helping them to understand these issues from a Christian
perspective.

The development of trusting relationships facilitated by this work was
one of the main ways of fulfilling the aims and objectives of the groups.

> From this process [two] distinct lessons seem to have emerged. First,
> trust and mutual understanding and appreciation do indeed develop
> within small groups of people who meet regularly and honestly, and
> openly share their own stories and beliefs, as well as their percep-
> tions, and sometimes misconceptions, of one another's traditions.
>
> Second, behind important differences of belief, structure and
> practice there are strong theistic core convictions which are shared,
> and upon which a durable peace, founded on mutual respect, can
> be based. We are in particular more aware of the injunction to 'love
> one another', and more confident of our ability to do so, if we will
> but try.[159]

In this, the Church Fora were similar to the other forms of inter-church
group working in the area in that internal trust and understanding had to
be developed before the group could move on to achieving its aims with
the wider community. The nature of this initial work demonstrates the
changes that had taken place in the inter-church landscape, as prayer was
no longer a central component of this process. The groups instead being
in a position to commence, with the help of facilitators, on a process of
understanding and dialogue that would not have emerged in other inter-

church fellowships until three or four years after their foundation.

Once this understanding had been developed amongst the members, they were then able to begin their work improving relations within the locality; the underlying theme of which would be to promote friendship and understanding in a safe environment. It is here that the individual personalities of each of the Fora emerges and it is perhaps from this that the idea has emerged that they are an entirely new phenomena which have suddenly appeared in Northern Ireland and are so peculiar that their work cannot be defined within a broad overarching framework. This stage of the Fora's work was characterised by the idea presented by a member that 'we try to focus in on those concerns which are common to all of us'.[160] However, despite the differences in approach, this stage of their work was 'an attempt by the churches to address some of the community issues that we feel need attention, not just sectarianism but also issues related to poverty, problems in the town specific to our situation'.[161] Two categories of this stage exist: the relational, which concentrated on increasing understanding and relationships between the Protestant and Catholic communities in the area; and the practical, which strived to tackle the problems of the local area such as high unemployment and drug abuse.[162]

The relational category consisted of the provision of courses and lectures on issues relevant to the situation both locally and within Northern Ireland as a whole. At the outset, this programme work was dominated by the political, looking in particular at the problem of sectarianism which is rampant within even the most bourgeois of Northern Irish communities. A member of one Forum based in an affluent town describes their reasons for starting with this topic thus:

> because we didn't have major problems in Larne during the worst of the troubles, most people said there is no such thing as sectarianism here and because they didn't feel affected by it, they thought there was no need to do anything. But we live in a divided community and the more the original clergy group talked about the situation and involved more people from their congregations in their discussions, the more realisation there was that we had to do something after all.[163]

One of the main techniques used by the Church Fora was the 'Open Discussion Evening' where speakers such as politicians, members of the Orange Order or local residents' groups[164] would be invited to speak about their work in Northern Ireland or the current political situation. For example, between 2004 and 2005 the Cookstown Forum were addressed by Simon Dilworth on the Orange Order, the Rev. Jim Rea, former President of the Methodist Church in Ireland, on issues facing the churches today, and Alf McCreary on his experiences as a religious correspondent for the *Belfast Telegraph*. Similarly, the Dungannon Area Churches Forum had speakers such as the Rev. Ken Newell, Moderator of the Presbyterian Church, Heather Ellis on human rights and Sean Brady, the Archbishop of Armagh.

The main aim behind the Fora's work was to promote understanding not only of the issues involved but also to humanise people who would previously have been demonised by those who did not agree with their world view:

> part of it was to hear the party line, it was also to get to know them as people: as the family man, or in his job as well, so that they are not just a face on the TV, so that next time you see them on TV we know a little bit more about who they are and why they are doing this and why they are prepared to stand up for this or that.[165]

The format of the programmes offered by the Church Fora was greatly affected by the existence of peace and reconciliation education initiatives within Northern Ireland and the types of programmes that they offered. Thus facilitators, such as the ISE and Mediation Northern Ireland, were used to provide courses on community relations and, in particular, biblically based reconciliation.

The methods used by the Church Fora to build community relations did not solely centre upon these 'discussion evenings' and some of the groups have engaged in innovative work that aims to bring their message of reconciliation to young people. This was primarily a result of the difficulties they had in attracting younger members. As one Forum member put it, 'it's just an awareness we have that when we look around, it is all people of a certain age'.[166] Amongst the youth groups and events aimed specifically at that demographic was one initiative, which attempted to bring the Religious Education curriculum to life for the Fora's local schools. This project, run by Ploughshare in Bangor, Co. Down, was constructed to help young people learn 'from each other and address the things that are common to us, as well as learning about our differences and addressing issues that we both as Protestants and Catholics are concerned about'.[167] This project brought GCSE pupils from the local Catholic and Protestant schools, both secondary and grammar, together for a number of one-day conferences, the themes of which reflected the Fora's broader desire to constructively deal with difference. During their involvement they took part in workshops dealing with sectarianism and racism, the intended outcome of which was getting the schools involved and make them aware, talking to them and getting them to talk to each other so that they know that these issues are not just foolishness, they know that community issues are bigger than just what they learn in the classroom. It gave them an opportunity to mix together. All of the secondary schools that serve this area were represented, there is good potential for filtering back with that.[168]

This form of programme work is the essence of the type of activity that the Church Fora envisaged on their foundation and further demonstrates the need for stable, trusting relationships within the core unit of the organisation as well as a long-standing presence within the local community. At the time of writing, all of the Church Fora find themselves at different stages in their development, and schemes like this one, whilst presenting a standard against which others may be set, demonstrate clearly the need for each Fora to be sensitive to the needs and wants of their own area. Many of the early Church Fora founded before 1999, tried to engage with the local community by adopting a more wide-ranging approach to its remit as a local-level inter-church body. They did so by adding a practical dimension which centred upon educating its members on issues of common concern. Consequently, information and discussion on issues such as drug abuse and unemployment were tentatively provided in order to 'encourage the churches to have some sort of social concern for those around them instead of just [concentrating upon] evangelism'.[169] However, despite a desire to engage in practical and informative community relations, by 2005 nearly all of the Church Fora in Northern Ireland had failed to fully develop this aspect of their work, instead moving towards a model in which they became 'the churches' voice'[170] within the local community. For example, members of a town's Church Forum would sit on some of the working groups or committees dealing with the issues that would affect people directly, such as the closure of the local hospital. Some of the Fora have also made submissions to parliamentary committees, for example, Ploughshare prepared a paper on the 'Mental Incapacities Bill' whilst nearly all of the groups made submissions to the consultation on the recent good relations document, *A Shared Future*.[171] By becoming the 'churches' voice' within the community, both locally and further afield, the Church Fora are trying to 'present what is a shared Christian perspective on social and political issues'.[172] In doing so they were demonstrating that, within the group at least, they have built strong enough relationships to feel able to speak as a cross-community group signalling that they are moving towards achieving their aims as well as developing strikingly similar methods.

Only one of the nine Church Fora, the Lisburn Inter-Church Project, which closed due to a lack of funding in 2003, progressed into the third stage of programme work: the provision of training for community relations workers. The premise was that by training members of the Church Fora to be trainers themselves, the work of the group could be expanded as these newly skilled people would be able to run more programmes in the local community. However, by 2003 only one group had been trained, and its impact upon the growth of its local Forum is therefore impossible to evaluate.

In theory, the Church Fora represent an amalgamation of the inter-church fellowships and SAPs operating within Northern Ireland throughout the 1980s and 1990s, bringing with it the involvement of the local Community Relations Officer and the CRC and taking advantage of the large amounts of peace-building funding that flooded into Northern Ireland after the ceasefires. They have thus been hailed as representing a new era in inter-church relationships in Northern Ireland, integrating local community relations work with biblically based principles of reconciliation within a highly organised structure to facilitate such aims. In practice, their programme work has not entirely matched their aims and objectives. Whilst they have achieved their aim of bringing the Churches together to work on issues of common concern, it is apparent that they had not been able to implement the more practical side of their plans by providing help on matters such as drug education or training for community relations facilitators which would help the work to grow. Their work clearlyrepresents the movement which has occurred in inter-church relationships in Northern Ireland since 1980, providing a strong distinction between church-based community relationship building and institutional ecumenism. However, in presenting such an idea they are joined not only by other local groups, but also by the leadership of the national level Churches who have formalised this distinction in their ecumenical structures for dialogue.

CONCLUSION

Although the experiences of each of these groups is unique, being moulded by the circumstances in which they were founded and the socio-economic status of the area in which they operate, it is clear that there is no such thing as an anomaly in local level inter-church relationships. During each phase similarities in method and structure have emerged with, for example, inter-church fellowships being popular in the early 1980s but being superseded by the Church Fora model that arose in the new context created by the paramilitary ceasefires, the influx of peace money and the growth of peace and reconciliation education initiatives. It is clear then that events and developments within local communities and churches have been central to the growth of inter-church relationships in Northern Ireland. It is in this arena that the separation of ecumenism from community relations was born, and without local level groups inter-church relations would not exist in Northern Ireland.

Local-level groups have taken on many forms and the landscape has constantly been shifting since 1980, with those involved adjusting their methods and outward appearances to take into account the relentlessly changing political situation in which they were operating, whilst always remaining committed to the values of Christian reconciliation upon which they were founded. Their contribution has, thus, been substantial. On the most basic level, in common with national-level dialogue, it facilitated an increase in friendship and understanding between members of the Protestant and Catholic Churches. However, as we have seen, local-level inter-church relationships have moved beyond the superficial contact witnessed at the national level and have contributed to the development of inter-church work in two key ways. The first and most important of these was its separation of theological ecumenism from community relations, which set the tone for all inter-church contact during this period. The methods employed by local inter-church groups were the main vehicle for such a change. Thus, it is evident that those organising inter-church contact understood the place of the churches within the local community, and allowed the contact between the two communities to grow organically, reacting to the need to improve community relations, rather than imposing a programme of theological dialogue upon groups, which would not have held their interest. This separation of community relations from theological ecumenism led to the second contribution made by local groups, as they pushed the boundaries of inter-church contact forward by challenging the apathy found at a national level and, once trust and understanding had been achieved, strived to develop projects that put the message of the Gospel into practice. The most blatant example of this can be seen in the Social Action Projects, which took the practical application of the Gospel to the extreme in their contribution to inter-church relations, whilst other groups, such as the Clergy Fraternals, engaged in more subtle methods which also challenged the national-level churches by addressing matters, such as the political situation, that the IICM were unable to engage with.

That is not to say that local level inter-church relations were perfect.

They were not, and they suffered from two main problems. The first of these was the nature of their growth. The groups discussed in this chapter were formed in a haphazard manner, mostly being the result of an individual's desire to improve relationships within the local area. Thus, there was no strategy behind their foundation and development, with, for example, their aims and objectives only being written either for funding purposes or for inclusion in the inter-church directory. This could possibly have affected their impact upon the local area, leading them to be misunderstood, being seen as an ecumenical prayer group, and therefore something suspicious, instead of something which might be of help, practical or otherwise, to the local area. Furthermore, this lack of strategy was translated into an uneven spread of inter-church projects across the province, and has made their involvement in the provision of services, such as unemployment advice schemes, patchy (although, the fact that each of the groups devised similar methodologies serves to further underline the influence that the ideas of Christian reconciliation, peace and forgiveness had upon the process). This lack of strategy was further highlighted in the post-ceasefire era, as a radical change occurred in local inter-church relations. From 1994 onwards, a great deal of planning went into developing inter-church relations in local communities; this caused the pendulum to swing too far in the other direction, promoting highly strategic organisations which, it could be argued, suffocated the organic nature of local inter-church groups. Thus, the groups began to mould themselves to fit in with the expectations of the funding bodies and the Community Relations Council, leading to the well-defined model of inter-church contact, in the form of the Church Fora, being established.

The second problem concerns the analysis of their success as, whilst there can be no doubt of the contribution made by local groups to the progression of inter-church relations in Northern Ireland, there is no means available at the present time to measure their impact upon their local communities, or indeed, upon the region as a whole. Thus, whilst their work is interesting and definitely contributing to the structural development of the inter-church movement, it could be the case that they are having no influence upon the Protestant and Catholic communities, and instead are something that is tolerated or ignored, except by those who actively participate. However, the fact that there is no organised opposition, in the form seen at a national level, to this contact, would indicate that there is at the very least a tacit acceptance of such groups or a belief that they are a benign presence within the area.

The success of inter-church groups within local communities has been, to say the least, varied: 'some have had more than a local habitation and a name, and some have had their day. Others struggle on with courage. Everyone has played a part and, all in all, they make one thing clear; they represent massive Christian concern and conviction about Ulster's troubles.'[173] However, it is clear that some, such as the Social Action Projects, have strayed so far away from the strict definition of inter-church relationships that it is questionable whether they could be defined as church-based projects at all, even though their aims and vision still retain an articulation of the need for Christian reconciliation in the province. Despite this, through the development of local level inter-church relationships can be seen a formalisation of the separation of institutional ecumenism from community relationships and peace-building issues to a degree not witnessed in any other form of inter-church relationships.

## CHAPTER FOUR

# Ecumenical Communities

The years since 1980 then have seen many people become committed to the idea of building peace in their own areas. This has resulted in the development of a form of inter-church work which reclaims the social imperative of the Gospel, with its emphasis upon the ideas of building peace, justice and reconciliation both through prayer and social action, replacing it at the heart of community life instead of the abstract theological discussion and comparison witnessed in national level meetings. Central to the phenomenon of local inter-church relationships has been the ecumenical community, founded in order to 'include Protestants and Catholics who share a common life and engage in activities marked by efforts towards reconciliation'.[1] Such communities have successfully combined groundbreaking work in the field of community relations and ecumenism with longevity. They were initially founded as a means of providing a respite from the violence of the late 1960s and 1970s, with the Corrymeela Community and the Christian Renewal Centre providing places of shelter, away from the inner cities where the violence centred. It was hoped that Protestants and Catholics could come together and pray whilst getting to know and understand something of each other's culture and faith.

As this period progressed, the form of the ecumenical community began to evolve, as newly founded groups began to concentrate upon a more geographically defined area, often working in places of deprivation and conflict, providing social welfare as well as opportunities for prayer and reconciliation. Thus, between 1977 and 1992 five new ecumenical communities were founded: the Lamb of God Community in 1977, the Columba Community in 1981, the Cornerstone Community in 1982, the Columbanus Community of Reconciliation in 1983 and the Currach Community in 1992. All of these communities operated on a much smaller scale than their earlier counterparts. Consequently, by the mid-1990s two types of community were in existence: the early pioneers (Corrymeela and the Christian Renewal Centre) and the peaceline communities (Cornerstone, Lamb of God, Columba, Columbanus Community of Reconciliation and Currach). Whilst the spirit of each of these seven communities has remained the same since their foundations, there is strong evidence to illustrate that an evolution has taken place within them as they have reacted to external political events, as well the failure of the Churches at a national level, with the early 1990s and the paramilitary ceasefires marking a turning point in the way in which they operated.

This chapter will examine the progress of each of these types of ecumenical communities, looking at the ways that they have reacted to the changes in the Northern Irish political and ecumenical landscapes. In addition to this, it will consider the way in which they have contributed to the development of inter-church relationships, by creating an environment in which ecumenism, community relations and reconciliation all work together in concurrent circles, instead of the separate spheres witnessed at a national level.

## THE EARLY PIONEERS: THE CORRYMEELA COMMUNITY AND THE CHRISTIAN RENEWAL CENTRE

Whilst the hierarchies of the churches in Ireland were embroiled in discussions concerning theological issues with the occasional glance towards the idea of community relations, many people, in the settings of their local parishes and university campuses, began to recognise the need for some form of Christian response to the problems facing the province. This resulted in the establishment of two ecumenical communities: the Corrymeela Community in 1965 and the Christian Renewal Centre in 1974. Both groups drew their members from all over Northern Ireland and were influenced by the new trends in spirituality, such as charismatic renewal, which were sweeping Christianity world-wide. In their establishment we can see the foundations of a new and in many senses groundbreaking inter-church movement. This new movement was separated from the national level dialogue of the period by its desire to move away from the discussion on issues, such as Marian theology or justification by faith, towards making practical steps on the road to reconciliation between the Protestant and Catholic communities brought about through their efforts to understand and accept the legitimacy of the opposing traditions based upon biblical witness and prayer.

## The Corrymeela Community

The name Corrymeela has come to epitomise inter-church relations in Northern Ireland being used by many as a byword for the development of healthy relationships and the attempt to heal the breaches that exist in society. They are by far the largest and most well established of all the ecumenical communities and, since their foundation in 1965, have constantly re-evaluated their aims and methods, taking into account the changing nature of the situation in which they were operating. They have thus, developed a form of reconciliation work based upon the visible example of Christian unity lived in their residential community in Ballycastle, Co. Antrim. Here they worked by removing people from their everyday environment and providing participants with effective ways of developing relationships. These worked by encouraging them to talk face to face rather than 'shout from a distance at one another', showing them that encounters with the 'other sort' could be both spiritually and personally enriching.

### Beginnings

The 1960s were years of renewal and change within the churches as the fledgling ecumenical movement in Ireland cultivated a desire amongst many young people to work for a 'wider vision of the Church'.[2] The early members of Corrymeela 'shared a deep commitment to the Church, but dissatisfaction with its contemporary structures and a longing to see something different'.[3] At the core of these new attitudes lay a desire to put into practice the ideals of a Christian community laid out in the Gospel. In order to do this, the founders of Corrymeela drew inspiration from two ecumenical communities, Iona in Scotland and Agape in Italy,[4] both of which were living according to the values of reconciliation and fellowship found in the Gospels. This vision was crucial to the development of Corrymeela as:

> It was in Iona that we began to recover the meaning of the Church as the whole people of God ... on Iona we found all the dimensions of the ecumenical movement held together in creative tensions – Unity, Mission and Renewal. All the rich traditions of Christian History were invited to contribute their insights, but it was in a context of an encounter with the real world today.[5]

These emerging ideals were strengthened by the group's contact with Agape. This presented them with a challenge to 'live and incarnate the problems and difficulties of men, be they hunger, unemployment or whatever, in order to bring them the message of the Kingdom of God which is the message of reconciliation, of service and of love'[6] prompting them to ask 'Could we not try to initiate an Irish Agape?'[7] The earliest members of the Corrymeela Community took up this challenge and in 1965 purchased the property in Ballycastle, that became the Community's residential base.

*Vision and aims*
Corrymeela's initial aims bear witness to the peaceful pre-troubles climate of their foundation, and they could have been transferred to any part of the UK. They aimed:

a) To help to train Christian laymen/women to play a responsible part in society and the church.

b) To provide opportunities for retreat, so that people under stress, or wishing to discover new meaning in their lives, may find quietness for readjustment.

c) To provide opportunities for industrial and professional groups to meet for conference and study.

d) Through work camps, to bring together crafts-people and voluntary workers in a realistic Christian fellowship.

e) Through youth camps, to provide a meeting place for young people of this and other countries.

f) To provide a meeting point for reconciliation work in the wider Community and in church life.[8]

Consequently, their vision was based upon a desire for ecumenical unity and attempted to translate the ideals of Iona and Agape into a Northern Irish setting, adopting:

> The growing Ecumenical vision which understood the church to be called to be a SIGN and agent of the purpose of Christ to draw all HUMANKIND INTO UNITY and not to be simply an agent for the salvation of individuals ... Complementary to this was the search for NEW WAYS of expressing Christian COMMUNITY.[9]

The Community quickly realised that reconciliation was going to have to lie at the very heart of anything they did,[10] and they thus incorporated this idea into their aims, whilst remaining faithful to their initial desire to provide a visible example of Christian Unity based upon the 'salvation of the whole person, rather than just the salvation of the soul'.[11] Accordingly, by 1980 Corrymeela had become a place for 'people of all

ages and Christian traditions who, individually and together, are committed to the healing of social and religious and political divisions that
exist in Northern Ireland and throughout the world'.[12] They felt that if
they were to build lasting relationships then the whole of society had to
be examined, and not just the pigeon hole of church.

From 1980, the Community continually reflected upon and refined
their objectives, taking into account the environment in which they were
working and building their aims upon their vision of biblically based reconciliation. By 1985 they were beginning to ground themselves firmly
within a Northern Irish context rather than in the general terms witnessed at their foundation. Thus, they began not only to see themselves
as an example of unity for the churches, but also as a beacon of reconciliation for the wider society, as they strived:

- To be a sign and a symbol in a divided society that Protestant
  and Catholic can share together in a common witness to Christ
  who transcends our divisions and leads us towards a large
  vision of reconciliation; to be a question mark to the existing
  structures of our churches in Ireland.
- To provide opportunities for people from all sections of our
  society for dialogue and encounter and learning in order to
  dispel ignorance, prejudice and fear and to develop new
  relationships of mutual respect, trust and co-operation.[13]

By the early 1990s, this vision had developed even further, as
Corrymeela became more committed to their belief that an undeniable
need existed in Northern Irish society for structures to be put in place to
facilitate the long-term healing of past inequities. Thus, in the mid-1990s,
they argued that '[a]s we struggle to find a basis for a pluralist society in
which both Irish and British traditions are recognised and given free
expression, and where all sections of our society can feel a sense of
belonging, ... we know that our deeper fears and wounds can always
block the way'.[14] Such a belief resulted in the production of a new set of
aims and objectives in the late 1990s, and again Corrymeela was seeking
to contextualise their aims and vision in the light of changing events within Northern Ireland. Thus, the political process from 1994 onwards
affected these new aims greatly and they wanted:

- To be a sign and symbol that Protestants and Catholics can share
  together in a common witness and ministry of reconciliation.
- To provide opportunities for meeting, dialogue and learning in
  communities to dispel ignorance, prejudice and fear and to

promote mutual respect, trust and co-operation.
- To support victims of violence and injustice; to enable the healing of personal and social wounds and to promote new initiatives for social and political change.
- To address contemporary issues of faith and ethics and develop new expressions of Christian community, life and worship.[15]

Furthermore, in this new set of aims were a number of significant differences to those that had gone before. Instead of presenting themselves as a body aimed principally at Christian reconciliation, Corrymeela preferred to place greater emphasis upon their role as a practical support network for those working in the field of reconciliation and peace building. In addition to this, they presented a more positive picture of the work of the Community as a place where reconciliation was actually happening, rather than expressing a hope that Corrymeela would be a place where reconciliation would occur. Nevertheless, despite these changes in the stated aims of the Community in the 1990s, their vision remained the same: 'essentially we are a group of Protestants and Catholics who are on a journey of reconciliation with one another ... [and] basically our centres are about places where people can come and join us on that journey of reconciliation'.[16]

In the development of Corrymeela's vision can be seen 'a much clearer sense of a journey, an exploration to find what reconciliation means, what peace means because [they] started before the troubles'.[17] However, even with the onset of the frantic violence and unrest of the early 1980s, it extended far beyond the promotion of a cessation of violence by religious means. The Community preferred instead to address the divisions rampant within society which caused the violence, an ethos which has remained constant throughout the thirty-five years of its work:

> what we were trying to do was something more fundamental than oppose violence. What we were trying to do was to find out what it means to live the lifestyle of Jesus in his footsteps. What does it mean in Northern Ireland today in the context that we live in? There is an inspiration in seeing what kind of friends Jesus made, they were always the outcasts, the downtrodden, how very often he opposed the people in power, particularly the religious leaders because they were about power and manipulation of the oppressed rather than the liberation. These are the things that life is really about, this is what we are called to do, no matter what the outward circumstances, these elements will still need to be addressed and thus there is a sense of sustenance and purpose no matter what the

circumstances.[18]

Corrymeela then is a living, breathing organism that reacts to its constantly changing environment with an extremely clear idea of its purpose and goals. As a result, it is dedicated to facilitating long-term and lasting reconciliation within Northern Irish society rather than just a cessation of violence.

### Programme work and methods

Throughout the late 1960s and 1970s, Corrymeela's work developed in a number of areas, which aimed to address the polarisation that was rife in Northern Irish society. They ran family weeks, work camps for young people, local cell groups[19] and conferences arranged for groups such as paramilitaries, politicians, teachers and clergy. As a result, the programmes offered by Corrymeela before 1980 initiated a new form of inter-church work in Northern Ireland, as they realised that 'far too often the participants in Ulster's communal struggles have shouted from a distance to each other'.[20] Despite this, it is evident that in common with most church groups, the value of the early programme work lay in its impact upon the Community itself:

> I am sure the real value of the early programmes ... was the impact they primarily had on the members of this young Community more than anything that was immediately achieved with those who came ... These early encounters opened our eyes not only to the religious and political divisions, but also the social and economic realities. Painfully we came to realise the almost complete lack of communication and began to struggle with what methods change could be brought about in these areas.[21]

Consequently, Corrymeela's programme work began to evolve, being based firmly upon its early experiences and a realisation of the need to enter 'a vast arena of conflicts and challenges which cried out to be faced'.[22] From 1980 onwards then, the Community adopted a reactive approach to their work with the methods and programmes constantly developing and changing according to the needs of those involved.

The Community's programme work can be divided into two categories: family and community work and youth and schools work, both of which illustrate their commitment to Christian reconciliation within Northern Ireland. Nevertheless, since 1980 both types of work have shared a common set of values and methodology that have been underpinned by the Community's Christian education work. The work of Corrymeela has always been based upon a holistic approach to reconciliation, interweaving both physically and metaphorically, where possible, all aspects of the Community's work:

> This has proved valuable in all sorts of ways since it often means that the Centre has groups from a variety of backgrounds and age groups meeting at any one time. The possibility of their interaction at the informal times or in the common activities of eating, recreation or worship has often added something special to the total experience. Many young people value the chance to relate to a wide variety of adults and not to be wholly encapsulated in a 'youth' culture (and vice versa). Community is about that kind of interdependence.[23]

The development of the methods and values behind the Community's programme work could be viewed as a journey shared by the members and participants alike. Thus, the Community has constantly reflected upon the methods employed, reassessing their usefulness and contribution to the continuation of Corrymeela's vision. Fundamental to this is the belief that 'reconciliation is a much broader concept than merely bringing the two traditions into contact'[24] an ideal which has guided those involved in developing their methodology. Corrymeela believes that it is possible to change the attitudes, beliefs and actions of an individual by addressing all of their relationships rather than just the Protestant/Catholic axis. Hence, their work is based upon the need to understand 'personal prejudices, recognising them in the future and trying to change behaviour or responses accordingly'.[25] As a consequence of these values, the programmes provided by Corrymeela were individualised according to the needs of the group, with 'each programme [being] designed ... for that particular experience and for those participating',[26] generally based upon the models available to their programme workers. In the early 1980s the Community used two programmes, which were employed by both the Family and Youth and Schools groups: the basic model and the seed group.

The basic model has provided the foundation for most of Corrymeela's methods since 1980, evolving to suit the needs of the participants and operating in three phases which moved from each individual sharing their own experiences to finding ways for the relationships within the group to develop.[27] Thus, the work of Corrymeela centres upon an experiential model, which encourages participants to form ideas concerning their own prejudices and life experience whilst building trusting, open relationships with the others in the group. This enables them to see that they can work with, and get to know, people from the other community. Such ideas concerning cross-denominational group work were employed in the second model employed by the Community, the seed group, which has been employed since 1981 with groups of young adults who are willing to make a commitment to work with Corrymeela for a period of six months.

During a process of reflection upon their youth work, the programme leaders recognised that the main strength of the Corrymeela experience was not in the structured learning that took place in group sessions, but was instead to be found in the encounters it provided for people with the other community. The consequence of this was a programme which aimed to provide the participants with gradual personal growth over a period of time, rather than the leadership training that had previously been offered. The new programme consisted of six monthly residential weekends with a group of approximately eighteen to twenty young people (aged 18–21),[28] along with four facilitators and aimed to guide them through a process that would see them, amongst other things '[b]uilding bridges of trust, understanding and personal friendship within a group spanning [a variety of] backgrounds'.[29] The participants followed a mixed programme, designed specifically to develop the trust and understanding needed to deal with the issues involved. One of the designers of the programme sums up its value by arguing that:

> Working with such a model has been a liberating experience. There is a design but not really any curriculum. There are topics for exploration, but no body of information to be absorbed. There are hopes but no explanations in terms of results. There is freedom for individual learning to follow different paths and also for the Spirit to work in ways that we can't programme or control. Perhaps the most exciting part, though, comes from the growth of a learning community, with trust caring and mutual sharing of gifts, so different from most models used in both secular and Christian education.[30]

By providing such a resource for young people, Corrymeela was in effect training them in their new form of holistic Christian reconciliation, recognising that the development of trusting relationships, rather than endless dialogue, was the key to conflict resolution.

Throughout the 1990s, Corrymeela built upon this work, taking into account new trends in reconciliation education, whilst remaining committed to their Christian ethos and desire to work with groups individually rather than superimposing rigid methodological ideas upon their participants. They began to develop new means of working with cross-community groups, in addition to those already in place. These included the use of methods already employed by other inter-church groups within Northern Ireland, such as single-identity groups, cross-border work and facilitating local inter-church contact. However, by far the most significant development in Corrymeela's work during the late 1990s was its attempt to work within communities as well as working with them at the Ballycastle centre. This new departure was represented by the Community Partners Project, established in 1997 to engage with interface communities. This programme works by looking 'at the needs of people whose life experiences, either personal or professional, are deeply affected because of the proximity to a sectarian interface'.[31] This project was based upon the fact that 'the people we are working with want to move forward and sometimes we are able to provide the contacts where they can find training and we can help them learn skills in terms of community development'[32] and took a more practical approach to Corrymeela's commitment to a holistic version of Christian reconciliation.

Community Partners works by supporting already existing groups and operating with them to achieve not only improved community relations, but also a sustainable and viable project for the area. The Corrymeela worker starts by exploring the needs of the local community before deciding how to help them, resulting in diverse approaches being taken with those involved. For example, one group builds relationships by engaging in activities, such as cooking and making Christmas cards, whilst another discusses the political viewpoints of the two communities and tries to explore ways of creating peace. Corrymeela uses its expertise in relationship building and all the means at its disposal to work with these communities, the most important of which is the use of its centre at Ballycastle to teach the groups how to work together and communicate with one another. The experiences of one women's group from Belfast, both in Ballycastle and subsequently, highlight the methods and effect of the Community Partners Project.

> This group comes from an Interface area that has seen some of the worst violence; they live with tension and the very real presence of paramilitaries, and experience high unemployment and deprivation. Their experiences at Ballycastle were significant for them not only in the short term as they contrasted so hugely with their normal lives, but also in how the group learned to relate to each other and the level of understanding and trust we all now have.
>
> Since the residential the women continue to meet and there is an increased willingness to look at what living within an Interface area means to them. Relationships have developed to the level where people can be honest and are prepared to be challenged on views that may be sectarian or racist. We recently took the open-top bus tour of

Belfast which took us onto the nationalist Falls Road, stopping at an IRA memorial and passing the Celtic supporters' bar. When I first started meeting with this group I would have been reluctant to take them on the tour and although this may seem like only a small step forward, it marks a beginning for other possibilities to develop.[33]

The project demonstrates the significance of taking a reactive approach to this type of work as the women involved would have been resistant to anything too rigid. As one of its workers put it, 'the Community Partners Project does not work to its own agenda. I do not go into an interface area with a ready-designed programme, but rather I go in and listen and then explore what support Corrymeela can offer; as the name suggests we come in as partners.'[34] In this, Corrymeela fell into the general pattern emerging in local inter-church work from the 1990s onwards, which demonstrated that the key to success lay in working in partnership with communities rather than prescribing them with a cure.

Corrymeela's programme work represents a tangible manifestation of their aims and visions, as they initially aimed to be a symbol of reconciliation within Northern Ireland. Through their work from their foundation until circa 1990, they did just this, as well as providing the means for a large number of groups to engage with one another in a neutral environment away from the conflict. However, Corrymeela did not remain static once they had achieved this model of reconciliation, rather growing and developing by trying to adopt new models, which were implemented in their work and provided a new means of engagement with the Protestant and Catholic communities.

### Membership and management

Since its foundation, Corrymeela has evolved from a small ecumenical community wanting to serve as an example of Christian reconciliation into a sophisticated body with a clear management structure in place for the facilitation of its programme of work. Consequently, due to its size and place as a province-wide ecumenical community, Corrymeela's management style was hierarchical and business-like, with a series of checks and balances to ensure the smooth operation both of its programme work and of its membership growth. In the 1980s and early 1990s, this meant that Corrymeela was totally unlike any other ecumenical community in Northern Ireland, with the others only following suit when the rigorous demands placed upon them by the Funding Bodies meant that they had, at least, to present a façade of structured management.

The Community's membership has grown vastly from the forty initial founding members in 1965 to 152 full members in 2005. 'Members commit themselves to support each other and the Community ... This commitment can manifest itself ... in their churches and in their own local community; as well as being focused directly upon the programmes and structures of ... Corrymeela ... per se.'[35] Although the work of the Community has changed, the route to membership has essentially remained the same. The candidate has to work through a set of guide-lines, which are designed to assess not only his or her suitability for the Community, but also whether membership would be of benefit to them. After an initial meeting with the leader, they are expected to undertake at least a year's provisional membership attending a number of weekend sessions focusing upon the work of the Community, whilst experiencing as much of the work of Corrymeela as possible. Once accepted, they take part in the dedication ceremony held in early January where they accept the member's commitment based upon the Community's vision.

The years since 1980 have been ones of enormous growth for Corrymeela and, as a result, a sophisticated organisational structure has had to evolve to take into account the growing numbers and variety of needs of those who wish to become involved with the Community's work, as not everyone was able to commit to working in the centre in Ballycastle. In order to cope with this growth, the 'cell group' model was refined to take into account the variety of membership. These groups have always been a vital component in building the Community in three ways: first, they aimed to deepen the members' encounter with Corrymeela by providing them with the sense of identity and close rela-tionships that the earliest members experienced. Second, they hoped to bring the work of Corrymeela to the area in which they were based and finally, they tried to live Corrymeela's vision of Christian reconciliation by experiencing and living their faith rather than just practising it. They argue that:

> It has been the interplay of these ... which gives the special flavour to our meetings. We are very much involved with the daily events of our world, both events which please us and those which we find very painful ... And it is for ourselves, our neighbourhoods and our country that we pray.[36]

However, the work of Corrymeela, and indeed membership of its cell groups, was not confined to its full members. The Friends of Corrymeela was founded in the mid-1970s to answer the needs of many of those who were interested in the work of the Community but were unable to commit to full membership, and by the mid-1990s there were approximately 2,300 people world-wide who had pledged to support Corrymeela's work by giving a small annual donation. By 2005, the Community had developed a number of membership strategies which were designed to fulfil a desire for Christian unity for a wide range of people whilst carrying out the practical vision of reconciliation through its work in Ballycastle and Belfast.

Accordingly Corrymeela developed sophisticated mechanisms to cope not only with the growth in human resources but also with the development in its vision and aims, thus as their programme work has flourished there has been a discernible change in the way in which the organisation is managed. Throughout the 1980s, the staff of the Ballycastle and Belfast offices managed the Community with the Council, elected by the members every three years, appointing the necessary staff and programme volunteers and overseeing the running of the two centres. In practice, the work of the Community was organised by line managers who were divided into a series of committees that answered ultimately to the leadership and the members of the Community. However, when the Community undertook a review of its structure and work in the early 1990s it was decided that the management structure needed to be overhauled as 'in the past there [had] been a degree of confusion as to how some committees viewed their purpose and task and this, inevitably, led to "grey areas"'.[37] The report suggested that 'committees should be grouped so that similar terms of reference can be made for each committee within a group'.[38] Five main groups were proposed and eventually implemented: the Council sub-committees[39] appointed by the Council and carrying out the work belonging directly to the Council, the Programme Staff Resource Groups, consisting of members who have experience in their work,[40] the Building, Domestic and Transport resource groups which would work alongside a staff member responsible to a line manager,[41] the Members' Involvement Groups[42] and finally the Staff Support Groups, which offered personal support to key members of staff such as the leader and field workers. In their willingness to reassess their structures and management, Corrymeela were illustrating one of the main components of their continued vitality. They demonstrated that they were willing to redesign and alter aspects of the Community whilst retaining that which had proved successful – an ethos continued from their programme work as they constantly tried to develop a programme relevant to the situation in which they were living.

Corrymeela occupies a unique place in the inter-church landscape of Northern Ireland, not only because of its longevity, but also because of its size. Thus, with an estimated 6,000 people taking part in its programmes each year, it is unrivalled and has constantly proved to be prophetic both in its reconciliation work with the two communities, and in the challenge of Christian living that it has presented to its members. It has moved from being a Christian community to an internationally renowned facilitator helping other groups to develop their own plans for reconciliation in the province. That is not to say, however, that Corrymeela is a flawless vision of how a Christian Reconciliation Community should operate within the context of the Northern Irish situation. And it is evident that their rigid management structure and distance from the communities with whom they work have prevented them from addressing some of the social aspects of the Gospel, such as deprivation, and it is only latterly that they have begun to go out into the community to work rather than expecting groups to come to them. Despite these problems, however, Corrymeela did pave the way for the other ecumenical communities in the province, developing many of the models of reconciliation used and providing the prophetic and critical voice needed, not only to challenge the hierarchies of the churches but also the complacency of many church-goers.

## The Christian Renewal Centre

In contrast to the extensive methods and influences of the Corrymeela Community, the other pioneering ecumenical community in Northern Ireland, the Christian Renewal Centre, had a much narrower focus in its development and consequently was not as influential in the evolution of inter-church relationships as all other ecumenical communities were. The Christian Renewal Centre used renewal and prayer as a means of transcending difference and has, since its foundation in 1974, remained firmly attached to its Charismatic Renewal roots, an attachment, which has radically affected their development causing them to stagnate whilst other communities branched upwards from their founding roots and extended their means of promoting Christian reconciliation.

### Beginnings

During the late 1960s and early 1970s, the Charismatic Renewal Movement[43] swept through Northern Ireland and at first was seen as a passing, and somewhat dangerous, phase in the church's history:

> So much has this become the case that one can detect the Hierarchy endeavouring to guide the faithful along safe paths and away from dangerous influences. Official Catholic concern is more than matched by unofficial opposition from theologically right-wing Protestants, who are equally determined to steer their faithful away

from danger.[44]

The Renewal Movement, with its gifts of liberation and spiritual revival to its adherents, was expected by many observers to have a profound effect upon community relations in Northern Ireland as 'the proclamation of the Gospel includes, for each and every Christian, the duty to contribute personally to that collective and essential righting of social justice'.[45] It was hoped that the relationships developed through Charismatic Renewal would help to transcend the fear and mistrust that was intensifying there by influencing political attitudes and paramilitary activity.[46] However, by the closing years of the 1970s it was becoming clear that many Charismatics had failed to embrace the social implications of their calling and had thus failed to make the impact that was expected.

Nevertheless, the experience of the Charismatic Movement during this period did contribute somewhat to the development of local-level inter-church relations[47] resulting in the foundation of the Christian Renewal Centre in Rostrevor, Co. Down in 1974 by the Rev. Cecil Kerr. The initial idea for the Centre came to Kerr whilst he was working as a Chaplain at Queen's University, where he was a member of a Charismatic prayer group and in 1973 began to feel the need for a centre of prayer in the province:

> As the vision focused more clearly I saw the need for a place where people from all backgrounds could come together, not to argue or debate but in an atmosphere of prayer to meet Jesus and allow him to lead us forward in his purpose for his Church and for our land.[48]

A discernment group was formed consisting of eighteen Christian leaders and students to decide whether the Centre should be established and as a result the Christian Renewal Centre was founded in Rostrevor in August 1974 as a place of prayer, renewal and reconciliation.[49]

*Aims and vision*
The founding vision of the Christian Renewal Centre was based upon the Charismatic tenets of prayer and renewal, which it was hoped would bring about reconciliation. However, this was not a community-based reconciliation but one which would allow the members of the Christian Renewal Centre, as well as others who came into contact with them, to transcend the labels associated with their traditions and the hurts of the past, thereby moving themselves away from sectarianism. Thus, everything that the Centre aimed to do was based upon the premise that 'at

the Cross the ground is level. The Catholic has nothing over the Protestant. The Protestant has nothing over the Catholic ... Meeting there makes all the difference.'[50] Since 1974, the purpose of the Community has always been:

1. To be a **place of prayer** where Christians from all backgrounds may come together in an atmosphere of love and prayer.
2. To be a **place of renewal** where people may encounter Jesus Christ as the Saviour and Lord who baptises in the Holy Spirit and renews his church to be an effective witness to his power in the world.
3. To be a **place of reconciliation** where those who have been separated by ignorance, suspicion and fear may find the reconciliation for which our blessed Lord prays.[51]

It was not until after a new leadership was installed in 2000 that the vision of the centre was redefined. They now wanted to: 'Grow in our understanding and practice of prayer and in particular intercession, Call Christians to come together for prayer and intercession, Equip Christians for effective prayer by: organising and developing training and promoting prayer strategies.' Whilst seeking to be a place: 'Of meeting and conversing with God, Of intimacy – of sharing our hearts with Him. This includes the possibility of personal encounter and change as we seek Him for that to happen in others, Where we listen to God as He shares His heart and mind with us, for others and Ireland.'[52] This new vision placed an even greater emphasis upon prayer than before and represented a culmination of the work undertaken by the Christian Renewal Centre from the mid-1990s onwards. Thus from its foundation, the Christian Renewal Centre sought to be an inter-denominational house of prayer, working towards reconciliation purely through the medium of prayer.

## Methods

Consistency has been the key to the work of the Christian Renewal Centre and, as its work developed, a programme was formed which sought to place prayer at the heart of everything they did. Thus:

This centre has brought together people from all traditions who have been separated by fear, suspicion and ignorance and has helped them to rediscover that they are brothers and sisters in Christ. It has given special emphasis to the need for the removal of deep blockages caused by past hurts, wounds and resentments as a vital part of the work of healing and reconciliation.[53]

Although those involved did not have a set plan, the Christian Renewal Centre initially began work in an impromptu manner, starting with a Charismatic prayer group for local people, and eventually facilitating days of renewal and retreats for both local and international Charismatic groups.

Despite the success of these, the only major project in the history of the Christian Renewal Centre was the establishment of the Prayer for Ireland initiative in 1994 as a response to the paramilitary ceasefires through which people would volunteer to join a twenty-four-hour prayer chain, committing themselves to pray for an hour a week for:

1. Renewal of the church in Ireland, through the power of the Holy Spirit – working individually and corporately in its members.
2. Unity of the church in Ireland, through repentance, forgiveness and reconciliation.
3. The evangelism of those who do not know Jesus as their Saviour.
4. Healing of the land. This is the fruit of a living vibrant church, manifested outwardly into society affecting family life, politics, ethics/morality, education, health care etc. (2nd Chronicles 7:14).[54]

This prayer focused upon the political process in Ireland with participants being given the names of political leaders to pray for. By continuing to use prayer as their sole method this scheme represented a complete attempt to fulfil the Centre's vision, addressing its three main components of prayer, renewal and reconciliation believing that this was the only method that could help Northern Ireland as the members were:

> very conscious that the struggles in Ireland are primarily of a spiritual nature (Ephesians 6:12) – that many, Christians and non-Christians, are blinded in mind and spirit and are therefore incapable of making the radical change necessary to bring about and enter God's peace in Ireland. Such a radical change has always and can only come about (and be maintained) through humble, specific and concerted prayer.[55]

The reconciliation found through the Christian Renewal Centre was deliberately spiritual and individual rather than relational and communal as those involved with the Community relied upon the gifts of the Holy Spirit rather than organised community relations programmes and discussion to fulfil their plan to reconcile Protestants and Catholics with one another. Consequently, in their promotional literature numerous instances of conversion experiences are recorded:

> People consumed by hatred, resentment and bitterness have been set free. Men and women of violence have been transformed by the power of Christ. Former enemies have openly embraced each other in moving acts of reconciliation. Not a few wounded and bereaved in the violence have found healing and comfort.[56]

This then is Christian reconciliation on a minute scale and it is in this attitude towards community relationships that the Christian Renewal Centre is very different to every other inter-church group operating within Northern Ireland. Thus, whilst they have remained true to their founding aims and vision, in doing so they have remained within a Charismatic vacuum, only reacting to the ceasefires in 1994 for example through prayer and have therefore prevented themselves from adopting any of the new methods of community engagement that have developed since 1980.

*Membership and management*
In common with the consistent nature of the Christian Renewal Centre's work, their membership and management structures remained the same between 1980 and 2005. Thus, membership of the Community consisted of three levels of commitment that were entirely dependent upon the members' personal circumstances. The first was Community members who dedicate themselves[57] to the Christian Renewal Centre for a year at a time, becoming 'committed to the dynamics of being a House of Prayer for Ireland, taking time out for personal and group prayer ... over and above the daily times of prayer which we hold',[58] in this they are connected to the Associate Members, who feel called to be a member of the Christian Renewal Centre but do not want to take any part in the running of the Centre. They are joined by the Helpers, who volunteer to aid the day-to-day running of the centre with a view to becoming members themselves. The management of the Centre has remained unchanged as it 'evolved during the early days of the ministry ... and seems to work fairly well'[59] by being divided into four main areas: General Administration, the Prayer Ministry, Catering and Housekeeping, and each member and helper is assigned to an area according to their experience and ability, at the weekly community meeting. The Christian Renewal Centre is run in a democratic manner and its relatively small size (never rising above fifteen members) enables it to work in such a manner. Furthermore, as the work of the Community centres solely upon prayer and has remained static since 1980 there is very little need for them to

adopt the sophisticated structures developed by Corrymeela or even the more fluid methods adopted by the peaceline communities.

In the development of these pioneering ecumenical communities can be seen two diametrically opposed groups both working for Christian reconciliation within Northern Ireland with entirely different ideas of how such an aim should be achieved. Thus, Corrymeela centred its approach to reconciliation upon the need for pragmatism reassessing their style and methods by taking into account the constantly changing environment in which they worked, whilst the Christian Renewal Centre remained faithful to its roots in the Charismatic Renewal Movement and concentrated solely upon prayer and personal conversion as a means of peace-building within the Province. Despite their failings, the development of these ecumenical communities certainly brought a new dimension to the question of ecumenical relations within Northern Ireland. Each in its own way helped people move away from the over-concentration upon doctrinal issues that had dogged and hindered relationships between the hierarchies of the churches, by introducing new methods of dialogue as well as the all-important issues of reconciliation and community relations into the equation. Whilst their impact may be incredibly hard to determine, it is clear that through their pioneering work they laid the foundations for the normalisation of this new form of Christian living within Northern Ireland which would see the establishment of a number of new ecumenical Communities in the early 1980s, all of which were to go on themselves to become permanent fixtures in the inter-church landscape.

## SAFE HAVENS ON THE 'PEACELINES': THE LAMB OF GOD, CORNERSTONE, COLUMBA, COLUMBANUS AND CURRACH COMMUNITIES

Through their work, Corrymeela and the Christian Renewal Centre demonstrated the value of providing a place to which people could retreat from the pressures of living in an area of ongoing conflict. However, by 1980 it was becoming obvious that retreat and removal from everyday life was not going to be effective for everyone and that some form of work *within* the Community needed to be undertaken, which would be able to encompass the more practical elements of the Gospel. This led to the development of the peaceline ecumenical communities which worked constantly to build trust and community relations in the urban areas in which they were based. One described themselves as:

a Christian Ecumenical Community ... on the peaceline. We are in the middle of Protestant and Catholic and that is really where we want to be and we feel that we are something of a parable of possibility for the peaceline with people coming together to pray and to share their faith and to work together doesn't make them into an amorphous mass. We still maintain our identities but we work together.[60]

Each of these peaceline communities were established through the vision and desire of a small group of people to begin the healing of their society by bringing the Christian message of reconciliation to their immediate neighbourhood and 'there was simply a strong desire to build relationships and encourage a faith journey together with people of different Christian Churches'.[61] Consequently, their value lay not in their pioneering work, although their sheer presence in their areas was just that, but in their commitment to longevity and consistency within the communities that they aimed to serve.

The location of each of these groups has been crucial to their role in the development of inter-church relationships and their membership and work has been constantly rooted in the area and community that they aim to serve. From 1977 onwards five of these ecumenical communities were founded: the Lamb of God community in 1977 in North Belfast, the Columba Community in 1980 in Derry,[62] the Cornerstone Community in 1982 in West Belfast, the Columbanus community of Reconciliation in 1983 in a middle-class area of North Belfast[63] and finally the Currach community in 1992 in West Belfast. These communities with the exception of Columbanus operate in extremely segregated areas, with social and economic deprivation characterising the life experience of both Catholic and Protestant residents and these circumstances have brought the added spectre of paramilitary violence: 'they are not fighting each other on the Malone Road ... There are two communities here, and one is involved in violence, suffering, unemployment and injustice. The demarcation is class.'[64] It was in this atmosphere of violence and deprivation, that the peaceline ecumenical communities were founded in order to promote a model of Christian reconciliation and living that had been developed through tentative contacts between a few people who believed that their faith in God should override ethno-religious labels.

Although the nuances of their experiences have been different, there have been a number of factors that have underlined the existence of these ecumenical communities and explain their development. First, with the exception of Columbanus, all of these communities were established by groups of people who had met one another through inter-church prayer groups and who had therefore already demonstrated a commitment to and understanding of local inter-church work that was to prove crucial to their success. Furthermore, although these communities were founded during periods of intense violence it would seem that, with the possible exception of the Columba Community, the primary impetus behind them was spiritual rather than a reaction to the surrounding events. Second, the rationale of each of these peaceline communities has been radically influenced by the local socio-economic deprivation and violence leading them to try and bring the Christian message of reconciliation into the heart of the community 'to feel what was going on'[65] rather than removing people from their own setting as Corrymeela does. Consequently, with each of these ecumenical communities the circumstances of their foundation were translated into their aims for and vision of their work with the communities who were living on the peacelines. Thus, each of them wanted their houses to be viewed as a 'safe haven' for both Protestants and Catholics, becoming a physical manifestation of their belief that people of different Christian traditions could live together without major conflict.

Their primary aim was to bring local Protestants and Catholics together and their methods were based upon a need to stress commonality whilst creating acceptance and, crucially, understanding of difference. Consequently, a common methodological model has emerged from the experiences of these ecumenical communities and whilst the schemes employed were not entirely the same, in their engagement with their local communities each has moved through three phases: prayer and outreach, community relationship building and social action, adding each of these new aspects to their work at roughly the same time and in doing so placing further emphasis upon the shift from pure ecumenism to church-based community relations witnessed in other local initiatives.

Through prayer and outreach they remained committed to their ecumenical origins with regular prayer groups, whilst establishing relationships with the wider community which enabled them to gain trust and acceptance within the area. These relationships allowed them to begin working on cross-community relationship-building and establishing social action projects whereby each peaceline community would implement some practical measures aimed at alleviating the problems of the area. It is no coincidence that these developments occurred at around the same time for each of these communities as it is clear that outside influences, such as the political peace process and the resultant influx of peace and reconciliation funding, had a profound effect upon the methods and work of these groups. As a result, during the years from 1980 to

2005 each of these communities developed links within their local areas and in doing so, created schemes through which they could bring their message of Christian reconciliation to the wider community, commencing with the idea that:

> We knew that we could not come in here and start doing what we thought that the area needed, that would have been unhealthy, what we needed to do was to come in here and be part of the community around here, talk to them and dialogue with them because we wanted to be part of the area as well and through that we would learn what would emerge.[66]

Finally, in order to achieve their overarching aim of Christian reconciliation each of these communities adopted a low-key approach to membership and management, allowing their organisational structures to evolve along side their work instead of permitting the structures to drive their engagement with the local community. Therefore, it is evident that each of these ecumenical communities would, because of their common commitment to Christian reconciliation, be strikingly similar. However, despite such glaring similarities, the way in which this aim manifested itself was unique to each community and the circumstances in which it found itself operating.

## *The Lamb of God Community, North Belfast*

The earliest example of the 'safe haven' ecumenical community was the Lamb of God Community situated in North Belfast. At points in its history, this community has been the largest of the peaceline communities, peaking at over seventy members during the 1980s. Consequently, they have been a dynamic force within their local community, evolving rapidly from an ecumenical prayer group into a group focusing upon social action and the inherent needs of the area. However, in their means of engagement with the local community they are unique, as they have failed to follow the path that other ecumenical communities have taken, instead responding to the environment in which they work and developing accordingly.

The core group initially responsible for the foundation of the Community in 1977 met at a mainly Catholic Charismatic Renewal prayer meeting that had been running in the Antrim Road area since the mid-1970s. From this meeting 'it transpired that a group of people expressed a desire to have another meeting and this meeting was to take place on another night'.[67] Those involved 'felt called to form a non-residential Charismatic Renewal Community'[68] and at the first meeting they created a core group to direct its establishment. 'During that year we ran life in the spirit seminars, days of renewal ... our leader Larry [Kelly], was deeply involved in the diocesan Charismatic Renewal so he decided after a while to give up his job and work for a while as a leader for us'[69] By 1977 they had purchased a premise in Duncairn Gardens in North Belfast, a place chosen 'because it was on the peaceline',[70] with the help of a mortgage which was paid off within a year through donations from their supporters.

The Lamb of God Community aimed to build up relationships within their own group, before attempting to address the issue of working in the wider community, an idea that was reflected in the original aims of the Community which have not changed since 1977:

> To encourage each other on the faith journey
> To build stronger relationships between different traditions
> To reach out together to the wider community.[71]

However, in the mid-1980s, as the Community grew, they felt that there was a need to articulate the way in which these aims had been implemented, resulting in the Community's Vision Statement:

> The Lamb of God Community is a group of people committed to the Christian Way of Life. Central to that way of life is Prayer, Praise, Worship and Service of others. The Community seeks ...
>
> • To be a light to those in darkness
> • To give hope to those in need
> • To work towards reconciliation in our troubled society.[72]

In this updated articulation of the Community's vision can be seen the development of its self-perception: they had become more outward looking, no longer feeling the need to focus on internal relationships, rather taking those relationships and using their understanding to aid their work with the wider community. Furthermore, this growth in the aims and vision of the Lamb of God Community also came from their experience of working on the peaceline as they realised that it should focus more on the practical, with prayer being used as a method to strengthen relationships within the Community itself. The result was a clearer representation of how they wished to work whilst retaining the spirit of their initial aims.

The Lamb of God Community was the only peaceline community that did not strictly adhere to three progressive stages of prayer and outreach, community relationship-building and social action in their interaction with their local community. Instead, they engaged with the community primarily through prayer and outreach and social action before latterly attempting to implement community relationship-building in the late 1990s. By adopting such methods they were demonstrating the need for trust and approval within their localities that each of these communities had to have in order to succeed and survive. They consequently developed, what they called, 'a quiet way of doing things'[73] which was in essence, a reactive approach to the needs of the local community, based upon their fundamental tenants of 'service, fellowship, worship and prayer'.[74]

Prayer was used as a means of interacting with local people before introducing new projects and has played a consistent role within the work of the Community by underlining all its methods of engagement within the area. In addition to the organised Charismatic Prayer gatherings, a prayer ministry was established aimed at helping local people affected by the troubles. Initially, the Community worked from the top two floors of a hairdressing salon in Duncairn Gardens and 'this provided revenue for the Community and also gave the vital means of contact with the surrounding area'.[75] Here they adopted a low-key approach to their relationships with the surrounding community, enabling them to build trust, and it was through the contacts made with the customers of the salon that Lamb of God was able to found its prayer ministry. As with most of its work, the Community took a simple and reactive approach to its development, waiting for local people to approach them before talking about its work or offering help. This led to a counselling programme, which was developed by a Catholic nun who, with the help of other Community members, answered the need in the locality for a place where people could go 'just to unburden and to talk and just to be listened to'.[76] Consequently, the Community began to be viewed as a safe haven within the area and through this their early work built up. By the late 1980s they had, through their prayer and outreach, fulfilled their initial aims and began to plan towards making a larger impact through practical schemes whilst remaining committed to their bedrock of prayer.[77]

The Lamb of God Community added social action work to their remit when they moved into new, larger premises in 1990. This move was prompted not only by the rapid growth of the group but also by a desire to expand the nature of the work:

> there seemed to be a lot of people coming to the house for counselling and prayer ministry, so the house became too small for what

> was required so we had to buy this house [Shalom House on the
> Cliftonville Road] ... and when we moved here ... there was more
> administration and we got into a wider spread of things that we
> were able to do because of having the premises.[78]

Hence, it was an internal event which provided the catalyst for the
Community to become more involved with social action work as they
moved from being a praying ecumenical presence on the peaceline into a
welfare service provider for the locality. The first stage was the foundation of the crèche in 1992 where local children 'would be taken care of
and allowed to play'[79] after an atrocity. By 2005, this crèche had become
one of the Community's central projects and was providing a regular,
rather than emergency, form of childcare for the area. From this initial
project Shalom House evolved, offering services to develop the 'emotional, social, personal and spiritual'[80] needs of the community. They
began to run GCSE courses in maths and English for people wishing to
return to education, a drop-in centre and a spiritual programme based
upon prayer and meditation. The social action offered by the Lamb of
God Community was holistic rather than purely material, and focused
upon alleviating the deprivation of the local community through positive
action rather than prescriptive charity. Their success was recognised by
the Eastern Health and Social Services Board, who now fund Shalom
Care, a satellite of the Community, which carries out domiciliary and
respite care work in North Belfast, working 'with the ethos of the house
in mind'.[81]

The Community's engagement with the local community was, then,
based upon the two pillars of Charismatic prayer and sensitivity to the
needs of those surrounding them. They initially aimed to bring a message
of Christian reconciliation to Protestants and Catholics in the area but
were diverted from this aim by the deprivation in which they found
themselves operating. By developing such a pragmatic approach to their
work, they seem to have been immune to the external factors such as the
ceasefires which have altered the operating methods of the other communities. It would seem that this was mainly due to their roots as a
Charismatic prayer group, as their changes in method were induced more
by prayer than worldly events. Indeed, their response to the peace
process and the need to build relationships has been addressed almost
entirely through prayer:

> Members were also taking part in regular Fellowship Breakfasts
> which were taking place in Belfast to which local politicians were
> asked to speak and at which there was prayer and praise. We were

also part of a 'Hope in the City' group which organised monthly meetings in the YMCA hall in the centre of Belfast. This group has since developed into 'Transformations', following on the Transformations videos depicting the ecumenical work being done in Africa and South America and other places. 'Transformations' ran the Belfast section of World Day of Prayer which was held in the grounds of Stormont Castle where the Northern Ireland Assembly meet (when in session!). We have also been part of prayer meetings held in parliament buildings.[82]

To the Lamb of God Community, their prayer and social outreach work were intimately entwined, with one informing the other to a greater extent than was seen in the other peaceline communities. Through this they remained wedded to their origins as a Charismatic prayer group, thereby setting themselves apart from the other peaceline communities by this unique interpretation of Christian Reconciliation and the form that it should take.

The Community's management structure evolved in line with the changes in its work, whilst its criteria for membership remained essentially the same. There have never been any formal structures for membership of the Community as, according to the Community's leader, 'there is no need for a commitment; it is written in your heart',[83] although by the mid-1990s, members were recommitting themselves each year to the Community in an informal ceremony. Due to the informality of the membership structures, very little information on the type of people who become Community members or indeed membership numbers themselves is available, but it seems that the Community has had a wide range of members. However, their membership has aged, moving from being predominantly young in the early 1980s to middle-aged by the late 1990s, possibly due to dynamics within the wider Charismatic Community. As the scope of the Community's work grew its management structures were forced to evolve to take into account the new demands being placed upon them. Initially, management duties fell to the Community's leader but it was then decided to establish a Service Team of six Community members who would be elected every three years to oversee the day-to-day operation of the Community. Hence, it is apparent that they do not have the sophisticated structures in place for membership and management that other communities, most notably Corrymeela, do. Thus each section of the Community's work tends to be semi-autonomous, being run by those who volunteer to facilitate the groups, leaving little need for elaborate structures and committees.

Innovation and adherence to their founding aims and vision have been the key to the development of the Lamb of God Community. However, they have been greatly influenced by the Charismatic Renewal Movement as their methods of engagement illustrate. Thus, whilst other communities have constantly reacted to the external political events surrounding them, the Lamb of God Community seems to have been operating in a vacuum, producing results which, whilst not entirely dissimilar to those of other peaceline communities, were based upon a different set of priorities, namely the welfare of those around them rather than being driven entirely by Christian reconciliation.

### The Columba Community, Derry

The Columba Community was inspired by the South American Basic Community model which can broadly be defined as an ecclesiastical community attempting to integrate with their locale.[84] However, these theological roots did not set it apart from the other ecumenical communities as they did not greatly influence the development of the Community's work beyond its foundation. Thus, in the growth of Columba we see a pattern and methods remarkably similar to its counterparts in Belfast.

The Columba Community was created because of its members' experiences of praying together but unlike the communities in Belfast, this group was established as a direct response to the violence that was increasingly controlling the city during the early 1980s as those involved wanted to experience a Christian lifestyle as an alternative to this. The main impetus for the establishment of Columba came from a Catholic priest, Fr. Neal Carlin, who felt that there was a need within the city for an alternative to membership of the paramilitary organisations and to aid those who had been affected by the conflict. In a reflection on his reasons for founding the Community he stated that 'some have suffered sever torture at the hands of legal forces. Others have promoted physical violence. Only in a loving Christian community with prayer and counsel can these memories be healed.'[85] A house was found in the centre of Derry, which they bought and renovated for £20,000 with the help of a benefactor and other volunteers.

The Columba Community saw their role as five-fold, incorporating prayer, community, evangelisation, repentance and reconciliation and thus presented the most developed founding aims of any of the peaceline communities.[86] Their aims stem from the desire to establish a basic community along the lines of those seen in South America and they saw themselves:

> As a group with a common experience of being 'held captive' in prison cells or by the forces of anger, guilt, fear and hatred, we are learning to appreciate each other's weaknesses and needs as well as developing each other's talents and gifts. We see Christian Community as a network of interpersonal relationships based on our common relationship with Jesus Christ as Rock and Cornerstone.[87]

Like the other ecumenical communities, they were aware of the need for internal strength in order to carry out their work successfully and whilst these aims and vision have not changed since 1980, their means of expression have.

The work of the Columba Community focused entirely on the Gospel's desire for reconciliation, based upon the notion that Jesus 'requires much more from us than platitudes and gestures at charismatic meetings and during the church unity octave each year'.[88] Through their engagement with the local communities, Columba were essentially trying to portray a living example of Christian reconciliation whilst simultaneously and consciously representing an alternative form of ecumenism to that practised by the national-level churches at the time. They did so by seeking to improve community relations rather than concentrating upon points of theology. Prayer was central to their ideal of reconciliation and was the mainstay of their work. Consequently, they followed the classic pattern of engagement with the local community: starting unobtrusively with prayer and outreach eventually intermingling it with cross-community relationship building, finally moving into social action projects once the opportunity presented itself.

Columba's prayer and outreach ministry began in 1980 with an inter-church prayer group for prisoners. Although it was quickly realised that such a scheme was too ambitious, the experience gained through this programme has greatly affected the direction of Columba's work prompting the foundation of their counselling services, which represented the continuation of their outreach and Christians Together, an inter-denominational prayer group, which signalled a move towards cross-community relationship building. The counselling service has been one of the Community's most vital contacts with the local area and was offered to all those who had been traumatised by the troubles. By the mid-1990s, the Community was able to secure funding for the service from the Community Foundation Northern Ireland and the Community Relations Council and it was consequently expanded through their work with other groups in the area, especially victims and survivors groups. 'The Community have actively participated on the trauma advisory panel and we work in co-ordination with a number of groups around the town specifically trying to address not only the spiritual needs but we are also open to those of differing or no spiritual or religious belief.'[89] Counselling was a vital tool in the Community's work and was valuable to its development for two reasons. First, it served as a means of integrating the Community into the local area as they provided 'an open ear and even if they needed something specially, that we couldn't give ourselves, we'd put them in the right track'[90] becoming successful 'because no matter, even if the problem was very small, and there is wound that is big to them and they'll always get an answer here'.[91] Second, and most importantly, it offered another way in which the Community could work towards reconciliation, as it provided an opportunity for the emotional and spiritual healing which they saw as the key to fulfilling this aim.

With the foundation of Christians Together in 1983 came an early attempt by Columba to move into cross-community relationship development as discussion between Protestants and Catholics played a key role in this programme which culminated with a service of repentance in Derry on Good Friday. However, as one of the participants points out, its value lay not in that symbolic act but in the preparation for it as by coming to know one another the participants felt more equipped to pray together, thereby achieving a spiritual reconciliation which was central to the ideal of Columba:

> So we meet for about six weeks and we made out lists of how we perceived others and what we really believed, so that the people who were doing it, I think that was the main part of the exercise: preparing for it, so that we began to see how other people see us and the things that we do that hurt them and the things that we do that hurt us. And we were able to be quite open about that.[92]

The experience gained from this was continually put to use by the Community from 1985 onwards and because of this desire to fuse prayer with outreach and reconciliation, a retreat centre, St Anthony's, was built in Donegal where guests could receive spiritual direction and join the Community in prayer.

However, with the advent of new methods of relationship-building occurring in the 1990s, Columba began to seriously consider their role as community relationship builders: a change in method which highlighted a shift from their single-minded focus upon prayer as a means to reconciliation towards one where an understanding of different traditions was developed in conjunction with the ability to pray together. They planned their methodology carefully preferring a proactive approach rather than the reactive schemes used by the other peaceline communities. Columba employed a reconciliation officer, Alex Bradley, who was funded by the Community Relations Council, to put their plan into action. The courses were started in Catholic parishes laying the foundations for a cross-community course to be established some eighteen months later. These courses were seen by Columba as another means of emotional release for their participants, a necessary step on the way to reconciliation, according to the ethos of the Community. Furthermore, these programmes were carried out with the help of pre-established services:

> What we did find from the groups of people who took part on the actual reconciliation programme were those who had been wounded physically and sometimes emotionally by the events of the past thirty years and the Columba Community have always had a counselling service here at Columba house and it was I suppose addressing a need to further develop that that we've provided ongoing counselling for those who have been traumatised.[93]

Columba's approach to this work illustrates clearly the way in which they were able to weave new techniques in with the old in pursuit of the accomplishment of their vision as, through their use of new methods of relationship building, Columba tried to achieve a marriage of their original aims of repentance, prayer and reconciliation with their practical work.

Nowhere is this seen more clearly than in the foundation of a rehabilitation centre for alcoholics in 2001, which represented a fulfilment of Columba's original objective of ministering to the marginalised people of Derry. The White Oaks Rehabilitation Centre was established as a result of a perceived need within the local community. As one of the members commented:

> Now I think the community felt that drink was a problem in the city, so we've moved into that area, because some lady came and banged at the door with her shoe, and broke the door in and said, 'Nobody is listening to me.' And I think at that stage we felt maybe we should listen to this. Anybody who comes breaking the door downstairs has something to say.[94]

The Centre offers a thirty-day residential programme designed to help addicts based upon the Twelve-Step programme used by Alcoholics Anonymous. 'The long term goals of [this] treatment are to encourage the person to live life free from mind-altering substances and to provide strategies that will help individuals in living creative, productive, happy lives.'[95] For the members of Columba, White Oaks represented a natural progression in their work, signifying a continuation of their engagement with prisoners and their later work with victims and survivors, enabling them to work towards reconciliation at a deeper level than before. Fr. Neal Carlin argues that this is the result of the outreach nature of the project: 'We're working for a third party; it's almost we pray more together in that, we're rubbing shoulders together in the difficulty. Working together for the deprived and for the needy is another type of ecumenism, which is more genuine because we're not into the niceties of doctrine and belief.'[96]

The programme offered at White Oaks is broadly based upon the spirituality of the Columba Community, with opportunities for silent prayer and meditation being offered: 'The ethos of the Centre is strongly influenced by the spirituality of Columba, believing that "those who wait on the Lord shall want nothing" (Psalm 31:1) As individuals we are cleansed, renewed and come close to "the Lamb of God who takes away the sins of the world" (John 1:29).'[97] In order to fund this Centre, the Community have had to enlist the help of Health Boards in the Republic of Ireland as well as other organisations such as the International Fund for Ireland. However, despite the involvement of outside agencies, as the treatment offered by the Centre demonstrates, the project has retained the spirit and Christian ethos of the Columba Community, helping it to achieve its founding aims of prayer, community, evangelisation, repentance and reconciliation.

Despite the constant growth and change in the Community's methods of working, its management and membership structures have remained almost constant since 1980, only being formalised when funding conditions required it. Membership is restricted to those who feel that they can commit to the Community's prayer life for a year at a time. Members have always taken an active role in the management of the Community, with responsibilities being decided at the annual AGM.

The performance of the Columba Community is hard to quantify. They have certainly provided support for those around them, becoming a lighthouse for those in trouble, but they have been reluctant to publicise their success stories, thus their accomplishments can only be measured by their practical achievements. One of their members sums up the evolution of their work thus: 'Our work is a Christian outreach: at one time to prisons and prisoners, later to reconciliation among denominations and more recently to alcoholics, but at all times towards the healing of society through the Gospel message and appropriate action.'[98] The Columba Community have fully utilised the methods available to them to facilitate each of these forms of work, which have, with the exception of prison work, been long lasting and well received in Derry and have been successful in remaining committed to their aims and vision, whilst using any innovations that were occurring within Northern Irish reconciliation work to their full advantage. They have become a place of prayer and reconciliation through their outreach and relationship building eventually finding new means of incorporating the marginalised back into society through their rehabilitation centre.

## The Cornerstone Community, West Belfast

The experience of Cornerstone is remarkably similar to that of its predecessors as it was based upon the need to replace the message of the Gospel at the heart of the community. The members of this Community have remained most closely allied to their roots as a praying presence on the peaceline and 'although [they] ... have changed many of the old structures [their] prayer life remains central to the Community and it is that which underpins [their] ... steadfast commitment to working for reconciliation and healing, our prayer in action'.[99] Thus, in the years since 1982, they have evolved from being a small prayer group into an organisation actively working for the betterment of their local community, both spiritually and materially.

The initial impetus behind Cornerstone came from an inter-denominational prayer group based in the Falls/Shankhill areas who felt the need to form an ecumenical community after their experience of the hunger strikes in 1981. 'They were [in Clonard] for about seven years ... [sharing and getting] to know one another ... during which time we had the hunger strikes which further divided [the] community ... At the end of that time the group felt quite strongly that they were being called by the Lord into a community.'[100] The group was subsequently able to buy two houses on the Springfield Road with the help of an English philanthropist, which have been the Community's physical presence on the peaceline since December 1983.

Unlike the other peaceline communities, Cornerstone did not produce formal expression of either their aims or vision until their funders demanded it. They described their initial aims thus: 'Prayer is at the heart and foundation of Cornerstone. *Being* is important to us. We want to be a people of prayer and a witness to God's reconciling love'[101] aiming through this 'to enable the people of the Shankill and of the Falls to discover the bonds that unite them and to respect their differences that arise from tradition and culture'.[102] This early vision has matured greatly: an occurrence that is a direct result of their instinctive understanding of their role within the area and the limits and opportunities it presents. The group now states its aims as follows:

> Cornerstone Community – Servant of God's reconciling grace in the Shankill and the Falls;
> The Cornerstone Vision – The people of the Shankill and of the Falls belong to one another in the family of God;
> The Cornerstone Goal – To enable the people of the Shankill and the Falls to discover the bonds that unite them and to respect their differences that arise from tradition and culture.[103]

By the beginning of 2005, Cornerstone were aiming to 'provide a model of change in people's attitudes to each other and to themselves'[104] and in doing so were illustrating the effect that their practical work has had upon their aims and ethos.

The work of Cornerstone has been radically affected by the fact that they were founded during a period of tremendous sectarian tension forcing them to begin their work in a low-key manner, only diversifying from prayer when the local community expressed a need. Cornerstone viewed its work as 'prayer in action, we do not separate the two. Our work has moved from being reactive to the needs of the Community to being both reactive and *proactive*'[105] which manifested itself in Cornerstone's partnership with Forthspring. Consequently, its work has developed through the three areas of prayer and outreach, cross-community contact and social action work.[106]

Prayer was initially the focal point of Cornerstone's work with the 'live in' members of the Community praying together twice daily and a large amount of time at the weekly Community Meeting being devoted to Scripture or prayer, through which they strengthened their relationships with each other. This was almost immediately translated into outreach work, which enabled the members of Cornerstone to become known within the area and allowed their activities to develop organically in response to events surrounding them. This they saw as an expression of their aims: 'We have tried to further our work of Peace and Reconciliation by having groups of Catholics and Protestants in to share views and prayer and by visiting local people and groups.'[107] The initial link between their prayer and outreach work came with the establishment of their bereavement and crisis visiting which was initiated by Fr. Gerry Reynolds after a member of the UDR had been killed by the IRA.

Thus, whenever a sectarian atrocity was committed locally during the 1980s a member of Cornerstone 'would go in and sit with the family and if [they] found it appropriate would say a prayer'.[108] In addition, Cornerstone became active in promoting inter-church prayer groups establishing a monthly women's prayer group. Gradually the members of the Community became involved in prayer initiatives outside the house itself: the most successful of these were the Shankhill pilgrimages founded in 1994, where members of the Catholic parishes of the Falls attended a service at a Protestant church on the Shankhill. Such schemes can be seen as a tangible manifestation of the reconciling vision of Cornerstone: 'We see our visits as planting new seeds of friendship and prayer between the congregations of the Church in the Shankhill and those in the Falls and as a communal response to Jesus' command *"Love one another as I have loved you"*.'[109]

Cornerstone's cross-community work was not directly affected by the advent of the peace and reconciliation educational initiative in the 1990s, as they were attempting to put formal community relations structures in place as early as 1986. They began by running conferences for groups, such as the clergy and women, aimed at promoting an understanding 'of one another and to seek God's way forward for our people'.[110] However, Cornerstone's chief means of promoting cross-community contact was developed though their family and youth workers, who were employed in 1990 and 1993 respectively as a response to a perceived need within the community, thereby highlighting the flexible and reactive approach that Cornerstone have taken towards their work. Thus, with the establishment of these posts Cornerstone began to offer services such as counselling as well as events such as an inter-community senior citizens' club and youth clubs. By the mid-1990s, with the establishment of Forthspring, the focus of Cornerstone's work began to change as these projects were transferred into Forthspring, providing the expertise for their successful continuation.

It has been suggested that Cornerstone has lost sight of its vision to be a praying presence on the peaceline in its work with the local community: 'much of the work is losing its Christian slant ... and its providing services for the general community'.[111] If one centred solely upon the social action work that Cornerstone carries out with Forthspring then this would be true as prayer does not seem to be central to the workings of after-school playgroups or mother-and-toddler groups. Yet it would seem that with the establishment of Forthspring in 1993, two separate Cornerstones emerged: Cornerstone, the service provider and Cornerstone, the ecumenical community. The latter remained faithful to its aims to be a reconciling presence on the peaceline, whilst the former demonstrated its understanding of and response to the needs of the local community. The work carried out by Cornerstone after 2000 serves to support this observation as they endeavoured to engage with local churches to promote reconciliation through prayer and dialogue. Through their community worker, Bridie Cotter, Cornerstone have carried on their efforts in much the same vein as before but chose to focus on the clergy as a means of bringing the communities together. Thus, they held meetings aimed at getting the clergy to talk to one another and discuss the relevance of the churches in modern society – a scheme which they believed to be successful, as two clergymen who lived in the same road spoke to each other for the first time. The adoption of such methods was based upon their belief that 'the Churches are called to do that work [reconciliation] and they haven't been ... They need to be seen working together',[112] further illustrating their commitment to their founding aims.

The change in Cornerstone's work was reflected in surface changes in the way in which they managed both their day-to-day running and their membership criteria. Initially, the Community adopted a relaxed approach to its membership being open to local people and, due to its position as a mostly non-residential Community, membership, mostly consisted of people from the Springfield Road area with almost equal numbers of Protestants and Catholics. However, with the arrival of international interest in peacemaking bodies in Northern Ireland and their consequent provision of funding, these communities found themselves subject to the constraints laid down to them by such organisations. This phenomenon seems to have been of particular significance to the Cornerstone Community, who have consequently drawn up more rigid guidelines on the admission of members to the Community, although these guidelines were only drawn up 'in case we ever need a safeguard'[113] and are generally ignored except when an application for a place as a volunteer is received. This relaxed approach to membership was also found in their management system, the uncomplicated nature of which allowed changes in its programme work to take place more easily than was the case in other communities, thereby enabling the Community to integrate into the area more swiftly.

At the outset there was very little structure in the management of Cornerstone,[114] a system which seemed to suit those involved and indeed the work of the Community: 'It's very flexible and it's not a place that you have to be in at a certain time or else you're asked questions. Because it's so flexible I think they're able to be flexible and respond to people.'[115] Cornerstone managed itself through weekly meetings attended by full members which were designed to allow:

- Practical business to be discussed
- Exchange of information about activities, ideas, requests, donations
- Matters of immediate and/or serious concern to be raised
- New projects or ideas to be discussed and decided upon
- Spiritual renewal to be maintained
- Strengthening of bonds among the members.[116]

The style of these meetings was informal and combined with their prayer meetings to keep the spirit of the Community alive. By the mid-1990s the management of the Community had become more formal on paper but in practice the earlier system remained in use.

Through their work, Cornerstone have become a symbol of refuge and safety to both Protestants and Catholics on the Springfield Road being seen by some as a 'nice wee religious group',[117] by others as a place in which they could meet the 'other sort' and by many as a place which was owned by the whole community.[118] This was achieved primarily through their reactive approach to the needs of the area and their willingness to become involved and offer support where they were needed resulting in the longevity of many of their programmes. By doing so Cornerstone were demonstrating a new model of reconciliation in which Protestants and Catholics could work and even worship together without the barriers of religious difference and sectarianism immediately being erected.

### The Columbanus Community of Reconciliation, North Belfast

> I had always felt was this Community invited or had it imposed itself? Largely it had imposed itself, although the local churches certainly owned it to a small degree being reasonably ecumenically minded and were therefore at the beginning welcoming and fairly open to involvement but that had decreased over the years. So my question was to what extent were we the nuisance factor?[119]

As this observation of Columbanus suggests, this Community has always been something of an outsider in the ecumenical landscape; a factor that has radically affected the way in which it operated, as it was not able to gain the trust of the local community as easily as its counterparts were. Its work never really progressed beyond ecumenical prayer with the eventual provision of reconciliation education. These problems were exacerbated by an overly hierarchical management structure and membership criteria which excluded the very people that the Community aimed to serve.

Columbanus did not set out to minister to a geographically limited area but rather wanted to 'have the whole wide world as its parish'[120] and was originally intended to be an all-male community. However, during the course of his feasibility study, Fr. Michael Hurley SJ, the founder of the Community, altered his initial plans and decided that membership should be temporary and open to both men and women.[121] After a complex recruitment and selection process, seven people (five women and two men). became the founding members of the Community, who then set out to find a precise location to live in Belfast. Eventually a property was found on the Antrim Road and in 1983 they moved in to begin their work. Although the membership of Columbanus was recruited from areas as diverse as Germany and Limerick and those initially involved had not actually engaged in a spiritual journey together prior to this, it is evident that once they came together, like their counterparts in other parts of Belfast, they displayed a commitment to reconciliation, peace and justice. This it was hoped would allow them to work in the immediate area to promote their ideal of 'unity in the Church, justice in society and peace on earth'.[122]

Whilst the other peaceline communities initially allowed their aims and vision to evolve slowly, Columbanus had highly developed aims from the outset. This was due to the circumstances of its foundation as it was modelling itself on an existing form of communities[123] and was therefore able to draw upon existing experiences of community work when deciding how to operate. The aims of Columbanus have thus remained constant, being:

> To give a practical example of what a more united church, a more just society and a more peaceful world would be like;
> To challenge the sectarianism, injustice and violence prevalent in Northern Irish society:
> - By adopting an opposite set of values – unity, simplicity and peace;
> - By living together according to these values in a mixed Community of men and women, of Anglicans, Catholics and Protestants.[124]

However, such clarity has not protected them from the need to constantly reassess their vision of how such aims should be put into practice, as, in common with all the other ecumenical communities, Columbanus have had to attempt, not always successfully, to understand the community in which they had placed themselves.

Consequently, Columbanus employed a slow, measured approach when developing their methods of engagement with the local community, preferring initially to engage in networking and prayer before trying to implement the more practical aspects of their aims and vision. It was envisaged that 'the life would be one of prayer, reflection and work in which members according to their vocations, age and training would help to service the works of other agencies, both secular and religious, rather than establishing specialised works within the community'.[125] Thus, Columbanus's projects would be borne out of the contacts made through the members' participation in parish life. The development of the Community's work did not follow the three classic phases of engagement mainly because they never became integrated into the local area in the way that the other communities did. Instead, their work can be seen as developing three phases: first, prayer, second, contact with the local community through prayer, which eventually led on to active involvement in community and reconciliation work.

Ecumenical prayer has been the most important aspect of the Community's life and work with its members praying together every day, whilst retaining active links with their own churches by attending services there on Sundays. The form of the Community's prayer has always taken into account the mixed nature of the membership, combining 'the essential elements of the [Catholic] Office with the freer tradition of Protestantism'.[126] Their focus upon ecumenical prayer and the lack of a Protestant minister initially allowed the Community to make contact with the local ministers as they were able to invite them to celebrate the Eucharist, thereby allowing them to get to know the Community and its aim of Christian reconciliation. Their emphasis on ecumenical prayer made a significant contribution to their work for reconciliation: 'ecumenism is the real key to Columbanus's contribution to reconciliation and there are many opportunities for participation in events throughout the city which draw people together',[127] and it was this participation that allowed the Community to move into the second stage of their work.

Due to their lack of roots within their area, Columbanus had to adopt a low-key approach to their integration into the local community. This process took longer for them than it did for the other communities and they remained a praying community until the beginning of the 1990s, when new methods in reconciliation work provided the opportunity for them to move on. In 1986 they stated that: 'at present we are still in the experimental, exploratory stage, trying to get a clearer picture of the colour and social patterns of our neighbourhood, finding out what is already being done and where there appears to be a lack or need'.[128] This was done in two ways: first, through their involvement in local inter-church prayer groups, meetings and conferences – by the early 1990s Columbanus itself was in a position to be able to offer a number of retreats, quiet days, Bible weeks and lectures with invited speakers as part of their ecumenical prayer programme. Second, and more crucial to the desire to demonstrate a model of Christian reconciliation, the members became involved in the surrounding area through their work in other local community projects, such as a project for ex-prisoners and a drop-in centre for the unemployed. This, as well as allowing them to take the values and ethos of Columbanus to those outside, promo-ted the very existence of the Community, enabling them to offer their rapidly expanding premises for use by community and church groups.

Thus, by 1992, the description of their work had altered somewhat from that set out ten years previously, and they had a much clearer picture of their role in the community and the vision and ethos that they wished to offer to those that they came into contact with:

> We challenge the prevalent sectarianism, injustice and violence of Northern Ireland society by just living together ... We pray to-gether and celebrate the Eucharist together and endure for the present the pain of not receiving communion together. We provide the premises, the faculties, the ethos in which small groups of Christians of different traditions can come together for meetings, for quiet days of prayer, for lectures and courses on issues of Christian unity and of peace and justice in our world. We assist the work of other organi-sations, which promote unity, justice and peace.[129]

Through their networking with local inter-church prayer and community action groups the early members of Columbanus were able to slowly lay the groundwork for a number of cross-community projects, which they aimed either to sponsor or run themselves, which promoted Christian reconciliation primarily amongst local schools through the use of the new methodologies emerging at this time. The first scheme was begun in 1988, funded by the Department of Education and run by a member of Columbanus, although by 1992 it had been decided to try to transfer the expertise of the schools worker to a project aimed at local youth groups and designed to help combat sectarianism and segregation. This eventu-ally led to an expansion of Columbanus's cross-community work as they began to run regular courses in conjunction with the ISE, which enabled them to promote their aims of peace, justice and reconciliation.

Columbanus has not been as successful in its work as the other peaceline ecumenical communities, only finding itself able to move into cross-community reconciliation work with the help of the formal structures of the peace and reconciliation educational initiatives. Much of this failure was caused by the perception amongst local people that the Community was 'above them because the Four Churches set it up'.[130] As a consequence, they were not been able to move as quickly in their engagement with the local areas as the other communities, having to wait almost a decade before some of their work became feasible, a problem which was exacerbated by their rigid management and membership structures.

An evolution in Columbanus's membership criteria began to take place almost immediately, as it became apparent that a permanent all-male community would have been unworkable. They decided instead to form a mixed Christian community, the membership of which would be temporary and open to 'both Protestant and Catholic, men and women, married and single, lay and clerical, young and old'.[131] This change in criteria was prompted by a realisation that participants would be difficult to find and that opening membership out would produce more positive results. From its foundation in 1983 until the late 1990s, membership of Columbanus was highly stratified. Thus, only those resident within the Community itself could be members and 'the in-house people had most of the power ... about what the programme involved and how it was expressed and who it involved and the locals were just associates or they were just patrons or were what we then called sponsors'.[132] Consequently, unless they were prepared to live with the Community, there was no real opportunity for the local people to become involved with Columbanus in a meaningful way which would have allowed them to own the work of the Community, such a policy providing a much-needed means of local integration. The constantly changing and international nature of the membership of the Community reflected this rule and despite the fact that Irish members, from both the North and South, dominated the founding group, the Community quickly became 'an international Community in residence',[133] with it becoming increasingly difficult to attract live-in members, both from Northern Ireland and elsewhere. However, when a new leader was installed in the late 1990s changes in membership criteria were put into place and as a result non-residential membership was allowed, increasing the membership figures fourfold as well as providing a means for local involvement in the Community. The Rev. Glen Barclay 'was very keen that the membership should not just be for residents who go through a process of application and then covenanting, I was keen that it should be open to everybody that was involved – all the committee people and the old associates'.[134]

Such rigidity was reflected in the management of the Community, which had the most highly organised managerial structure of all of the peaceline communities, with a number of sub-committees, such as the finance and property committee, reporting to a council responsible for overseeing the running of the Community. Furthermore, all of the authority rested with the leader of the Community, leading to confusion:

> The founder who lived here for ten years, and was leader for nine of those ten years, had set up a system whereby ... he was the major link person between committees. There was no authority in any of them – not the final authority, except to do with property and finance, which the Trustees had. Everybody seemed to think it was the other committee's responsibility to make that particular decision. So, in the end, the authority rested with the founder come leader who moved between the committees and that seemed to work in that period. Then, the next leader came and there was the same sort of line management.[135]

With the arrival of a new leader in 1997, it was realised that such a system of management, and indeed membership, was hindering the Community's work, as a small group of people held the power undemocratically. After a consultation, that involved people from the local churches, she established a more democratic and de-centralised system of management, which, it was hoped, would enable the Community to grow in the post-Peace Accord era. An AGM was established for the first time at which the members could voice their opinions on the direction of the Community. In addition, whilst the patrons and trustees remained, a new executive council comprised of both clergy and lay people was put in place to oversee the work of the Community. Each of these groups' roles in the management of Columbanus was closely defined: 'The Patrons meet when desirable and guarantee Columbanus Community of Reconciliation's credibility as a genuine inter-church community. The Trustees meet at least twice a year. They have the material and spiritual guardianship of the Community. The Executive meets bi-monthly with the Leader and set up sub-committees as necessary.'[136] However, these changes in managerial structure were unable to prevent the closure of the Community in 2003. The leadership structure suffocated Columbanus Community of Reconciliation from its very beginning. The failure of Columbanus was brought about by its over-hierarchical management system in two ways. First, the Community's structure appeared to adhere closely to the rigid structure of the Catholic and Anglican Churches, which, in effect, created a further barrier between the Community and the local area, as the inhabitants already felt that

Columbanus had been imposed upon them. As well as this, the managerial structure also prevented the growth of the Community itself, both physically and in the type of work it was able to undertake. Thus, any new ideas for working within the local community could not be acted upon quickly and Columbanus was not able to evolve organically in the same manner as the other peaceline communities.

Columbanus, then, can be seen as the hierarchies' attempt at establishment of an ecumenical community, rather than an endeavour to provide an alternative to the theologically driven ecumenical dialogue of the time by promoting inter-church contact as a means of improving community relations. However, in its attempts to work with the local community, it was unsuccessful, as its closure so clearly highlights. Columbanus was trying to provide a model of Christian reconciliation for the area in which it operated, but instead of listening to the wants and needs of the local inhabitants, tried to impose its own vision and, consequently, failed to make any substantial impact. From the outset, it was seen as something remote, rather than an integral part of the local community, and the leaders neglected to do anything to rectify this problem. As a result, even without its closure, it can be seen as the least successful of all the peaceline ecumenical communities.

## The Currach Community, West Belfast

The Currach Community was the smallest and most recent of the ecumenical communities in Northern Ireland. It was formed in 1992 in a period when the operating methods of the peaceline communities were beginning to alter. The experience of Currach provides a reflection of these changes as they were able to establish successful cross-community ventures relatively easily as well as becoming almost immediately involved in social action work.

Currach was founded by a Dominican sister, Noreen Christian, who was drawn to Cornerstone's ethos of being integrated into local society. In 1989, after a new housing estate was built in the area, she gathered together a group of people, including two female members of Cornerstone, to explore the idea of a new ecumenical community as she 'was aware that there was a whole new interface of a peaceline being set up so I knew that in order to maybe serve in someway it would be good if there was a community actually here'.[137] After a process which took two years, the group decided to form a community on the Protestant side of the peaceline, behind a Methodist church and next to the peaceline's gate, with the first members taking up residence there in May 1992.

The experience of the Currach Community, founded over a decade after the other peaceline communities, illustrates clearly the nature of the development of such groups, highlighting the need for them to take a low-key approach in the initial stages of their establishment. The initial aims of Currach provide a reflection of this fact: 'we felt that there was need for a small presence or cell group in this area so as to help people hold the difficulties of living on an interface and to try to maybe make some contribution towards making that a more constructive reality'.[138] However, by 1997 the Community had become sufficiently integrated into the local community to allow them to build upon the nuances of their aims and develop a more proactive vision of Currach's work: 'Our *raison d'être* is to bring people together, to help them discover what they have in common, what their differences are and to begin to value the commonness and the difference.'[139] This change was possibly due to their close ties with the Cornerstone Community, as they were able to draw upon their experiences, and illustrates clearly that as entities each of these peaceline ecumenical communities needed to go through a period of settling into their local community before a clear vision of what their Community should be about could be developed.

Currach itself does not engage in much organised programme work, instead working and eventually amalgamating with the Forthspring project – a collaboration which represents its social action work. Even though the Community was founded ten years after all the others they still had to take a reactive approach when dealing with their local community waiting 'to hear a need expressed before stepping in'.[140] A year after their foundation, Currach's leader was asked if she would consider starting a women's group in the house. This group was Currach's only official programme work but serves as a clear illustration of the need for careful planning and understanding when engaging in work of this nature. Indeed, much of the work done in the early stages was very practical, dealing with cooking and crafts: 'it took us two to three years before they would do anything serious, even look at their own stress levels'.[141] Once trust had been established, the group felt able to do more serious work looking, for example, at their own identity and that of their families. For the participants these meetings 'stand out as times when we took risks with each other in expressing our fears and prejudices. While each of the courses encouraged us to be articulate about our own beliefs and traditions we also learnt to listen respectfully and to appreciate the experience of others'.[142] The experience of Currach's attempts at programme work in the post ceasefire organisation era demonstrate that each of these communities had to go through a 'settling in' period within their local community. For some this has been a shorter exercise in trust building than others but these foundations needed to be established before bolder attempts, such as work looking at identity, can be made. Furthermore, Currach's experience with the women's group prompted the change in their aims and vision as they realised that they could make a much stronger contribution to the area than being a praying presence on the peaceline.

Currach's management structures are under-developed when compared to those of the other ecumenical communities in Northern Ireland, being as informal and unobtrusive as their work for Christian reconciliation within the surrounding communities. Their membership has tended to be drawn from outside Northern Ireland, with the only permanent member of the Community, its leader Noreen Christian, recruiting through American and German charities which place young people on their 'gap year' or national service. As a result, the selection process is simple:

> When people hear about it, they apply either by writing or phoning and they ask questions on the finances and lifestyle etc. Ideally they should come and live here for a couple of days to get the feel of it and for us to get a feel for them and the feel of Forthspring. The volunteers coming through those organisations will have a process that they will have gone through of talking through a liaison person about the living conditions and expectations. We would just really be told that they think them suitable.[143]

Currach are the only example of a totally residential ecumenical community in Northern Ireland and their membership, which never rises above seven, thus changes from year to year, as those who join make their commitment annually. As a consequence of their short lifespan and their relatively small membership numbers, their management structures are extremely informal with decisions being made by the Community as a whole:

> Our Community is reconstructed every year, someone leaves or others come. You have to begin again when people leave or when they come so that everybody feels when they come that they have a say in how we live and how we pray, how we plan our timetable, what is required of us regarding the sharing of our lives, when do we have community meetings, who is cooking, cleaning etc. Everybody piles in to decide that together and our prayer changes according to the people in the group.[144]

The informality of their management structures not only reflects the size and age of the Currach Community but also provides a clear indication of the way in which it works with the community it serves. Currach has consistently worked in a low-key manner, supporting and working in partnership with the other inter-church projects in the area, and their management and membership mirrors this. Furthermore, as their membership has not grown and their work has not yet evolved in the way in which that of the other ecumenical committees has, they provide a tangible and contemporary example of the unobtrusive methods and management that need to be employed by a peaceline community before they can proceed to the establishment of the larger projects.

Although Currach has benefited from the experience of Cornerstone and its involvement with the Forthspring project,which has allowed it to progress into social action work more swiftly than would otherwise have been the case, there are two unique elements in its work which have made it successful. First, its size and uncomplicated approach to management issues has allowed it to adapt to the needs of the surrounding community, leaving it at liberty to start cross-community groups and engage with other community groups in the area without long processes of internal consultation. Second, Currach have demonstrated an innate understanding of the area which has prompted them to take a reactive approach to the needs of the local community thereby gaining their trust and most importantly their acceptance.

CONCLUSION

Each of these ecumenical communities, then, has made a unique contribution to the landscape of inter-church relationships in Northern Ireland by presenting a form of Christian reconciliation, which blended community relations with ecumenical prayer, to the area in which they operated. However, their success is hard to quantify. Their longevity does provide an indication of their acceptance into their localities, whilst the use of their programmes, such as the women's group, indicates that there is a tacit agreement within the area that reconciliation is needed. This was a direct result of the way in which they put their aims and ethos into practice: aiming to exist and support those who came to them through the medium of prayer, rather than adopting a proactive approach by immediately setting up schemes that may have been totally inappropriate to the needs of the area. Furthermore, in endeavouring to provide solutions to problems that may not necessarily have been of much importance within the area, they would have alienated the very people to whom they wanted to speak. This desire to start off quietly as 'a praying community of different denominations'[145] on the peaceline was reflected in the founding aims of each of these safe haven communities, as were their early experiences as ecumenical prayer groups. The aims of each of these communities remained constant but their ideas of how these aims would function changed with their understanding of the reality of the situation in which they worked and affected them in two key ways.

First, whilst the structural development and programmes that each of these peaceline communities had in place by 2005 may not have developed in entirely the same way, their methods of engagement with the local community in the years immediately after their foundation were strikingly similar. Hence, by circa 1993, members of each of these communities were actively involved in ecumenical prayer groups, having used the contacts made during these meetings to further their outreach work. In addition to this, they were all involved in working with social outreach agencies, outside the sphere of their own ecumenical communities, which allowed them to gain knowledge of conditions in the local area, thereby providing a clear idea of what contribution they could make as a community. Such engagement also enabled them to establish their houses as a neutral venue in which local people could meet, a factor that was to prove crucial in developing trust within the local community. Ultimately, the birth of new methods of community-relations work in the early 1990s afforded most of them a chance to build further upon their reconciliation work, efforts which were to come to fruition in the aftermath of the paramilitary ceasefires of 1994. These similarities in approach and experience were due, in part, to the ecumenical basis of their group with its emphasis on prayer and their commitment to the need for reconciliation, unity and justice. They were also caused by the fact that they were all operating in arenas which had been both physically and psychologically scarred by paramilitary violence, and latterly by the reality that, although those living near these peaceline communities were separated by their sectarian attitudes towards one another, they were all suffering some of the highest levels of socio-economic deprivation in the UK. This meant that they could all potentially benefit either from practical help or through encounters in discussion or prayer groups, which would help to alleviate their common difficulties.

Finally, unlike the highly structured and organised management and membership structures of the Corrymeela Community, these peaceline communities have always operated in an informal manner preferring to keep their membership numbers below fifty and engaging a less stratified method of management for the day-to-day running of the Ecumenical Community and its work. This is not to say though, that the peaceline communities have stagnated structurally, instead it is evident that their methods of management have evolved alongside their methods of engagement with the local community. Indeed, in the years immediately after their foundation, the structure and, perhaps more importantly, the criteria for membership, has changed as those initially involved became fully aware, not only of the demands that their work in peaceline areas placed upon them, but of the type of people who would be called to such work. Furthermore, as they have become more involved in bringing their message of Christian reconciliation to the areas that they serve, they have had to become more organised to cope with the demands being placed upon them. However, this phenomenon seems to be linked to the direct experience of the communities themselves, rather than trends in inter-church activity or political events. Hence, the larger and the more established they became within the local community, the more need there was for a tighter control on the day-to-day running of the place. In short, the structure and membership of the peaceline communities has underpinned the evolution of their aims, vision and methodology.

Due to the development of the peaceline communities in the early 1980s, a divergence in the work of the ecumenical communities is evident, with Corrymeela and the Christian Renewal Centre working on a large scale within the entire province, and the peaceline communities concentrating upon small-scale projects in geographically defined areas. Nevertheless, despite the initial changes in method by these new forms of ecumenical communities, there is a great deal of continuity in their work. Whilst the methodology of each of these groups may have changed, their aim of replacing the biblical values of peace, justice and reconciliation at the heart of the two communities in Northern Ireland has not.

## CHAPTER FIVE

# Peace and Reconciliation Education Initiatives

Inter-church relationships in Northern Ireland were fluid rather than fluent; operating on an *ad hoc* basis, with those involved being forced to constantly assess the situation in which they were working, resulting in their methods developing in a reactive rather than proactive manner. For the national-level churches this resulted in both ecumenical and institutional stagnation, with those involved being prevented from making any tangible progress by the more conservative elements within the Protestant Churches and a reluctance to act upon the recommendations that were being produced by the IICM. At a local level, inter-church groups were becoming increasingly organised and focused in their provision of services to their communities. By the early 1990s, it was becoming obvious that some form of support network was needed to sustain and promote the inter-church action which was occurring at both a local and national level, thereby providing a new 'professional class' of inter-church workers with the necessary expertise to facilitate dialogue and practical measures at all levels.

Such organisations have been given a number of different labels: for example, resource agencies and facilitators and have taken many forms, ranging from locally appointed reconciliation officers to province-wide government-funded agencies.[1] Whilst each of these groups worked alongside various inter-church groups, and were characterised by a commitment to peacebuilding, they were independent of institutional church control and became autonomous inter-church bodies, which were underlined by the ethos of providing 'resources for training, advice, information and support for developing community-relations work within the churches sector'.[2] They have been instrumental in developing and promoting new forms of inter-church work by interacting with local groups, as well as sponsoring rigorous research into issues such as sectarianism and reconciliation from an inter-church perspective.

Such groups have been in existence in some form since the foundation of the Irish School of Ecumenics (ISE) in 1970 and can be classified into three groups: the Irish School of Ecumenics, which promotes ecumenical education and research as a means of reconciliation,[3] the resource providers, who provide training and resources for local groups and, finally, the supporters who have evolved into an over-arching province-wide body aimed at supporting all types of work. This chapter will examine the evolution of groups associated with these categories, looking at the aims and methods of the organisations involved, assessing their contribution to the development of reconciliation and peacebuilding work in Northern Ireland especially at a local level.


## THE IRISH SCHOOL OF ECUMENICS

The 1970s saw a number of innovations in the field of ecumenical and inter-church education, which for the most part were developed in order to facilitate informed discussion, mutual understanding and exchange between Protestants and Catholics. Three such initiatives were founded during this per-iod: the ISE, the Integrated Education Movement and the Churches Peace Education Programme.[4] Of these, the ISE stands out as having had a sustained influence upon inter-church relations in Northern Ireland, first through its longevity and second, and most importantly, through its teaching, academic research and the input it has made to local communities through its programme of ecumenical education.

The ISE was the brainchild of Fr. Michael Hurley SJ and the years before the school's formal inauguration in November 1970 were spent developing this vision and building up the contacts needed for such an endeavour.[5] The resulting ecumenical institute was founded in Dublin as 'an independent, unofficial, interdenominational institute',[6] academically affiliated to the University of Hull (a role assumed by Trinity College Dublin in 1983), and initially funded by the Irish Flour Millers Association[7] with patrons from the four main churches in Ireland.[8] Its main desire was to build a student body which consisted of equal numbers of Catholics and Protestants and to develop 'applied research at the intersection of politics, theology and religion'.[9] The ISE has made a substantial impact upon both in Ireland and further afield, by providing opportunities for postgraduate education on Ecumenism, International Peace Studies, and Reconciliation Studies, engaging in academic research and offering community relations courses to local communities. Each of these constantly informs the other and is underlined by a commitment to interdisciplinary research aimed at the three constituencies of the church and religion, academia and society.[10]

*Aims and vision*

Although there was no formal articulation of its vision, the primary aim of the ISE was to fill the lack of ecumenical teaching, which was believed to be hindering ecumenical relationships and understanding. During the 1960s, theologians were debating whether ecumenism should be seen as 'a dimension of all disciplines [within theological education] or a special discipline by itself'.[11] Hurley believed that in order for ecumenical relationships to flourish that this challenge needed to be addressed and that: 'The special discipline was necessary for the sake of the dimension and that an institute such as the ISE was necessary for the sake of both. It would meet "the present need for ecumenically competent personnel"; it would educate and train those who would teach the discipline and who by doing so would help to create the dimension.'[12] During the 1970s and early 1980s, the ISE aimed to be a training institute providing an ecumenical education for ecumenical leaders with MPhil degrees being offered in Ecumenical Studies and International Peace Studies. This was combined with academic research programme.

In the 1990s they produced a formal articulation of their aims:

> The Irish School of Ecumenics is an international academic institute, Christian in its inspiration and ethos, interdenominational in structure and personnel. It exists to promote through research, teaching and outreach activities the unity of Christians, dialogue between religions and work for peace and justice in Ireland and abroad. Its resources are available to churches and other appropriate bodies committed to unity, dialogue and peace.[13]

Such aims were broad and deep enough to include, alongside the focus on teaching and research, a programme of community based courses. It is significant that amongst the ISE's alumni are those that have made an important contribution to the field of inter-church peacebuilding as it was offering training for leaders of cross-community groups, as well as working on the development of community relations courses. Such courses aimed:

> To develop greater understanding between people from the traditions in local communities; To raise awareness of and explore key community, religious, cultural, political, social and reconciliation issues; To empower the participants to be actively involved in the practice of reconciliation within local communities; To promote the practice of equity, diversity and interdependence between the traditions; To enable participation in the building of an integrated and inclusive civic society through the practice of active citizenship.[15]

These statements demonstrate a development in the focus of the ISE as they, in parallel with inter-church bodies, widened their outreach approach to ecumenical relationships. This particular programme taking a highly contextual approach, sensitive to the expressed needs of those taking part. In doing so they have established themselves as a source of community-relations training which is firmly grounded in the research and teaching experience.

## Programme work

By definition, the ISE has always been an educational establishment contributing to inter-church relations by providing a place in which people could work on matters related to inter-church concerns in an academic environment. They offered postgraduatee degrees in Ecumenical Studies, International Peace Studies and from 2001 in Reconciliation Studies. Initially by working as a research and postgraduate-education unit they were making themselves inaccessible to the majority of those engaged in local level inter-church work in Northern Ireland. However, the early 1990s brought a sea-change in the way in which the ISE's multi-dimensional approach to their pioneering work in the ecumenics was practiced. Consequently, they began using the critical perspectives and analytical tools developed through their teaching and research to implement contextually sensitive Christian reconciliation courses for local communities in Northern Ireland.

### 1973–93

During the initial phase of its existence, the work of the ISE included both teaching and research, both of which made a contribution to Christian reconciliation in Ireland. The School concentrated mainly upon the theological issues surrounding ecumenism in line with the ISE's founding vision. A one-year course, the Ecumenical Studies MPhil Programme,[16] was envisaged for students who had already completed some form of basic theological training, with options in comparative Christianity, the history of the ecumenical movement, the methodology of ecumenism, and inter-church conversations with fieldwork to be undertaken either in the USA or Geneva.[17] This course was designed to 'introduce and explore all three currents of the modern ecumenical movement – justice and peace, inter-religious dialogue, and inter-church dialogue'[18] – whilst aiming to 'reflect critically on major issues and insights of the ecumenical movement and to lay a theological foundation for the vision of ecumenism, engagement in issues of justice and peace and inter-faith dialogue'.[19] Through the provision of such a course, the ISE was contributing to an improvement in ecumenical relationships in an practical manner by providing a solid academic grounding in the key issues of Ecumenics and Peace Studies which, when combined with the practical  elements of the field work, prepared the School's graduates for their future roles within the ecumenical movement.

It would seem that Hurley had envisaged a much wider role in reconciliation work than the earliest offerings of the school would indicate. He stated that 'August 1971, was to see the introduction of internment without trial. Just six months later on 30th January 1972 came Bloody Sunday. The need for what the ISE was offering became even more glaring.'[20] He wanted the remit of the school to expand into the related area of reconciliation as:

> Fr. Hurley was deeply conscious of the need for the Churches to break free from their sectarian history. The widespread ignorance, stereotypes and distrust of each other's tradition and the lack of awareness in Ireland of the world wide development of dialogue, co-operation and theological convergence, was seen to be a major obstacle to the work of reconciliation in Ireland.[21]

However, despite the underlying understanding of the basic methods of improving community relations, once more such work was carried out in an abstract and academic manner, first through an early research project and, second, through the provision of another degree course on International Peace Studies.

The first research project undertaken by the ISE was carried out in co-operation with the Centre for the Analysis of Conflict (CAC) in London in 1970, which introduced the model of relationships which have gradually (from circa 1985) onwards been adopted by inter-church groups working on improving community relations. The project was designed with the help of the CAC to be a controlled group communication between Northern Irish Protestants and Catholics.[22] They engaged 'in a face to face situation presided over by a group of social and political scientists who would contribute their knowledge about the nature of the conflict and help the parties to a conflict to make accurate assessments of the motivations of each other'.[23] The results were generally agreed to be exciting and influential as they produced a clear understanding for all those involved.[24] However, the most positive aspect of this for the ISE's work, and indeed for inter-church relations in general, was its introduction of the 'gradualist' or lowest-common-denominator-approach to community relations to Northern Ireland. This was 'a model of conflict resolution that encouraged people to work together on functional matters in which they had a common interest, until they built up enough trust to deal with the more decisive issues'.[25]

In the early 1980s, ISE introduced a certificate in International Peace Studies, which was later to become the MPhil, this course was designed to cater for a wider range of participants and worked intandem with the peace and reconciliation elements contained within the Ecumenical Studies programme.

> The idea behind the proposal … [was] rooted in the concept of reconciliation and in the view that the fundamental inspiration of the School [was] the study of relations between the two communities, and the analysis of the principles guiding their harmonious development. While Ecumenical Studies focuses on religious communities, and their relations with society, International Peace Studies addresses the problem of reconciliation at the level of state and secular groupings within and across state boundaries.[26]

Thus, with the implementation of this course came the expansion of the disciplines covered by the ISE to include, for example, sociology and politics. However, once more, the emphasis of the course was on academic research rather than the implementation of practical schemes of reconciliation within Northern Ireland, which rendered it inaccessible to most local inter-church participants. Nevertheless, throughout this period, both through their ecumenical education programme and their attempts to build a reconciliation based research programme, the ISE did make a contribution to the development of inter-church relations in Northern Ireland by preparing people, in a controlled environment supported by academic research, for the challenge of leading those wishing to build relationships at all levels, providing them with the skills and knowledge necessary to facilitate local attempts at reconciliation.

## 1994–2005

With the paramilitary ceasefires, and the subsequent peace process, came fundamental changes in the practice of inter-church relationships in Northern Ireland, and this period saw the ISE build upon their success in educating the future leaders of peace and reconcilaiation groups. They began to provide resources and training for those wishing to become involved in local inter-church and community development work, in addition to their research and theological courses. Consequently they established the *Learning Together: Education for Reconciliation Programme* and the Certificate in *Reconciliation Studies Programme*, both taught in Northern Ireland; second, through the five-year research project *Moving Beyond Sectarianism*, which after its conclusion in 2000 resulted in new means of engagement with Northern Irish communities including the *Partners in Transformation Project*.

The basis for these programmes was summed up by Johnston McMaster:

> The changing context and the peace process challenge the churches to educate for reconciliation. The cultural disestablishment of the churches and the consequential experience of being pushed to the edge of society create a new context for being church.[27] The challenge now is; what shall we teach and how shall we teach it? ... The last few years have seen the explosion of the School's Northern Ireland base ... All of these programmes, diverse in their content and styles, are essentially about education for reconciliation. [28]

This led to the establishment of two courses aimed at promoting reconciliation within Northern Ireland: *Learning Together: Education for Reconciliation* and the *Certificate in Reconciliation Studies Programme*, both of which were specifically designed to address 'the needs and experiences of people in Northern Ireland'.[29] The *Learning Together* programme was essentially a series of courses on themes related to reconciliation, such as *Where are we going? Important Current Issues in Church Relations*, *The Politics of Faith – Exploring the Bible as a Political Text* and *Knowing Ourselves? Knowing Others? Exploring Our Christian Traditions*. It was designed to:

> Introduce a whole new set of dynamics in relation to inter-church and peace and reconciliation issues. It is largely a focus on ecumenical issues, on churches trying to understand one another, on exploring peace, reconciliation, and justice issues. That means trying to tackle some of the political questions, the social questions and it is about enabling people to make a journey together so that trust and confidence as well as knowledge is increased.[30]

Admission to these courses was open to anyone and they were run in areas throughout Northern Ireland, such as Enniskillen, Belfast and Dungannon. The *Certificate in Reconciliation Studies* as more formal in nature and required a two-year commitment from its participants, being designed to 'address the challenge of developing a fuller, more complex, and more systematic understanding of the theoretical and practical approaches to reconciliation'.[31]

The form of these two courses illustrated a growing awareness on the part of the ISE that a more contextual approach to the issue of reconciliation was needed if they were going to make a valuable contribution to reconciliation and peacebuilding in church and society.

> There is a growing realisation that people need to understand each other's religious, cultural and political identities. There is also a growing awareness of hard questions and the need to tackle them. Reconciliation itself is slowly moving up the personal and denominational agenda for some, and with it the realisation that reconcilers require to be skilled. The Adult Education Programme is addressing the need for encounter, knowledge and skills.[32]

Those facilitating the courses implicitly understood the importance of the local setting and experience in the development of the Education for Reconciliation Courses. They consequently adopted a reactive approach to the needs and level of relationships already in place: The style and the context are always local. The local group ... is essentially designing the programme. We take it away, give it shape and unpack the content.'[33] This work, when combined with their postgraduate degree provision, highlights their evolution into a successful ecumenical body, taking into account nuanced experiences at a local level, rather than just concentrating upon the leadership training witnessed prior to 1994. Such a change in focus was further strengthened by their research project *Moving Beyond Sectarianism*. This project developed the pathway of community-based processes to an even greater degree and adhered to Hurley's founding vision by being based upon research in this instance into the dynamics of sectarianism within Northern Irish society.

The *Moving Beyond Sectarianism* project was run by Cecilia Clegg and Joseph Liechty from January 1995 to June 2000[34] and 'was initiated to examine the causes, expressions and consequences of sectarianism in Ireland, as well as develop insights and models for moving beyond it'.[35] Through this project we can see the maturation of the ISE as a contextually-focused organisation, as well as its commitment to its academic origins by contributing to an understanding of the conflict in Northern Ireland from an ecumenical perspective:

> Sectarianism is widely recognised as a significant aspect to the conflict in Northern Ireland, and yet very little of the voluminous literature on the troubles has given serious attention to sectarianism. And when sectarianism is discussed, the role of religion receives little attention; remarkably little, given that the popular understanding of sectarianism associates it with a destructive

mingling of religion and politics. A church focused approach to sectarianism addresses an important gap in understanding conflict in Northern Ireland.[36]

The methodology employed was comprehensive, including reviews of literature on religion and conflict in Northern Ireland, focus groups 'which brought together groups from neighbouring Catholic and Protestant congregations to address issues of sectarianism and identity',[37] interviews, focused consultations, conferences and 'a social science survey to test attitude change in group work participants'.[38] The final report presented an analysis of sectarianism from a religious viewpoint, looking at its origins, definition and manifestation within society. However:

> What came to dominate MBS ... was a kind of work not even mentioned in our original job description. Early in the project groups started to ask if we would say something to them about sectarianism or help them think about how they could address sectarianism. While it did not fit our initial understanding of our work, we did not feel free to say to people who were willing, even eager, to tackle such a crucial issue as sectarianism, 'Give us a few years to finish the research, and we'll get back to you.' ... By the end of MBS, we had led hundreds of sessions, sometimes a single session intended largely for information, more often multiple sessions for one group with a practical outcome in mind.[39]

This aspect of *Moving Beyond Sectarianism* led to the development of a number of new ISE projects attempting to deal with the issue of sectarianism within local communities. This work defines the development of the ISE in the post-1994 period as it demonstrates the beginnings of a union between academic research and education provision with community relations work, underlined by a desire for Christian reconciliation. *Partners in Transformation* was the most prominent of these projects and was undertaken as an ISE partnership with Mediation Northern Ireland. From its foundation in 2001 until its funding ran out in 2004, it worked 'with church leadership teams to enhance, nurture and support the capacity of churches and faith communities in their calling to be peacebuilders and agents of transformation'.[40] It did so by addressing 'the need for systematic work with churches and faith communities around generating a new vision and strategies for peacebuilding [working] with church leadership teams at all levels from national to local; [with a] remit that covers the whole island with a particular focus on Northern Ireland'.[41] Thus, project workers, Doug Baker and Cecilia Clegg, and latterly Geraldine Smyth worked in collaboration with organisations, such as the Church of Ireland and Catholic clergy groups, to develop tailor-made programmes for groups which, amongst other things, would enable 'clergy from the two traditions to get to know their local counterparts more deeply, understand more fully the context and challenges of each other's ministry, identify specific manifestations of sectarianism in their settings and explore practical steps they can take individually and together to address them'.[42] In addition, the project also provided consultants who worked with church groups to develop large-scale programmes. This project represented a maturation in the ISE's continued commitment to the education facilitation and resourcing of local groups, illustrating their ability to build upon the academic aspects of their work and produce schemes which represent the intersection between theology, the social sciences and community relations.

The work and achievements of the ISE since its foundation in 1973 have been mixed to say the least, and they have only begun to make a far-reaching contribution to the development of inter-church relationships since 2000. Prior to this, their work was carried out on what can only be called an abstract level, based upon academic research and postgraduate course provision in Dublin and latterly Belfast. It was inaccessible to the majority of those who wished to engage in reconciliation work in Northern Ireland. During the pre-1994 period, the value of their work lay in their research which laid the foundations for the low-key approach to inter-church relationships employed both at a national and local level during the 1980s. However, after 1994 the School began to provide training for those wishing to lead inter-church groups and developing analytical models and practical tools for use in local areas and in doing so has achieved its aim of promoting teaching, research and outreach amongst inter-church groups.

## THE RESOURCE PROVIDERS

In contrast to the formal and multi-centred approach of the ISE, the largest group of peace and reconciliation education initiatives were initially founded as informal bodies, which 'weren't really intended to be the start of a process, they were intended to be one-off things and ... right through until around 1994 there was always a sense that [they] were basically an *ad hoc* group going from one thing to the next'.[43] From 1983 to 1991, three such groups were founded: the Faith and Politics group in 1983, Youth Link in 1990 and Mediation Northern Ireland in 1991. With the exception of the Faith and Politics group, these new groups developed in three stages with 1994, once more, marking a turning point in the way in which they operated. Initially, they worked by providing resources for discussion, such as booklets looking at events and issues from a biblical perspective, moving into facilitating courses on these issues and eventually providing training for those who wished to organise cross-community courses themselves. Each of these groups have made a substantial contribution to inter-church relationships in Northern Ireland by developing the main core of professional inter-church workers in the area. Furthermore, they have also provided the means and expertise needed to support the expansion of local level initiatives by developing tools and models for cross-community relationship building, which guide those involved through sensitive areas, such as political and cultural identity issues, whilst remaining committed to the need for Christian reconciliation.

## The Faith and Politics group

The Faith and Politics group was an inter-church initiative founded in 1983 as a result of discussions that had taken place at the Greenhills Ecumenical Conference:

> I thought that it was silly that we were having a meeting on Faith and Politics: what we needed was a structure to look at it and deal with it. The proposal that I put [to Greenhills] was that there would be a formal inter-church structure to deal with it; fortunately the churches were highly opposed to that proposal and didn't want anything to do with it. But had they been involved well we wouldn't have the freedom we do in the Faith and Politics group to explore stuff.[44]

Faith and Politics was founded as a religio-political think-tank to reflect theologically upon the conflict in Northern Ireland and the problems that it posed for Christians. Their work contains implications for inter-church relationships for two reasons: first, through their advocacy of the need for reconciliation via cross-community contact, calling on people to 'leave the safe, secure and familiar places to reach out to the other community, even when it involves risks',[45] and second, by the use of these publications as discussion tools by local level inter-church groups, especially clergy groups.[46]

The Faith and Politics group define themselves thus:

> Our group has tried to move beyond what we perceived as the Christian criteria for politics in Ireland to see what political con-

sensus we had among ourselves ... A different group of Christians might come up with a significantly different set of opinions and proposals based on the same criteria. Our project is of necessity a provisional and tentative one – designed to promote discussion and response, rather than to come to definitive and biding conclusions.[47]

Since the production of their first document in 1983, they have maintained their primary objective of producing theological reflections upon political issues which are consequently used as resources by local groups. Nevertheless, the content of their work has reacted constantly to the changing atmosphere in Northern Ireland, and has produced resources which are a reflection of the society that they are attempting to help:

The documents produced between 1995 and 1997 highlighted the new opportunities and context following the paramilitary ceasefires of 1994. They deal with the sensitive issues of forgiveness, dialogue and parity of esteem and sovereignty, and go on to explore the key issues of weaponry, policing and security and prisoners.[47]

Their work centres upon the political and the need for a Christian response to the conflict in Northern Ireland, and this is reflected in the work produced by Faith and Politics between 1983 and 1999.

The Faith and Politics group met between 1983 and 1999, producing twelve documents,[49] working on the interface between theology and politics.[50] As with the work of other organisations, there is a discernible shift in the group's focus in the post-1994 era. From 1983 until 1993 their work concentrated upon producing ideas for the settlement of the conflict in Northern Ireland, whilst from 1994 onwards their pamphlets began to centre upon ways in which Christians could contribute to the success of the peace process by looking at key issues, such as reconciliation and issues relating to territory.

The initial stage of Faith and Politics' work was one of self-definition and understanding:

the interesting thing is we came to solve the problems of the world but eventually looked at each other and said there are some problems in this room and we had to find space for each other ... that was an interesting process because we were squirming round maybe for a year trying to find a focal point and when we did find it we said we have to write a reflection on ourselves and what we believe theologically, politically and that led to the publication of *Breaking Down the Enmity*.[51]

The resulting document looked at the role that Christians had played in the continuation of the conflict in Northern Ireland, arguing that 'the conflict is a judgement that we have brought on ourselves by worshipping the false God of sectarian interests and not the God who is revealed in Jesus Christ'.[52] They concluded that true Christian faith should present a challenge to sectarian mindsets, with reconciliation being:

> People finding a way of living together in difference. It means the restoration of broken relationships. It means wanting the other to be with us and not wanting to destroy, dominate or separate from them. It means being able to take the other community into account and sharing power, responsibility and resources. It means going beyond the 'right' and 'wrong' of the conflict – the vicious circle of action and reaction – to create a new and creative relationships.[53]

By emphasising a requirement for Christians to transcend sectarian mindsets, *Breaking Down the Enmity* was setting the tone for the first period of the Faith and Politics group's existence. The next five publications stressed the need for an equitable solution to the situation in Northern Ireland based upon their definition of 'true politics'.[54] For example, they looked at the Anglo-Irish Agreement, asking 'How should Christians of different traditions respond to the Agreement and its implications?'[55] Their answers to this question examined the role of the churches and the challenges facing them, as well as the implications of any political agreement for a number of groups within Northern Irish society. It then went on to discuss the role that violence, memory and identity play in the perpetuation of the conflict: 'We need to break out of the vicious circle of seeing the "other" side as always to blame and ourselves as always righteous, the innocent and the good ones.'[56] The entire tone of the Faith and Politics group's work during the initial period from 1983 to 1993 centred upon the idolatry of sectarianism and the need for Christian reconciliation as a solution to the problems facing the area, and later pamphlets echo this language:

> Christian reconciliation needs to be based on what God has done for us and therefore what we must do ourselves. This should challenge us to respond in a new way. Remembering the past as a Christian means remembering with a desire to forgive and a will to change things for the better today.[57]

However, the ceasefires and the peace process brought a new dimension to this work as, whilst Faith and Politics remained committed to an advocation of Christian reconciliation, their means of creating theologically based politics for the province changed, as they began to focus on concepts such as forgiveness rather than using events such as the Anglo-Irish Agreement and reactions to 1916 as the driving force for their analysis.

As with *Breaking Down the Enmity,* the first pamphlet produced during this stage in the life of Faith and Politics, *The Things that Make for Peace,* served as an overview of the situation post-1994 from a Christian viewpoint.

> Over the past ten years ... we have tried to bring to our reflections the perspective of faith ... The ceasefires and the publication of the Framework Document seem to us to be ... landmarks inviting our further reflection. We outline in this document the principal themes that we feel are important to consider at this time.[58]

So, for example, they look at forgiveness, dialogue, parity of esteem, sovereignty, policing and prisoners, matters which were each the subject of individual publications in following years. The publications that followed this were expositions of a number of the key themes facing the political situation in Northern Ireland at the time, whilst retaining the founding ethos of the group. For example, *Forgive us our Trespasses ... ?* focused upon the themes of reconciliation and forgiveness, both major focal points prior to 1994. They centred upon the relationship of forgiveness and repentance to reconciliation, assessing what this relationship meant for the peace process in Northern Ireland, concluding that 'reconciliation only happens when *both* aspects – forgiveness and repentance – come together in a new and just relationship'.[59]

Their next publication, *New Pathways Developing a Peace Process in Northern Ireland*, provided a model for such a relationship. Once more, they centred upon the need for forgiveness, repentance and reconciliation, pointing out that the people of Northern Ireland need to take ownership of the peace process, rather than just seeing it as something political and removed from their experiences and lives. Thus, 'there needs to be an organic process of change at all levels of society. Unless change takes place in a way that involves wider participation, ownership and responsibility, new structures are likely to be unstable and non-inclusive.'[60] Here, they are arguing for the involvement of the churches and other agencies of civil society in the peace process, presenting this as their biblically based model of reconciliation for the area. 'Political compromise does not sell out the transcendent God who is beyond all our political aspirations. What God requires is new and just relationships between persons and communities.'[61] In the provision of such a model, Faith and Politics remain committed to their roots as Christian commentators on the situation in Northern

Ireland and are emphasising the need to promote relationships based upon the principles of Christianity.

The Faith and Politics group did not present themselves as a classic resource provider, remaining fixed to their initial plan to provide Christian reflections upon the situation in Northern Ireland and in doing so were lending themselves more to the creation of a political theology for Northern Ireland rather than the promotion and facilitation of community relations. However, in their consideration of the situation from a theological viewpoint, they have produced a series of pamphlets which have been used by local parishes and clergy groups as a focal point for the consideration of the role that Christianity has to play in the perpetuation and amelioration of the conflict. In doing so they have placed themselves within a category of resource providers whose reach and influence cannot be determined.

## Youth Link

Youth Link was the indirect result of a document produced by the IICM on *Young People and the Church*, as those involved in its production wanted to try and translate its findings into a tangible form by developing a 'particular approach to training and empowering youth workers and young adults for cross-community work'.[62] The result was the foundation of Youth Link in 1990 by the four main churches as a resource for young people and their leaders in Northern Ireland. It involved 'the four larger Churches officially ... in "developing better cross-community relations through a Christian understanding of society"'.[63] In the development of its work, Youth Link has displayed all of the key characteristics of a peace and reconciliation education initiative, moving through the stages of resourcing, facilitating and training, with the peace process, and the Good Friday Agreement, in particular, marking a turning point in their modes of operation.

### Aims and vision

Youth Link's founding aims indicated that an organisation was envisaged which would provide community relations resources and training for youth groups. In the fifteen years since its foundation, Youth Link's aims and vision have been interchangeable and their evolution demonstrates the manner in which the organisation matured and learnt from its experiences within cross-community groups. In 1990, their vision was viewed as separate to their aims, but by 2005 their vision had become their aims, as they had established themselves firmly within inter-church work and sought to articulate a picture of the future which they intended to help facilitate.

Youth Link wanted to improve the quality of the community relations training for young people being carried out by churches and other Christian groups. This purpose was clarified through its vision, pointing out that 'Youth Link is not engaged in evangelisation, still less proselytisation ... The Christian faith underlies Youth Link's purpose and ethos, but the organisation is not directly concerned with faith sharing and the invitation to the faith journey.'[64] Instead, the vision that lay behind its work was one of empowerment as:

> Youth Link is primarily concerned with the development of better community relations. In the wider faith context, that in itself is a response to God's kingdom present here and now, and it is the kingdom that gives content and meaning to the Christian understanding of society which is fundamental to Youth Link's approach to community relations.[65]

Once they had achieved the clarification of its vision and ethos, Youth Link developed a set of aims which reflected this and centred completely upon the practical ways in which it intended to work. These aims evolved as Youth Link increased their understanding of how best to put their vision into practice. Initially they were basic, and represented a sketch of the work that the group were to carry out before 1994. They sought to: 'Facilitate funding; Initiate projects; Share role models; Produce resource material; Develop programmes; Liaise with other bodies; Listen to and empower young people.'[66]

The events of the mid-1990s prompted a reassessment within the organisation, which led it to centre more upon the training and facilitating aspects of its work promoting an alteration of the aims. Youth Link now concentrated upon:

- Providing skills and training for those involved in Youth Ministry, including community-relations work.
- Ensuring that professional youth ministry and community relations work is informed by best practice.
- Encouraging Youth Leader networking at local, national and international level to share information, ideas and resources.
- Meeting Churches' needs with respect to Youth Ministry and community relations through dialogue with Church Youth groups.
- Providing a 'prophetic voice' to the Churches and wider community in relation to issues in youth ministry and community relations.

- Providing support to the Churches in providing opportunities for young people of different traditions and cultural backgrounds to develop mutual understanding, tolerance, acceptance and respect and be active contributors towards reconciliation.[67]

Thus, whilst they no longer saw themselves as resource providers, Youth Link had become more confident in its ability to provide community relations training programmes. These aims demonstrated that they were hoping to begin to form a role as advocates for the improvement of the sector, an idea which was articulated in the vision espoused by Youth Link post-2000 as they set forward their aims for the future:

Youth Link's vision of the future is one where:

- The Churches together act as a role model in the development of youth ministry;
- Youth work is integrated into the heart of each Church's Ministry;
- Equity, diversity and interdependence are integrated into all aspects of policy and practice in youth ministry;
- The voice of young people is valued in both the Church and society;
- Youth Link is seen as a source of excellence in all aspects of leadership in youth ministry and community relations youth work.[68]

Although these aims and vision indicate how Youth Link perceived their work, in practice this work has not been an instant manifestation of each of these but rather, like all the other organisations, has built up slowly commencing with resource provision.

### Methods

In their approach to working with young people and the churches, Youth Link followed the three stages of resource provision, facilitation and training closely, beginning with the production of booklets on community relations issues and translating these theories into practice after 1994 with the provision of courses and training. Between 1993 and 1994, Youth Link produced a series of booklets on issues relating to young people and community relations in Northern Ireland. Through these booklets, we can see the expansion of the organisation's vision to bring a Christian dimension to the practice of reconciliation and community relationships. These booklets can be divided into three categories: the first puts for-

ward an argument in favour of community relationship-building,[69] whilst
the second looks at the nature of young people's attitudes and analyses
the way in which relationship-building can contribute to their development, thereby providing a starting point for the planning of their training courses.[70] The final category provides historical analyses of the conflict in Northern Ireland.[71] It is the first two categories which hold the
most importance for the development of Youth Link.

In the first category of publications, Youth Link offer an outline of
their argument in favour of improving community relations through the
churches and, in doing so, provide an articulation of the religious basis of
their work. The first of these two booklets examining the role that the
churches had to play in community relations looking closely at the reasons
behind the need for this role. Thus, they present an analysis of the issues
facing those who wish to engage in such work, looking at problems such
as stereotypes, prejudice, sectarianism and similarities and differences,
arguing that each of these problems need to be addressed by the churches
because to do so would be 'to explode myths, reduce prejudice, overcome
ignorance and develop understanding and better community relations'.[72]
Furthermore, through this booklet we can see the beginnings of the form
of cross-community relationship building used by Youth Link, as they
attempted to translate the need for church involvement into a tangible
form which resulted in a set of guidelines being produced which they
believed 'should facilitate maximum benefit from a project'.[73] These were:

Pre-Project – set agreed goals and objectives
– outline nature and essential elements of the Project
– identify participating groups
– prepare participating groups
– prepare project in partnership

Project – ensure equality between groups
– acknowledge similarities and differences
– address stereotype images
– share self-images, fears and concerns
– provide for inter-group as well as inter-personal
relations

Post-Project – ensure follow-up activity
– evaluate project in light of aims and objectives
– highlight learning and developmental experiences
– identify the next project.[74]

This demonstrates that Youth Link had developed a framework for community relations courses, the content of which they would provide after consultation with the group themselves. However, such analyses and community relations courses were not based upon the broad notion that churches should get involved in community relations work, but rather have at their root an exposition of the biblical principles involved, an articulation of which is provided in *A Biblical Basis for Cross-Community Work*. They argue that:

> Cross-community work aimed at reconciliation here in Ireland or in any other setting is not simply a response to the pain of division, nor is it simply an objective established by various voluntary groups and government departments. It is intimately linked with God's purpose and plan for creation and participation in it is a response to the initiative for reconciliation God has already taken.[65]

Through this analysis, it is evident that Youth Link has gained an understanding of the faith-based foundations of their work and in the next category of booklets we can see the development of their understanding of the sector with whom they aimed to work and the benefits that such work would have for those involved.

The three documents within this category looked at the role of sectarianism in the lives of young people, and the way in which a faith-based approach to community relations could enhance their lives, whilst contributing to the development of Youth Link's approach to relationship building. Youth Link argue that it is important to understand fully the nature of the sector with which it is attempting to work:

> It is all too easy for the Churches to make the generalised statement or assumption that young people are anti-sectarian and, if given the chance, will cross the divides and build a new community. This is undoubtedly true of an element of the youth population, but it may represent a pious hope on the part of some adults within the Church. It ignores the fact that a significant number of young people are, in fact, guardians of sectarian tradition, it is this expression of youth culture in Northern Ireland that poses one of the greatest challenges to Church-based youth work.[76]

Through the creation of such an understanding, they were laying the foundations for the development of their work as they demonstrated their belief in the need to work with the whole of society rather than just with 'more middle class and socially acceptable young people'.[77] Such work would be a two-way process, benefiting both the young people involved and their churches. Thus, as 'the Church's essential mission is community building and community relations. Its programmes from pre-natal to the grave ought to enable people to move with maturity though the stages of development on their life journey',[77] whilst, through their work with young people, the churches would be given an opportunity to move away from their sectarian stances of the past towards the anti-sectarian position expected of them by the Gospel:

> The Churches, historically over-identified with sectarian politics and loyalties of their respective communities, may find difficulty in appropriating an anti-sectarian role. But if the Gospel of the Kingdom of God is the ultimate claim to loyalty for the Christian community and provides the community of Faith with a critical perspective on all human institutions and ideologies, then the Churches have no option but to live as an active anti-sectarian community.[78]

These publications, then, play a three-fold role in the development of Youth Link's methodology: first, by presenting us with a proactive approach to community relations within Northern Ireland based upon an understanding of the sector in which they wished to operate; second, when combined with an exposition of the form that they intended their training and facilitational work to take, by providing a clearer picture of the ethos behind it than their aims and vision, whilst finally acting as resources for those wishing to work with young people.

Unlike the other peace and reconciliation education initiatives operating in Northern Ireland during the early 1990s, Youth Link saw themselves 'as a professional Inter-Church Youth Service Agency'.[80] This was the result of the involvement of the national-level church leadership in their foundation, which meant that they began with a formal constitution and the approval of the Department of Education.[81] Consequently, the implementation of their training programmes began before 1994, with 1998 marking a turning point in the work of the organisation, as they believed that the Good Friday Agreement presented them with a new context in which they could enable local churches to work together in much the same way as the ceasefires prompted other organisations to rework their methods of engagement with their participants.

From the outset, then, Youth Link's work with local churches represented a blend of training and facilitation with their 'general youth work training receiving formal and professional recognition to the level of NVQ. Cross-community training at both single identity and contact level developed a wide-ranging modular approach dealing with the key issues at the heart of community division and conflict.'[82] The facilitation work undertaken by Youth Link is best defined by the development of two of their courses: the *Kairos Project* and *Education for Peace*, whilst their training work initially aided the development of single identity training *Building Confidence* which was designed to be used by workers in parishes who had undertaken the training programme offered by Youth Link.

The training work offered by Youth Link to youth workers was planned in conjunction with its participants and centred on an ethos of understanding: 'Youth Link: NI: training in the skills and issues of cross-community work will help you understand your own tradition a little better and appreciate the diversity of Christian tradition in Northern Ireland. All our training and events operate with a distinctively Christian ethos.'[83] Training was offered in a three-step format: Initially those interested would take the *First Steps* or *Single Group Preparatory Work*[84] course, which was an introductory-level, single-denominational course run through two church youth work agencies, Cathog[85] and CYSC.[86] Although the nuances of the courses run by these two agencies were different, their tone was similar as they were both designed to prepare participants by developing the 'skills, knowledge and vision required for youth ministry'.[87] These courses looked at issues such as spiritual development, prayer, the role of the media in society and pastoral issues, whilst also teaching the skills necessary to lead a youth group such as programme planning and evaluation. Once this stage had been completed, youth leaders could then take the next course in the scheme *One Step Beyond* or *Cross-Community*,[88] which focused upon inter-denominational youth work and which looked at the issues covered in *First Steps* in more depth, along with others such as team building and communications skills whilst working towards a certificate in Youth Work.

It was in the final stage of its programme that we can see the bridge between Youth Link's training and facilitational work, through the *Further Steps* or *Peace Builders*[89] programme. This was based upon the idea that:

> Nobody finds cross-community work easy and all of us can be hindered by fear and apprehension. Youth Link can help young people and adults confront those fears and move beyond them. Consultation is often the first step. Youth Link staff will visit your area to facilitate: an exploration of cross-community possibilities; designing a cross-community programme or project; resourcing cross-community work; developing a training programme; setting up a cross-community youth group.[90]

The courses facilitated by Youth Link within local churches were based around three models which involved working with young people in conjunction with their youth leaders. Each of these programmes were linked intrinsically to the training that they offered to youth workers, as they allowed them to put the skills learnt in *First Steps,* such as programme planning, into practice. The first to be developed was the *Kairos Project,* which was designed as a 'relationship building' course, through which young people would have the opportunity to consider and discuss issues such as identity, culture, faith and politics in a mixed group whilst 'developing trusting relationships and ... working together on a project which impacts positively on community relations'.[91] This course was followed by the establishment of *Education for Peace,* which was 'designed to enable young people to be active participants in the promotion of a plural, just and democratic society'.[92] They thus addressed issues such as reconciliation and human rights in a manner which was designed to develop meaningful inter-denominational relationships.

However, Youth Link stressed the need for their work to adapt to the requirements of their participants, arguing that 'education in cross-community partnership [should] enter into partnership with young people in ways appropriate to the different stages of personal development'.[93] This belief led to the development of *Building Confidence – A Single Identity Programme for Church-based Groups,* brought about by the fact that 'a major blockage to making contacts and building bridges across the community divide in Northern Ireland is a lack of confidence. This usually means a lack of confidence in one's own identity.'[94] The result was a six-week programme designed to be undertaken by single-denomination groups, which guided them through a series of discussions on issues such as political identity and religious belief. It culminated in a biblical reflection upon the role that religion has played in the conflict in Northern Ireland and the way in which it can contribute to reconciliation.

Youth Link expected their facilitation and training work to be a starting point for church-based youth groups, stating that 'where it leads to will be decided by participants in the final session'.[95] In the post-Good Friday Agreement period, a change in the focus of Youth Link's work came about, as they began to perceive themselves as advocates for the needs of the Church youth sector: 'The changing context of the post-Agreement Northern Ireland ... provides a forum for Churches to work as partners together sharing problems, opportunities, responses and resources. Youth Link is therefore a visible witness to common Gospel values and a shared commitment to the total well being of young people within the community',[96] going on to state that Youth Link's role should be as 'a prophetic voice with young people within church and society'.[97]

Youth Link believes itself to be playing a unique role within inter-church relationships in Northern Ireland, as they say of themselves that 'it could be said that Youth Link and its member churches were almost a decade ahead of the developments that have now taken place within the wider community'.[98] However, a close examination of their aims and work would prove such an assertion to be an exaggeration at best, and false at worst, as their work was developing in line with that of other organisations operating in the area at the time. Instead, Youth Link should be viewed as a conventional peace and reconciliation education initiative providing training and resources for the youth sector, based upon a desire to promote an understanding not only of young people in Northern Ireland, but of Northern Irish society as well. As trainers and facilitators they have been quite successful in meeting some of their aims as, for example between 1996 and 1999, 1,225 youth leaders participated in their programmes,[99] but the assertion that they have contributed a 'prophetic voice' to community relations and youth work issues is doubtful and incredibly hard to measure.

*Mediation Northern Ireland*
Mediation Northern Ireland was the last of the peace and reconciliation education initiatives to be founded, coming into existence in 1991. Unlike the other organisations working with the Protestant and Catholic Churches, it was not created with a specifically Christian ethos in mind, but rather to promote peace building which they believed 'must be "organic" going on across society'.[100] Mediation Northern Ireland identified 'six sectors of Northern Ireland society in which to promote meditative activity: the community; the justice system; the churches; political affairs; public bodies and in the business world'.[101] The nature of their engagement with society meant that the churches constituted about one-sixth of Mediation Northern Ireland's work. Furthermore, due to the multi-sector focus of their work, Mediation Northern Ireland's methodological development has not followed exactly the same model as the other para-church organisations. They have focused instead upon mediation services and the provision of training courses, often in partnership with ECONI and the ISE, aimed at training people within the churches to become mediators and community relationship trainers themselves. Their work has remained constant since 1991 and the peace process served to reinforce Mediation Northern Ireland's understanding of their practices.

*Aims and vision*
The vision of Mediation Northern Ireland centred upon mediation within Northern Irish society, defined as 'the process in which a third party

becomes a facilitating presence to people affected by conflict with a view to their moving through a designed process in the direction of a resolution'.[102] This was encompassed in their vision: 'Our vision is to assist reconciliation in our society by supporting a culture in which conflict is dealt with constructively ... [Mediation Northern Ireland] promotes the use of Third Party intervention in disputes and supports creative responses to conflict in Northern Ireland'.[103] From the outset those involved in Mediation Northern Ireland, probably due to the fact that they were all experienced mediators, had a clear idea of how this vision should be put into practice. Consequently, their aims have remained the same: 'We assist reconciliation in Northern Ireland by: the provision of training in Community Relations, Conflict Intervention and, in particular, Mediation. Building and maintaining a corps of mediation practitioners. Supporting individuals, localities and organisations in developing their capacities for constructive intervention in conflict [and] providing mediative assistance in disputes.'[104] In their translation of these aims into a programme for church work, Mediation Northern Ireland have been creative, adopting a cause-and-effect approach rather than just dealing with consequences, such as the results of sectarianism. In doing so they have been at the forefront of the move towards a more holistic and empowering approach to inter-church relationships by training 'clergy and lay leaders for constructively handling conflicts',[105] rather than an imposition-based approach presenting them with a generic set of guidelines for relationship building.

## Methods of mediation and training

The work of Mediation Northern Ireland was two-fold: 'Mediation in disputes with a community relations significance and training',[106] in areas such as peace building and societal change and community relations practice. Their work rests upon understanding, and is directed by a need to comprehend not only the conflict in Northern Ireland, but also the dynamics and needs of those groups that have sought their mediative skills. They argue that 'mediation must be tailored to the desires of those engaged in conflict. This might mean that they do not want to compromise; they simply want to live in safety with the enemy without making him/her a friend.'[107] As a result of this commitment to understanding, Mediation Northern Ireland's work with the churches is underlined by a clear philosophy concerning their place within Northern Irish society and, more importantly, their role in the conflict:

> There would be a number of reasons why we are doing this work: first of all, religion is a historic theme in society and therefore it is

important to address that element. Secondly, churches remain very strong institutions in society and they have a lot of impact on their membership and so they are an important group through whom to work in terms of reaching people and influencing programmes.[108]

It is these ideas that have informed the development of their programme work since 1991, and which have lead them to work in partnership with other groups in the implementation of their church-centred courses, promoting them to centre upon training rather than mediation. In their work with the churches, Mediation Northern Ireland focused upon four elements: first, their clergy' and lay church leaders' training work; second, the creation of an understanding of special areas of concern for ministers, such as sectarianism; third, their work with individual denominations to encourage them to develop their own peacemaking capacities, and finally, the support of local inter-church initiatives which began with the implementation of the Church Fora model after 1994. After 2000, Mediation Northern Ireland's work with the churches was completely amalgamated with the ISE's programme work, further demonstrating their commitment to community-relations training.

The main focus of Mediation Northern Ireland's work was on training clergy and lay leaders to handle 'conflict within the church, which is training clergy and laity from all denominations to understand how conflict operates and tools and skills for addressing conflict within church life which is important in its own right; it is also important in that it is where many of the church people are more motivated to begin to explore things'.[109] In the formulation of this training programme, Mediation Northern Ireland took a lowest-common-denominator-approach, based upon their conviction that conflict resolution training can only be successful if it starts with something that the participants are interested in before moving on to the wider context of the role of churches in peacemaking and reconciliation.

Mediation Northern Ireland ran a series of courses for churches which illustrate this approach. The first, *Handling Conflict in the Church*, was designed 'to assist participants enhance skills for handling conflicts within the church – and to begin to appreciate how such skills might also help to address wider conflicts in society'.[110] The second course in the series, *Processing Conflict in the Church*, aimed to build upon the first, by looking at approaches which may prevent conflict, whilst enhancing the 'awareness and skills necessary to intervene in conflict and to help process conflicts'.[111] This was followed by *Facilitating Decision Making*, which aimed 'to enhance awareness and skills needed

in facilitation'.[112] Once these three courses had been completed participants then moved into the area of inter-church contact and cross-community relationship- building with *Skills for Transformation,* which was
aimed at equipping 'participants to be leaders and facilitators in work
with local inter-church groups by exploring ways of moving beyond sectarianism; transforming ourselves and groups; contributing to the transformation of society'.[113] It was in this phase of the courses that we can see
the implementation of Mediation Northern Ireland's second form of
church work. This looked at issues that were particularly pertinent to the
churches as 'all ministries or church work takes place in a particular backdrop where the background to the ministry is divided'.[114]

The content and form of these training courses were quite significant
for the development of inter-church work in Northern Ireland, as they
acknowledged and formally articulated the need for participants in such
groups to prepare themselves for encounters with the other community.
Furthermore, they also provided a capacity for those who would be
resistant to such work to develop an interest in inter-church relations:

> The conviction is that if people do not have positive experiences of
> church life and dealing with diversity, they can't be expected to go
> out and apply this in a wider context. If you were to offer training
> on the wider context as a starting point not so many people would
> start but when you offer it later it may catch their imagination.[115]

Finally, in their provision of such courses Mediation Northern Ireland were
concurrently engaging in the final two phases of the methodological model
employed such organisations, moving from the facilitation of courses into
the training of future facilitators in the last stage of the programme.

The final two methods employed by Mediation Northern Ireland in their
church work were intertwined and focused upon building the capacity of
denominations and local congregations to interact with those from the other
community. It was this aspect of their work that they concentrated upon
after 2000, when they founded the *Partners in Transformation* Project with
the ISE.[116] They have been described as 'helping to persuade those within the
church structure to make peace making a positive resolution within the
wider society a higher priority ... [whilst] supporting local inter-church initiatives to be available in what ever way is appropriate to support the grass-
roots things'.[117] It was through this service that Mediation Northern Ireland
practised most of their facilitation work, as they built local inter-church connections for groups in segregated areas by matchmaking. Once a suitable
match has been achieved Mediation Northern Ireland became facilitators
for these groups as:

what they are conscious of is that polite contact and they are not getting to the point of discussing what might be difficult issues with one
another and they are saying if there is going to be real healing in this
relationship we have to get into those difficult topics and they say we
don't know how, and we are afraid if we do what might happen and
how to deal with that. So, they look for outside facilitators who can
come in and get them talking to one another in a new way, someone
who is comfortable doing that but also someone who is neutral.[118]

In line with Mediation Northern Ireland's ethos of conflict resolution,
once they had been invited into an inter-church group, their facilitators
adopted a low-key approach to enable the group to communicate with
one another, helping participants to think about issues like their identity
and perspectives on certain issues either through the use of examples
from their direct experience or through role playing based upon biblical
stories such as Ephesians 2.[119] Doug Baker sums up Mediation Northern
Ireland's approach to facilitation when he says 'I think that the biggest
role as a facilitator is giving them some handles through which to talk
about their experience and giving them permission to do so.'[120] Thus, in
common with the methods employed in their training programmes,
through such work Mediation Northern Ireland were empowering those
involved in local level inter-church relationships to understand their
situation by adopting an unobtrusive approach to relationships. This was
achieved by starting at each group's level and allowing them to explore
issues, rather than dealing with local-level church groups by providing
a pre-determined model, as has sometimes been the case. In the
post-ceasefire era, this work continued to grow and was joined by another
aspect of Mediation Northern Ireland's work with local level inter-
church groups, whereby they would provide an evaluation service for
groups, such as the Lisburn Inter-Church Project who were applying for
the newly available funding, such as the European Peace and
Reconciliation Fund. Such work initially involved helping them to refine
their vision and develop a strategic plan but, once they had gained confidence in this area, moved into supporting and helping them wherever
possible in the application process.

Through their work Mediation Northern Ireland have built up a register
of over seventy people who have been trained as mediators within Northern
Ireland, and in doing so have added a new aspect to inter-church relationships in the area by providing a professional class of people trained to enable
relationships to be built in a meaningful manner, rather than through the
polite contact which was so often the case in the 1980s. Furthermore,

through their partnerships with groups, such as the ISE, Mediation Northern Ireland have contributed to the growth of such services by providing a model of community relations work which understands the limitations of local churches within Northern Ireland and prepares them fully for contact before cross-denominational relationships occur.

The content and approach of each of these three peace and reconciliation education initiatives have been built upon a similar framework. Thus, each of these groups have been engaged in an attempt to improve community relationships within Northern Ireland through the employment of Christian reconciliation by presenting an argument based upon biblical values for Protestants and Catholics to work together and, in the cases of Youth Link and Mediation Network, translating these arguments into practical measures, such as relationship-building courses and leadership training, which are designed to do just that. Furthermore, unlike their counterparts at a national level, these organisations have been in a position to react quickly to events and trends, using events, such as the paramilitary ceasefires, as an opportunity to introduce new aspects to their work. However, in order to carry out such aims, these organisations have been compelled to remove themselves from their own denominations functioning instead outside the immediate sphere of the churches, thereby presenting the leaderships with a challenge to take up their 'biblical responsibility for peace'. By working in such a way they have been aligning themselves with the ethos of the inter-church groups operating within local areas and have helped to crystallise the separation of theological ecumenism from community relations. However, in order to achieve their aims both the organisations, and the different forms of local level inter-church groups, needed a support network which was provided for them by the Community Relations Council.

## Supporting the Peace and Reconciliation Education Initiatives: The Community Relations Council

Since its foundation as a charitable organisation in 1990, the Community Relations Council has played a unique role within the voluntary sector in Northern Ireland, providing funding, resources and support for groups working within the area on issues related to community relations. It aimed to 'assist the development of greater understanding and co-operation between political, cultural and religious communities in Northern Ireland and to help the people of Northern Ireland recognise and counter effects of communal division'.[121] It was not until the mid-1990s that it began

to take the role of the churches in improving community relations seriously. They, subsequently appointed a churches' Project Officer in 1996, who
stated that 'when I started there was very little going on in terms of inter-
church contact and my post was aimed at trying to increase inter-community contact within and between the churches – on a single-identity basis and
a cross-community level'.[122] This led to the establishment of the Churches'
Advisory Group (CAG), which operated until 2001, consisting of 'representatives from clergy, laity and interested individuals'[123] designed to enable
the Community Relations Council to fulfil its organisational aims within the
churches' sector. Although the Community Relations Council initially provide a number of resources for the churches in Northern Ireland, their most
substantial contribution to the development of inter-church relations has been
through their provision of funding. The role of the Community Relations
Council within the development of inter-church relations in Northern Ireland,
then, was one of supporter rather than facilitator, as although they themselves
did not provide any form of community-relations training, they offered assistance to those who did.[124]

Even before the Churches' Project Officer post was created, the
Community Relations Council was interested in the role that the
churches had to play in the promotion of reconciliation in Northern
Ireland. They commissioned a research report, the results of which were to
lay the foundations for their church-work policy over the next five years.

The report presented a series of recommendations to the Council:

1. Discussion with the relevant people in the Churches with a view
   to suggesting the introduction of community relations into the
   training of clergy at college level and beyond.
2. In-service training in the form of conferences, workshops, study
   days/retreats. Through the training networks of the Community
   Relations Council, to develop possible models of community
   relations training geared to the needs of the clergy. Similar
   induction courses for laity committed to or prepared to take the
   lead in community relations are also suggested.
3. Provision of community relations information and teaching
   material with models of good practice particularly at parish and
   congregational level.
4. Compilation of a Directory of all inter-church groups.
5. Compilation of information about Resource Groups.[125]

Each of these recommendations was implemented in some form, beginning with the compilation of a practical guide for churches in Northern
Ireland, which was followed a few months later by the recommended

directory of inter-church groups, both of which were updated in the late 1990s. This, when combined with the funding support offered by the Council to local inter-church initiatives, represents their contribution to the development of inter-church relationships during this period.

The first publication of the Community Relations Council aimed at the churches' sector was a resource document: *Churches Working Together*,[126] published in March 1994 'to encourage involvement, build confidence and enhance skills in work for better community relations'.[127] This resource was essentially designed to guide churches through community relations courses by providing a series of models which aimed to take into account the diversity of experience in Northern Ireland; these were interspersed with case studies concerning a variety of existing inter-church groups, which 'illustrate what is possible and hopefully encourage others'[128] as well as providing a snapshot of the form that inter-church work was taking at the time.[129] In addition, the booklet also provided lists of contacts for those who wanted some form of professional help with their groups, giving details of the services and resources available. This resource guide was quickly followed by *An Inter-Church Directory for Northern Ireland*,[130] the form of which was simplistic, dividing the groups into three categories: Protestant–Catholic Groups, Protestant–Catholic Social Action Projects and Ecumenical Communities, providing contact details and a list of their main aims and activities. However, by the late 1990s it was becoming obvious that these two resources needed to be updated to take into account the growth that had occurred both in size and form within inter-church relationships since the peace process:

> It hadn't been done for a couple of years and there are people within the church background actually expressing an interest in having resource material that they can use, the sort of things that can show them how to get started and what sot of approaches can be used and some materials that they can actually copy to use.[131]

The new inter-church directory was published in 1999 and, as well as providing a list of inter-church projects, illustrates clearly the changes that had taken place in the field since 1994. It provided a more comprehensive list by taking into account all forms of inter-church work rather than just prayer and social action projects. Although they were fairly comprehensive, when compared to the resources being provided by agencies such as Youth Link, those offered by the Community Relations Council were meagre,[132] providing ways of initiating discussion rather than discussion material itself, and it became increasingly evident that their main aim was not really to provide resources but to support those who were through their funding initiatives.

The influx of funding into Northern Ireland in the post-ceasefire era was a significant influence upon the development of inter-church relationships. The funding came from a number of sources, most notably Europe and the British and Irish governments, and was intended to support any group promoting peace and reconciliation within the area.

> We have a core funding budget and a European budget both from the government ... Through our core funding budget we support salary costs for groups like Cornerstone, Corrymeela, Mediation Network ... and we also fund premises. Through the European Fund we fund the Armagh Church Forum and the Lisburn Inter-Church Project and as well as that we have two grant-aiding budgets which is small for grants up to £10,000 but normally a group would only get a couple of thousand.[133]

The funding provided by groups like the Community Relations Council drove the development of inter-church relations forward, especially within local communities, as it provided local groups, and some peace and reconciliation education initiatives with the resources to develop their work and community relations programmes. The provision of funding was to a large extent responsible for the form that many of the church-based community-relations courses took in the post-ceasefire era. Such courses would not have developed as quickly, or as fully, without the impetus supplied by the money and its demand to produce material for use in local communities. Furthermore, it could be argued that the influx of funding aided the formalisation of the separation between ecumenism and community relations, as the funders provided an agenda (through their criteria) which indicated the direction in which they envisaged inter-church work going. Nevertheless, too much weight should not be placed on this because, as we have seen, this separation had been occurring in the decade before the major influx of funding commenced and it is unclear how the funders developed their criteria.[134] Despite this, much of its significance lay in the fact that the Community Relations Council were the main funders for inter-church projects in Northern Ireland,[135] and it is in this provision of funding, combined with their involvement in the establishment of the Church Fora, that their contribution to inter-church relations lay.

Through their management of these funding programmes, the Community Relations Council have enabled the growth of inter-church relationships in Northern Ireland, particularly since the paramilitary ceasefires of the mid-1990s. However, in spite of this success, they have failed to sustain the measures put in place after the Radford Report, with, for example, their commitment to the provision of resources for inter-church groups totalling four publications. It would seem, then, that after 1995 the work of the Community Relations Council changed direction as they placed all their resources in supporting other inter-church groups through the establishment of their funding schemes and subsequent monitoring of recipients, thereby moving them further away from the traditional work of the peace and reconciliation education initiatives into the role of supporter and supervisor of the development of all forms of local-level inter-church relationships in Northern Ireland.

CONCLUSION

The establishment of the peace and reconciliation education initiatives in Northern Ireland radically altered the direction of inter-church relation-ships, especially at a local level, by introducing a more proactive and strate-gic approach to the issue. They introduced planning and structure to local inter-church contact, primarily through their courses, which were tailored to suit the individual groups. Furthermore, through their provision of com-munity- relations courses to local churches, they have established a new, 'professional class' of inter-church workers who have the expertise, and critical distance from the group, to help local inter-church organisations improve relationships. Although these organisations and their work are still in their infancy, their provision of external moderators for inter-church groups has the potential to encourage the growth of the movement, by enabling inter-church groups to be established in areas where they had pre-viously failed, due, for example, to a lack of leadership.

The main benefit has been their contribution to the formalisation of the separation of ecclesiastical ecumenism from community relations in inter-church relationships. Consequently, they concentrated upon devel-oping methods of community relationship building that centred upon the need for Christian reconciliation between the Protestant and Catholic communities, instead of working on matters related to theological ecu-menism, thereby building upon the foundations that had been laid for them by earlier local-level inter-church groups.

However, the contribution of organisations such as Mediation Northern Ireland and Youth Link to the development of inter-church rela-tions has not been as substantial as outward appearances would suggest. Indeed, it could be contended that inter-church relationships would continue to grow at a steady pace, even without the assistance of such initiatives and their community-relations courses. They have a number of inherent problems. First, through their implementation of strategic planning for local groups and set ideas of how relationships should be developed within communities, peace and reconciliation education initiatives have, in many ways, disturbed the rhythm of local-level inter-church relations, which, prior to their creation, had developed in an organic manner. This has meant that many of the well-established groups within the area found their work being taken in a direction that they might not previously have thought of, or indeed have wanted to explore, possibly at the expense of projects that were already in existence. In addition, through their provision of community relations courses, it is clear that these organisations made a substantial contribution to the establishment of Church Fora in Northern Ireland, which, in recent years, have become the dominant model of inter-church contact, thus further damaging the organic and fluid nature of relationships. Furthermore, in their desire to promote inter-church relationships, these initiatives seem to have swung the pendulum too far in favour of a community-relations-based approach, and, in doing so have failed to identify opportunities that may have been present within some groups to discuss more theologically based matters. This, it could be argued, was in opposition to the holistic approach to inter-church relations that was established by local-level churches and taken on board by the IICM. However, this particular problem may be rectified once the initiatives become more firmly established and develop a more nuanced understanding of the needs of those using their services.

Peace and reconciliation education initiatives, then, have provided a final layer in the development of inter-church relations in Northern Ireland and, despite their drawbacks, through their development of community relations courses, which emphasise the need for Christian reconciliation and their availability to groups as facilitators, they have provided a new dynamic in inter-church relationships in Northern Ireland. They have helped them to move into the new phase of operation presented by the ceasefires by offering a space to participants, which has enabled them to take advantage of the more open atmosphere and attitudes to cross-community contact in a structured manner designed in conjunction with their needs and wishes.

# Conclusion

This book has aimed to examine the ways in which the Protestant and Catholic Churches have worked together in Northern Ireland by looking at the aims and outcomes of each of the different forms of inter-church co-operation that they developed since 1980. In doing so, it has illustrated that three different levels of inter-church contact exist: at a national level, between the leadership of the Protestant and Catholic Churches, at a local level, between ordinary church-goers and through the medium of the peace and reconciliation education initiative, which represents the growing professionalism of such work since the mid-1990s. Furthermore, although it could be expected that some co-operation would exist between the national and local levels, it is evident that the participants viewed them as two completely separate movements with broadly similar aims but vastly different methods and results. Thus, whilst at each level the premiss of this inter-church co-operation was based upon the need for reconciliation, an idea which makes up one of the key tenets of the Christian faith, it was the means of achieving this aim which caused the complete separation of the two forms of co-operation, with the activities that were occurring at a local level proving to be more successful than their national level counterparts.

It has been commented that 'historically, Irish religion and Irish politics and culture have been so closely inter-related that the latter, "non-theological factors" have had a profoundly adverse effect on inter-church relations'.[1] When assessing ecumenical relations prior to 1980 such a comment is true, however, between 1980 and 2005 'non-theological factors', such as Northern Ireland 's political culture, have had a constructive influence upon the practice of inter-church relations combining with other factors to change its very definition. In doing so, they have provided a model of co-operation that adheres closely to the principle of Christian reconciliation upon which the aims of this work were founded. Thus, since 1980 the very function of inter-church relationships in

Northern Ireland has changed, moving from abstruse theological discussion to a movement which understands the place of the church in civil society and the contribution that it has made to the creation of identity there and attempts to address the problems that this has caused.

Therefore, by far the most fundamental development in inter-church relationships in Northern Ireland has been the change in its definition and function. From its inception, dialogue between members of the Protestant and Catholic Churches, both in Northern Ireland and worldwide, has always been a comprehensive affair, dealing with matters of common concern, as well as those points upon which the denominations differ. However, prior to 1980, the balance of these conversations in Northern Ireland, both at a national and, to a certain extent, local level, weighed heavily towards theological matters, with an over-concentration upon issues such as Marian theology and justification by faith, which led to a disengagement from those that the clergy involved were working for. From 1980 onwards, this arrangement began to shift, as participants in inter-church dialogue were forced by external criticism and events such as the hunger strikes, the ongoing violence and peace talks, to reassess what church-based dialogue with the 'opposing side' actually meant. This prompted the balance of inter-church dialogue to be redressed as groups, such as the newly founded peaceline ecumenical communities, began to follow the lead of pioneers such as the Corrymeela Community and some local inter-church discussion groups, to include matters relating to the situation in Northern Ireland and community relations into their prayer and dialogue with one another. However, throughout the 1980s and 1990s the balance of inter-church relationships continued to shift even further in favour of a more holistic approach, which has moved discussion away from matters relating to theology, Bible study and prayer, towards those concerning community relations which were examined in the context of the participants' Christian faith.

Consequently, the years between 1980 and 2005 have witnessed a complete change in the definition and function of inter-church relationships in Northern Ireland, as they moved from theological discussion into working in a manner which addressed the issues of identity and communal relations from a Christian perspective. Thus, as a result of the work and innovations made by members of the Catholic and Protestant Churches, especially at a local level, inter-church relationships can no longer be seen as a generic term for ecumenism, but instead have been transformed into a movement in its own right which combines the three elements of community relations, Christian reconciliation and ecumenical dialogue in a manner unique to each of the inter-church groups and levels operating in Northern Ireland throughout this period. This change in definition of inter-church relationships was caused by two key factors: the biblical imperative for Christian reconciliation, which provided the key motivation for these interactions, and a growing realisation that in order to fulfil this need that the issue of identity in Northern Ireland would have to be addressed by the churches. This, when combined with a growth in friendship and understanding and external events, most notably the paramilitary ceasefires and the subsequent peace process, led to development of a more nuanced understanding of the practice and implications of such inter-church contact.

The need for reconciliation lay at the core of all inter-church contact in Northern Ireland throughout this period, and it was this idea which provided the key inspiration for the change in definition of inter-church relationships, as it became the link between ecumenism and community relations. As one anonymous interviewee commented:

> What they are trying to do now is separate peacemaking[2] from ecumenism, because a lot of people who would be involved in peacemaking might not necessarily be ecumenical and might not be even church-goers or whatever ... So it is ... trying to draw the line between that [and] not separate them because they are inter-linked, but not necessarily so that they feel that to be into peacemaking you have to be into ecumenism. To have peace you have to have reconciliation, and reconciliation would be the link between them [peacemaking and ecumenism] but there are a lot of things that have to be reconciled to make peace but one of the things... that would apparently seem to be at the root of this is the church thing- its got all embroiled with it.[3]

As a result of such observations, which were commonplace at each level of inter-church contact, those involved argued that reconciliation between the churches, as well as between the Protestant and Catholic communities, was needed in order to bring some form of solution to the problems in Northern Ireland and that as Christians they were compelled to work towards this by the teachings of the Gospel.[4] Thus, Christian reconciliation has been defined as a move from animosity and hatred to a relationship underlined by forgiveness and understanding, and, from the evidence of inter-church relationships presented, it is apparent that those involved in such contact were trying to work towards reconciliation from such a blueprint. This led to inter-church work progressing into community relations as it was in this sphere that reconciliation was most necessary, due to the prevalence of the sectarianism that the churches had played a part in perpetuating. This was especially true of local level inter-church relationships and, as their work progressed within local communities, it became apparent that the need for reconciliation between Protestants and Catholics at a communal level was far more pressing than the need for agreement on forms of church worship and other ecumenical matters. It soon became evident that a community relations based approach to inter-church contact would be more successful with those who would otherwise have been resistant to such work, as it removed issues such as joint worship which many Protestants strongly objected to. This led to the establishment of a reactive approach to inter-church work within the community, with schemes only being established when those involved felt that the local community would accept them. Practical schemes, such as unemployment advice centres, became the forerunners to discussions relating to communal identity which, as we have seen, only became a widely used means of reconciliation after the 1994 ceasefires and the advent of the peace and reconciliation education initiative. At a national level, this commitment to communal reconciliation led to a change in the nature of topics under discussion, as the leadership of the Protestant and Catholic Churches tried to reach an understanding with each other on matters, such as sectarianism and the role of young people in the church, which they hoped would promote more positive relationships between the two communities. Thus, the reconciliation attempted by inter-church groups at all levels was holistic, based not only upon small groups but also upon a recognition of a need for a wider societal reconciliation, which those involved hope to contribute to through their inter-church endeavours.

Closely linked to the idea of Christian reconciliation was the issue of identity. It is clear that the concept of inter-church contact was based upon the creation of an understanding of identity, be it communal or theological, between Protestants and Catholics. This was crucial to the achievement of reconciliation and, therefore, to the success of inter-church relationships themselves. At every level of inter-church contact this need for recognition and understanding of the other's identity was based upon the Gospel and the shared goal of Christian reconciliation. This creation of understanding was based upon a de-demonisation of the 'other side' through the use of various methods, which developed not only with the political culture of Northern Ireland, but also with events local to the groups that were engaging in such work.

Once more, the differences between the methods employed by the local and national levels to achieve this understanding were vast. At the national level between the leaderships of the churches' contact was based upon a need to enable the stabilisation of the identity of each group through an articulation of the key tenets of faith and communal identity. This was combined with some attempt to breach the gaps between the churches on crucial matters, which would, in effect, represent a recognition, not only of the need for contact, but also of the validity of some of the theological differences between the Catholic and Protestant Churches. At a local level, however, the process of inter-church contact was one of normalisation, which used whatever means were available and acceptable to the local community to promote the idea that contact with the other side was tolerable and beneficial to the local area, both physically and communally. Such ideas eventually manifested themselves in the foundation of some of the larger peace and reconciliation education initiatives, such as Mediation Northern Ireland and Youth Link, who developed and ran courses aimed at promoting such an understanding of identity. Thus, the growth of this recognition of the need for identification and empathy aided the change in function of inter-church relationships throughout this period, as it became clear to the churches that, as one of the key components of identity creation in the province, their work for reconciliation needed to concentrate upon the issue of identity and, more crucially, the lack of understanding between the two groups especially at a local level.

This commitment to the need for Christian reconciliation and understanding of the other community's identity was strengthened by the development of friendships between those involved, and these provided one of the main lynchpins of inter-church contact in this period. From the emergence of relationships between the Protestant and Catholic Churches in Northern Ireland, friendships were paramount, being as important to the development of national-level ecumenical dialogue as they were to small clergy-led prayer groups, as without the trust inherent in such relationships discussion on sensitive issues, such as sectarianism, could not occur. This wish to build friendships between Protestants and Catholics became one of the main objectives of inter-church contact, as it was surmised that it would prove the founding-stone for better community relations and the development of Christian reconciliation. Consequently, just as understandings of the process of Christian reconciliation changed, so did the participants' understanding of how such friendships were developed, leading to a more community-relations based approach to inter-church contact. This was founded upon the lowest-common-denominator approach, which enabled those involved to work towards reconciliation in a manner that did not directly impinge upon their religious beliefs concerning, for example, joint worship or theological matters.

These changes in definition and understanding took place against a backdrop of constant political change, which itself was to have ramifications for the practice of inter-church relations, especially within local areas. By far the most important of these were the paramilitary ceasefires of 1994 and the Peace Process, which led to the Good Friday Agreement in 1998. Thus, as a result of the atmosphere in the province from 1994 onwards, inter-church relationships blossomed, with contact taking place in a more structured and open manner. The growth in contact took place for two reasons: first, people were no longer afraid to be seen engaging in contact with the other community, and thus began to take advantage of the opportunities being offered to them. Second, as the issue of reconciliation became an important component in the peace talks, many people felt compelled to engage in some work towards reconciliation themselves.

The concept of inter-church relationships in Northern Ireland, then, has radically altered since 1980, with its definition, function and motivation changing as the participants' understanding of the issues and problems involved deepened. It moved from being a concept related to ecumenical prayer and dialogue to a holistic vision of inter-church practice, encompassing the ideas of community relations, ecumenism and reconciliation, which were balanced according to the needs of those involved. But how successful were each of the three levels in their practical implementation of this new vision of inter-church contact and how should such success be measured? The standards for measuring the success of the programmes carried out at a national and local level and those of the peace and reconciliation education initiatives were vastly different due to the expectations of such work, and the examples and models available to practitioners. Despite its complete lack of formal aims, the expectations for national-level dialogue were much higher than those for the other two levels, due to the higher standards set for those involved. Such standards were created for them by trends in world-wide theology and the actions of other inter-church groups in areas such as South Africa. Thus, it would be expected that in working together the churches in Northern Ireland, mindful of their contribution to the identities of the two communities there, would become a force for leadership, providing the prophetic voice necessary to encourage reconciliation and better community relationships, not only highlighting the normality of contact between the Protestant and Catholic communities but also supplying a theological blueprint for such interaction. The standards for local-level and peace and reconciliation education initiatives were slightly lower as, whilst their aims of Christian reconciliation and the promotion of better community relations were the same as their national-level counterparts, they were not, and indeed did not set out to be, examples of leadership except within the confines of their immediate area (a role which they only assumed when it was offered to them by the local community). Those involved in working within local communities were operating on a day-to-day basis, reacting to events both locally and nationally and changing their methods accordingly, which eventually resulted in the development of different forms of community relations work and a fledgling theology of reconciliation for Northern Ireland.

It could be expected, that this change in definition and function from the practice of inter-church ecumenism into church-based community relations would have had the greatest effect upon the hierarchies of the Protestant and Catholic Churches and, therefore, radically altered the practice of national-level ecumenical dialogue. However, this has not been the case, as the years since 1980 have been ones of consistent disappointment as the churches at a national level have failed to rise to the challenge offered to them by international examples of inter-church practice, the situation in Northern Ireland and the development of inter-church relations at a local level. Despite this, there is some evidence of attempts by those involved in national-level ecumenical dialogue, under the auspices of the IICM, to move towards a more community relations-based approach to their work, as they did commission numerous reports on matters of common concern, which were related to the need for better community relations in the province, as well as redesigning their structures to emphasise the distinction between formal ecumenism and practical community relations. However, commissioning reports on community relations issues was the limit of the IICM's work, as the recommendations were never built upon and no attempt was made to fuse the work of the two departments to develop an understanding of the need for Christian reconciliation in Northern Ireland. Furthermore, in their failure to address the issue of reconciliation from a theological point of view, the IICM was demonstrating its paralysis, caused by the more conservative elements within Protestantism and the hierarchical authority structures of a number of the churches involved, which prevented them from moving away from the exercises in comparative theology that had characterised Protestant and Catholic engagement at a national level in the 1970s. It is evident from the results of the IICM's work that they did not fully enter into the development of the new form of inter-church relationships, seeing ecumenism and community relations as two clear-cut issues, which whilst of relevance to the work of the meeting, were rarely allowed to combine. Thus, the record of national-level ecumenical dialogue since 1980 has been one of mediocrity, with its value lying in the symbolic gesture that it provides for the people of Northern Ireland, rather than any tangible movement towards reconciliation between the Protestant and Catholic Churches. Furthermore, instead of providing a positive example that each community's identity could be enriched by contact with the other, it merely serves to reinforce the image of such gestures as futile talking shops.

In direct contrast to this, inter-church activity at a local level, and through the medium of the peace and reconciliation education initiatives, was more successful in its promotion of Christian reconciliation and creation of an understanding of the 'other side's' communal identity between Protestants and Catholics. Thus, it was at a local level that the redefinition of inter-church relationships took place as those interested in such work were not constrained by the authority and attitudes of their church's hierarchy and instead, were able to develop schemes which blurred the lines between community relations, reconciliation and ecumenism in a way which allowed for wider participation in inter-church schemes than a rigid adherence to prayer and dialogue on religious issues would have allowed. Consequently, numerous schemes were developed from 1980s onwards, which continually pushed the boundaries of inter-church relationships by presenting new ways in which Christians could bear witness together to the imperative of reconciliation presented to them in the Gospel, without facing the compromises to their faith that ecumenical discussion caused. Schemes were established as a response to the needs of the area in which these inter-church groups were operating, with Social Action Projects running after-school play groups and community relations courses being provided by ecumenical communities for example, all of which centred upon the ethos of Christian reconciliation and identity recognition, which provided the foundation for all inter-church work in Northern Ireland. Thus, instead of the parallel lines witnessed at the national-level meetings, local-level inter-church relations became the concurrent circles of ecumenism, community relations and Christian reconciliation, which enabled participants to take as much or as little of each as their attitudes to the elements involved allowed.

By the 1990s these changes, when combined with the Peace Process, brought about the development of the peace and reconciliation education initiative which represented the formalisation of this new brand of inter-church relations, providing training on matters related to community relations and reconciliation whist retaining the Christian ethos and spirit so central to the practice of these relationships. This, in turn, brought with it changes to the practice of local-level inter-church relationships as they provided the equipment and support for those involved to tackle issues, such as sectarianism and politics, in the broader arena of their local communities, rather than just in the immediate sphere of the inter-church group itself, through the use of models designed with the help of local practitioners themselves.

Each of these three levels of contact view themselves as completely separate movements, with those involved in national-level dialogue believing themselves to have more restraints placed upon them than their local-level counterparts. It is generally held by participants that 'the national level scene has some symbolic importance but it doesn't make any significant impact at local level. Local Councils of Clergy, etc., are in many places quite strong groupings and it is a pity that that strength cannot be reflected in a national body.'[5] It is evident that the period since 1980 has witnessed a complete turnaround in the status of national – and local-level dialogue and their attitudes to one another, as the local-level churches no longer view themselves as a direct challenge to the failure of the national-level structures, being motivated instead by local events and needs, whilst the national- level churches now look to local groups for inspiration. Thus, the 1984 structural reorganisation provided evidence of the IICM's attempts to follow the trend within community-based groups to work towards an improvement in community relations. Hence, the change in definition that has occurred in inter-church relationships has not been the same at each level, and has been caused mainly by groups in local areas, with national-level dialogue presenting a weak replication of their work, and the peace and reconciliation education initiatives being generally founded as a result of a need expressed by those working within local communities.

Since 1980 the churches, as groups of people rather than institutions in Northern Ireland, have been attempting to embrace their place in civil society in a cross-community rather than mono-communal way, and in doing so have redefined the concept of inter-church relationships in a way that is uniquely Northern Irish. Whilst this study mapped the development and form of these relationships, it was unable to quantify the full impact that inter-church relationships have had in Northern Ireland, thus it is unknown how many people have attended the activities offered by local level groups or whether their experiences have had any impact upon their attitudes to cross-community contact, as the groups studied did not have the means at their disposal to monitor the impact of their work fully. Furthermore, whilst the impact of the anti-ecumenical movement on national-level ecumenical dialogue is evident, very little is known concerning their impact upon local-level activity, as inter-church workers there were unwilling to discuss the issue. Such gaps in knowledge have prompted a number of further research questions in the fields of theology, social policy and history. First, despite the failure of the national level churches to work towards the creation of a reconciliation or political theology for Northern Ireland, a form of grassroots theology is starting to emerge, the nature of which is entirely dependent upon the life experiences of those living in the different areas in which it is developing. There is a need for this newly emergent theology to be recorded, as it would go some way towards rectifying the need for a serious theological consideration of the situation in Northern Ireland. Second, as most of the inter-church groups working in local areas have been unable to measure the impact of their work, a quantitative audit looking at the role of these groups within local communities and the dissemination of their work, when combined with a comprehensive mapping exercise of post-1994 local-level inter-church work, would prove invaluable to future researchers. Finally, the impact of peace and reconciliation education initiatives upon the practice of inter-church relationships has yet to be realised, and a discussion of their methods and development of models of church-based cross-community relationship building would contribute greatly to a fuller understanding of inter-church relationships in the post-Good Friday Agreement era.

Although their methods and outcomes have been vastly different, each of the three levels of inter-church contact has, with varied success, been working towards the same goals of promoting Christian reconciliation and the normalisation of contact between the Protestant and Catholic communities. In 1980 such contact was almost non-existent, but by 2005 numerous groups existed under a number of guises throughout Northern Ireland, the full impact of which have yet to be quantified. In the light of increased secularisation and the current post-conflict situation such work needs to be developed further by every form of inter-church group as in order to remain relevant:

> Churches have a choice. They can choose to play a role in the public and ongoing healing process in Northern Ireland or they can choose to be consigned to oblivion through denial, through privatisation, or through scapegoating. If they are to play a role then it is crucial that they lead the process of 'necessary judgement', starting with themselves. This will require not only courage and honesty, but also a process of sustained reflection around a number of issues ...[6]

And the most crucial reflection will be of their role in the creation of identity and a continued promotion of the concept of the normality of contact between the Protestant and Catholic communities.

# References

PRIMARY SOURCES

*Annual reports*

Churches Voluntary Work Bureau and Churches in Co-operation, *Annual Report*, 1997–98.

Churches Voluntary Work Bureau and Churches in Co-operation, *Annual Report*, 1998–99.

Community Relations Council, *Annual Report*, 1998–99.

Forthspring Inter-Community Group Ltd., *Annual Report 2001, The Community Together.*

Forthspring, *Annual Reports*, 2002–04.

Irish Council of Churches, *Annual Reports*, 1980–2005.

Irish School of Ecumenics, *Annual Reports*, 1999–2004.

General Assembly of the Presbyterian Church in Ireland, *Report of the General Assembly of the Presbyterian Church*, Belfast and Dublin, 1980–2005.

General Synod of the Church of Ireland, *Annual Reports of the General Synod Committee for Christian Unity*, Dublin, 1980–2005.

PAKT (Lurgan), *6th Anniversary Report*, December 1999.

PAKT, *10th Anniversary Report*, (2003)


*Author's interviews*

*Rev. Doug Baker*, Mediation Network, Belfast, 4 October 2000.

*Rev. Glen Barclay*, Leader of the Columbanus Community of Reconciliation, Antrim Road, North Belfast, 15 February 2002.

*Group Interview with Members of the Belmont and District Council of Churches*, Belfast, 10 November 2005.

*Mr Alex Bradley*, Columba Community, Derry, 17 January 2000.

*Rev. John Braithwaite*, Presbyterian Minister, Dunmurray, 21 October 1999.

*Rev. Jim Campbell*, Presbyterian and member of the Ballynafeigh Clergy Fellowship, Belfast, 6 October 2000.

*Rev. David Chillingworth*, Church of Ireland 'Think Again' Project, 1 February 2000.

*Sr. Noreen Christian*, Leader of the Currach Community, Belfast, 21 October 1999.

*Sr. Noreen Christian*, Leader of the Currach Community, West Belfast, 13 February 2002.

*Mr Philip Clarke*, Community Relations Officer, Dungannon, Co. Tyrone, 28 June 2005.

*Dr Cecelia Clegg*, Irish School of Ecumenics, Dublin, 13 June 2004.

*Mr Liam Cluskey*, Lamb of God Community, Belfast, 9 November 2005.

*Community Relations Officer (anonymous)*, Northern Ireland, June 2005.

*Mr Roy Crowe and Mr Martin Murray*, Journey in Understanding, Carrickfergus, Co. Antrim, 8 November 2005.

*Rev. Dr Eric Culberton*, Church of Ireland, Dungannon, 4 October 2000.

*Cardinal Cahal Daly*, Belfast, 3 February 2000.

*Cardinal Cahal Daly*, Belfast, 22 June 2005.

*Group Interview with Members of the Columba Community*, Derry, 17 June 2005.

*Interview with a Member of the Columba Community*, Derry, 14 February 2002.

*Group Interview with Members of the Cookstown Christian Churches Forum*, Cookstown, Co. Tyrone, 10 November 2005.

*Mrs Bridie Cotter*, Cornerstone Community Worker, Cornerstone Community, Belfast, 9 November 2005.

*Rev. Tony Davidson*, Convenor of the Presbyterian Church's Inter-Church Relations Board, Armagh, 13 January 2000.

*Rev. Dr John Douglas*, Free Presbyterian Church, Gilford, 11 October 2000.

*Anne Doyle and Margaret Huston*, PAKT, Lurgan, 8 November 2005.

*Rev. Dr John Dunlop*, Presbyterian Minister, Belfast, 14 January 2000.

*Rev. Dr John Dunlop*, Retired Presbyterian Minister, Whiteabbey, 15 June 2005.

*Rev. Michael Earle and Mr Rob Fairmichael*, Irish Council of Churches, Belfast, 11 November 2005.

*Rev. Dr Ian Ellis*, Church of Ireland's Church Unity Committee, Newcastle, Co. Down, 12 January 2000.

*Rev. Dr Ian Ellis*, Newcastle, Co. Down, 23 June 2005.

*Bishop Anthony Farquhar*, Auxiliary Bishop of Down and Connor, Belfast, 26 January 2000.

*Bishop Anthony Farquhar*, Auxiliary Bishop of Down and Connor, Belfast, 20 June 2005.

*Maire Foley and Graeme Thomson*, Ploughshare, Bangor, Co. Down, 9 November 2005.

*Mrs Therese Gallagher*, Lamb of God Community, Belfast, 14 October 2005.

*Mr George Glenn*, CEO of Churches in Cooperation and the Churches Voluntary Work Bureau, Derry, 25 January 2000.

*Rev. Ken Good*, Church of Ireland, Lurgan, Co. Armagh and founding member of PAKT, Lurgan, Thursday, 5 October 2000.

*Rev. Gordon Graham*, Church of Ireland, Newcastle, Co. Down, 16 October 2000.

*Mr Tom Hannon*, Leader of the Cornerstone Community, Belfast, 28 January 2000.

*Mr Tom Hannon*, Former Leader of the Cornerstone Community, Belfast, 15 February 2002.

*Rev. Robert Herron*, Convenor of the Inter-Church Relations Board, Presbyterian Church, Omagh, 24 January 2000.

*Rev. Robert Herron*, Omagh, 7 November 2005.

*Mrs Isobel Holmes*, Dungannon Area Churches Forum, Dungannon, 7 November 2005.

*Fr. Michael Hurley SJ*, Dublin, 12 June 2004.

*Mr Glenn Jordan*, Research Consultant, ECONI, Belfast, 17 May 2001.

*Rev. Tim Kinahan*, Church of Ireland, Belfast, 14 January 2000.

*Rev. Tim Kinahan*, Church of Ireland, Belfast, 11 November 2005.

*Group Interview with Members of the Lamb of God Community*, North Belfast, 12 February 2002.

*Rev. Charlie Leeke*, Reconciliation Officer of 'Think Again' Project, Church of Ireland, Down and Dromore Diocese, Belfast, 12 February 2002.

*Fr. Brian Lennon SJ*, Community Dialogue, Belfast, 26 January 2000.

*Fr. Brian Lennon SJ*, Community Dialogue, Armagh, 7 November 2005.

*Mr Stephen Lynas*, Presbyterian Church's Information Officer, Belfast, 27 January 2000.

*Mrs Michaela Mackin*, Community Relations Council, Belfast, 10 October 2000.

*Mr Derek Matthews*, Community Relations Council, Belfast, 10 October 2000.

*Rev. Norman McAuley*, Presbyterian, Magherafelt, 6 October 2000.

*Rev. David McCarthy*, Evangelical Alliance, Belfast, 9 October 2000.

*Rev. Dr Johnston McMaster*, Irish School of Ecumenics, Belfast, 27 January 2000.

*Rev. Dr Johnston McMaster*, Irish School of Ecumenics, Belfast, 14 February 2002.

*Bishop James Mehaffey*, Bishop of Derry and Raphoe, Derry, 17 January 2000.

*Bishop Harold Miller*, Bishop of Down and Dromore, Belfast, 11 January 2000.

*Bishop Harold Miller*, Church of Ireland Bishop of Down and Dromore, Belfast, 12 February 2002.

*Fr. Padraig Murphy*, Director of Ecumenism, Archdiocese of Armagh, Armagh, 4 February 2000.

*Rev. Ivan Neish*, Presbyterian, Newtownabbey, 10 October 2000.

*Mr Kerry Nicholson*, Project Worker, Lisburn Inter-Church Project, Belfast, 12 February 2002.

*Rev. Ruth Patterson*, Restoration Ministries, Dunmurray, Belfast, 21 October 1999.

*Rev. Ruth Patterson*, Restoration Ministries, Dunmurray, Belfast, 27 June 2005.

*A project worker for an inter-church group,* February 2002.

*Rev. Jim Rea*, Methodist Church, Portadown, 3 October 2000.

*Mrs Phyllis Skillen*, Belmont and District Council of Churches, Belfast, 17 October 2000.

*Dr Geraldine Smyth*, Director of the ISE, February 1995–April 1999, Dublin, 7 March 2001.

*Dr David Stevens*, Irish Council of Churches, Belfast, 18 January 2000.

*Dr David Stevens*, Irish Council of Churches, Belfast, 13 February 2002.

*Dr David Stevens*, Corrymeela Community, Belfast, 13 June 2005.

*Mr Alwyn Thompson*, Research Officer, ECONI, Belfast, 16 May 2001.

*Msg. Tom Toner*, Belfast, 1 February 2000.

*Rev. Trevor Williams*, Corrymeela Community, Belfast, 11 January 2000.

*Rev. Campbell Wilson*, Presbyterian, Portadown, 3 October 2000.

*Rev. Dr Harry Uprichard*, Presbyterian, Ballymena, 9 October 2000.

### Church documents

*Catechism of the Catholic Church* (London: Geoffrey Chapman, 1994).

*Decree on Ecumenism: Unitatis Redintegratio*, Solemnly Promulgated by His Holiness, Pope Paul VI on November 21, 1964, N.C.W.C

Translation (Boston: Pauline Books and Media, 1964).

The Irish Episcopal Conference, *Directory on Ecumenism in Ireland* (1976).


## Community relations council reports and directories

*Beyond Sectarianism? The Churches and Ten Years of the Peace Process* (Belfast: Community Relations Council, 2005).

Churches Advisory Group, *A Directory of Cross-Community Church Groups and Projects in Northern Ireland 1999* (Belfast: Community Relations Council, 1999).

McMaster, J., *Churches Working Together – a Practical Guide for Northern Ireland* (Belfast: Community Relations Council, March 1994).

McMaster, J. and Higgins, C., *Churches Working Together – A Practical Resource* (Belfast: Churches Advisory Group, Community Relations Council, February 2001).

McMaster, J., *An Inter-Church Directory for Northern Ireland* (Belfast: Community Relations Council, 1994).

Morrow, D., 'It's Not Everyone You Could Tell That To' A Report on the Churches and Inter-Community Relations to the Armagh Church Forum (Belfast: Community Relations Council, 1997).

O'Neill, J., *My Faith, Our Faith Inter-Faith in Practice – An Overview. An examination of Various Religious-Based Initiatives and Religious Faiths within Derry/Londonderry* (Derry: Yes! Publications, Derry City Council, 1999).

Williamson, D., Brown, D. and Irvine, G., *Dreams Judged on Delivery: A Report on the Work of Church Based Groups Supported by the Community Relations Council* (Belfast: Community Relations Council, n.d.).


## Conference proceedings, papers and speeches

Community Relations Council, *Community Relations and the Churches, Conference Report*, Newtownabbey, 20 May 1998.

Community Relations Council, *Community Relations and the Churches, Conference Report*, Omagh, 27 May 1998.

Daly, C., *Ministering the Peace of Christ in a Divided Community*, Address in the Abbey Presbyterian Church, Dublin, 8 June 1983.

McMaster, J., 'Reconciliation: The Irish Experience', *Church and Peace Conference*, Amerdoun, June 2000.

## Letters to author

*Rev. David Chillingworth*, 7 March 2002.

*Fr. Michael Collins*, 10 December 1999.

*Geraldine Connolly*, Administrative Officer of the Cornerstone Community, 10 December 2001.

*Cardinal Cahal Daly*, 12 March 2002.

*Rev. John Dunlop*, 8 March 2002.

*Mrs Joan Hannon*, Member of the Women in Faith Group, Downpatrick, 9 December 2000.

*Robert Herron*, 12 March 2002.

*Bernie Laverty*, Programme Co-ordinator of Forthspring, 15 August 2002.

*Rev. Gary Mason*, Founder of Forthspring, 8 August 2002.

*Tommy McCay*, Columba Community, 10 February 2002.

*Rev. Stephen Nelly to the Presbytery of Dromore*, no date but part of a letter sent to author, 12 October 2000.

*Rev. David Nesbitt*, 19 March 2002.

*Rev. John E. C. Rutter*, January 2000.

*Harry Smith*, Leader of the Christian Renewal Centre, 13 November 2001.

*David Stevens*, 15 March 2002.


## Miscellaneous information leaflets

Baker, D., *Learning Together in Northern Ireland: The Seed Groups of the Corrymeela Community*, The Corrymeela Papers (Belfast: Corrymeela, 1984).

Campaign for Complete Withdrawal, *The World Council of Churches and Reformed Doctrine*, Pamphlet no. 1, *c.* 1979.

Columba Community, *Columba House* (Information Leaflet, n.d.).

Columba Community, *Good Friday Repentance Service* (1985).

Columbanus Community of Reconciliation, *An Introduction* (Information Leaflet, n.d. but *c.* 1994).

Columbanus Community of Reconciliation, *Draft Copy of an Introductory Leaflet* (n.d.).

Columbanus Community of Reconciliation, *We Plough the Fields and Scatter* (n.d.).

Cookstown and District Inter-Church Forum, *Constitution* (May 2004).

Cornerstone Community, *Information Leaflet* (n.d.).

Iona Community, *Information Leaflet* (n.d.).

Irish School of Ecumenics, *Learning Together: Education for Reconciliation* (Information Leaflet, 2000).

Irish School of Ecumenics, *Postgraduate Programmes* (2005).

Irish School of Ecumenics, *The Achievements You Are Promoting Through the Irish School of Ecumenics* (n.d.).

Kerr, C., *Reconciliation Breaking Down Divided Walls* (Christian Renewal Centre Leaflet, n.d.).

Lamb of God Community, *Shalom House* (Information Leaflet, n.d.).

Morrow, J., *Aims and Objectives of the Corrymeela Community* (Corrymeela Leaflet, n.d.).

Morrow, J., *The Corrymeela Community* (Corrymeela Leaflet, n.d.).

Ploughshare, *Ploughshare's Aims* (2003/4).

Young, C.M., *Draft History of the Belmont and District Council of Churches* (unpublished, 2002).


### Newspapers and magazines

*Belfast Telegraph*
*Church of Ireland Gazette*
*Cornerstone Contact*
*Corrymeela Connections*
*CRC News*
*Derry and Raphoe Vision*
*Evangelical View*
*Fortnight*
*Irish News*
*Irish Press*
*Irish Times*
*Link:Up*
*Lisburn Inter-Church Project Newsletter*
*Presbyterian Herald*
*Presbyterian News USA*
*The Reformer: Magazine of the Movement for Presbyterian Reform*


### Nelson Papers, Library of the Irish School of Ecumenics, Dublin

*The Inter-Church Meeting Organisation and Structure*, Form approved at Meeting of Inter-Church Committee, 5 December 1984.

*The Inter-Church Meeting, Ballymascanlon*, Version of the Inter-Church Meeting Organisation and Structure presented to the Inter-Church Relations Board of the Presbyterian Church in February 1985 and subsequently reproduced in the *Report of the General Assembly of the Presbyterian Church* 1985, p. 115.

O'Hanlon, G. *The Agenda of the Department*, 25 November 1992.


*Pamphlets (all Belfast unless otherwise stated)*

Baker, D., *A Biblical Basis for Cross-Community Work* (Youth Link, 1994).

Carlin, N., *Freedom to the Captives* (1983).

Forthspring, *The Hurt the Peace the Love and the War Living in West Belfast* (2004).

Inter-Church Group on Faith and Politics, *Breaking Down the Enmity Faith and Politics in the Northern Ireland Conflict* (1993).

Inter-Church Group on Faith and Politics, *Breaking Down the Enmity* (1985).

Inter-Church Group on Faith and Politics, *Burying Our Dead: Political Funerals in Northern Ireland* (1992).

Inter-Church Group on Faith and Politics, *Doing unto Others Parity of Esteem in a Contested Space* (1997).

Inter-Church Group on Faith and Politics, *Forgive Us Our Trespasses ... ? Reconciliation and Political Healing in Northern Ireland* (1996).

Inter-Church Group on Faith and Politics, *Liberty to the Captives? The Early Release of Politically Motivated Prisoners* (1995).

Inter-Church Group on Faith and Politics, *New Pathways: Developing a Peace Process in Northern Ireland* (1997).

Inter-Church Group on Faith and Politics, *Remembering our Past: 1690 and 1916* (1991).

Inter-Church Group on Faith and Politics, *The Things that Make for Peace* (1995).

Inter-Church Group on Faith and Politics, *Towards an Island that Works: Facing Divisions in Ireland* (1987).

Inter-Church Group on Faith and Politics, *Towards Peace and Stability: A Critical Assessment of the Anglo Irish Agreement* (1988).

Inter-Church Group on Faith and Politics, *Self Righteous Collective Superiority as a Cause of Conflict* (1999).

Inter-Church Group on Faith and Politics, *Understanding the Signs of the Times* (1986).

McMaster, J., *Building Confidence: A Single Identity Programme for Church Based Groups* (Youth Link, n.d.).

McMaster, J., *Cross Community Goals and Personal Development* (Youth Link, 1993).

McMaster, J., *The Churches and Cross Community Work with Young People* (Youth Link, 1993).

McMaster, J., *Historical Perspectives on a Divided Community* (Youth Link, 1994).

McMaster, J., *Living Through the Troubles* (Youth Link, 1994).

McMaster, J., *Young People as the Guardians of Sectarian Tradition: The Challenge to the Churches* (Youth Link, 1993).

White, P. K., *The Needs of Young People in Northern Ireland* (1993).


### Publications of the Irish Council of Churches and the Irish Inter-Church Meeting

*Being Church in the New Millennium, A Discussion Document* (Dublin: Veritas, Department of Theological Questions, Irish Inter-Church Meeting, 2000).

*Ecumenical Relations in Ireland* (Belfast: ICC pamphlet, June 1999).

*Ecumenical Principles* (Dublin: Veritas, Department of Theological Questions, IICM, 1993).

*Freedom, Justice and Responsibility in Ireland Today* (Dublin: Veritas, Department of Theological Questions, IICM, 1997).

*Salvation and Grace* (Dublin: Veritas, Department of Theological Questions, IICM, 1993).

*Sectarianism, a Discussion Document: The Report of the Working Party on Sectarianism* (Belfast: Department of Social Issues of the IICM, 1993).

*The Challenge of the City*, A Report to the Churches (Belfast: Department of Social Issues, IICM, 1990).

*The Dearest Freshness Deep Down Things, Papers from the Working Party on Spirituality* (Belfast: Irish Inter-Church Meeting, 2005).

*Report of the Working Party on Young People and the Church*, A Report to the Irish Inter-Church Meeting and its Department of Social Issues (Belfast: IICM, 1990).

*Violence in Ireland: A Report to the Churches* (Belfast: 1976).

Gallagher, E., 'Northern Ireland' in *Ecumenism in Ireland Experiments and Achievements, Survey Papers Commissioned for the Inter-Church meeting at Ballymascanlon, Co. Louth, on 6 March 1980* (Dublin: A Joint Publication of the Irish Catholic Bishops' Conference and the Irish Council of Churches, November 1981).

Hurley SJ, M. and Ellis, I., *The Irish Inter-Church Meeting: Background and Development* (Belfast: IICM, 1998).

Ledwith, M., 'Ecumenism in the Republic of Ireland', in *Ecumenism in*

*Ireland Experiments and Achievements, Survey Papers Commissioned for the Inter-Church meeting at Ballymascanlon, Co. Louth, on 6 March 1980* (Dublin: A Joint Publication of the Irish Catholic Bishops' Conference and the Irish Council of Churches, November 1981).


### Questionnaires

*Questionnaire on the Experiences of Ecumenical Communities: The Lamb of God Community*, Belfast, 11 September 2001.


### Strategy documents, evaluations, reports and reviews

Carey, M. and Roulston, C., *The Cornerstone Community, A Report for the Annual Review* (University of Ulster, September 1996).
Colraine Borough Council of Churches Forum, *Draft Summary of Origins, Aims and Progress of Colraine Borough Council of Churches Forum* (n.d.).
Cornerstone Community, *Strategic Plan* (October 2001).
Forthspring, *Application for Grant Aid* (n.d.).
Fowler, C., *The Corrymeela Community and its Programme Work: Part one, a description* (July 1995).
Irish School of Ecumenics, *A Report on Graduates* (April 1999).
Lisburn Inter-Church Project, *Strategy 2002–2005.*
Macaulay, T., *Action Research Project: Inter-Church and Church Community Relations in Newtownards* (April 2003).
McMaster, J., *Report on the Work and Development of the Belmont and District Council of Churches* (January 1996).
Rourke, S., *PAKT Lurgan Strategic Review of Activities and Operations, Summary of Conclusions and Recommendations* (May 2000).
Stevens, D., *The Corrymeela Community: Way Forward* (1992).
Tipping, B., *Parents and Kids Together, Lurgan, Final Evaluation Report,* (March 1999).


### Websites

Belmont and District Council of Churches, *Response to the Shared Future Consultation*, http://www.asharedfutureni.gov.uk/pdf_documents/belmont.pdf, accessed 27 December 2005.
Central Community Relations Unit, *Project Directory entry for Forthspring*, http://www.ccruni.gov.uk/research/directory/srmcccc.

htm, accessed 8 August 2002.

Christian Renewal Centre, *Prayer for Ireland*, http://www.crc-rostrevor.org/pr_4_irl.htm, accessed 21 June 2002.

Christian Renewal Centre, *Our Vision*, www.crc-rostrevor.org, accessed 12 January 2006.

Columba Community, *White Oaks Centre for the Treatment of Individuals Addicted to Drugs or Alcohol*, http://www.columbacommunity.homestead.com/files/wobrochurenew.htm, accessed 8 February 2006.

Community Relations Council, http://www.community-relations.org.uk, accessed 29 September 2002.

Conflict Archive on the Internet, *1991 Census: The Religion Report*, http://cain.ulst.ac.uk/ni/religion.htm, accessed 4 April 2002.

The Corrymeela Community, *The Corrymeela Community – Who we are*, http://www.corrymeela.org/Who_we_are/who_we_are.html, accessed 17 June 2002. Forthspring, *Vision-mission-aims*, http://www.home.btconnect.com/Forthspring/home.htm, accessed 4 January 2006.

Irish Council of Churches, *A Shared Future: A Consultation Paper on Improving Community Relations in Northern Ireland*, http://www.asharedfutureni.gov.uk/pdf_documents/irishcouncil.pdf, accessed 29 November 2005.

Irish School of Ecumenics, *Ecumenical Studies Programme: MPhil Degree and Diploma Programme*, http://www.tcd.ie/ise/degree_diploma/esp/index.html, accessed 10 September 2002.

Irish School of Ecumenics, *Reconciliation Studies Programme: MPhil Degree and Diploma Programme*, http://www.tcd.ie/ise/degree_diploma/rs/index.html, accessed 10 September 2002.

McEwen, S., *Protestants on the peace line*, http://www.corrymeela.org/Articles/protestants_on_the_peace_line.html, accessed 12 January 2006.

Mediation Network, *Annual Report*, 1997/1998, http://www.mediation-network.org.uk/html/programme_of_the_m_n_.html, accessed 5 April 2000.

Mediation Network, *Home Page*, http://www.mediation-network.org.uk/ accessed 5 April 2000.

Mediation Network, *Services*, http://www.mediation-network.org.uk/html/services.html, accessed 24 September 2002.

Mediation Network, *Training for Conflict Transformation*, http://www.mediation-network.org.uk/html/training.html, accessed 24 September 2002.

Northern Ireland Census 2001 Key Statistics, http://www.nisra.gov.uk/census/pdf/Key%20Statistics%20ReportTables.pdf, accessed 26 July 2005.

PAKT, *Strategic Aims*, http://www.paktlurgan.com/strat.html, accessed 4 January 2006.

Presbyterian News Service, http://www.pcusa.org/pcnews/old-news/1999/99300.htm, accessed 9 May 2002.

Ploughshare, *A Shared Future – Responses*, http://www.asharedfutureni.gov.uk/pdf_documents/ploughshare.pdf, accessed 30 November 2005.

SEUPB, *Programmes*, http://www.seupb.org/prog.htm, accessed 29 December 2005.

Youth Link, *Cathog*, http://www.youthlink.org.uk/cathog.htm, accessed 27th September 2002.

Youth Link, *Further Steps ... Exploring difference and diversity*, http://www.youthlink.org.uk/kairos.htm, accessed 27 September 2002.

Youth Link, *Kairos Menu*, http://www.youthlink.org.uk/index.cfm?id =35, accessed 4 April 2006.

Youth Link, *New Opportunities for Young People and Youth Workers*, http://www.youthlink.org.uk/ylni_courses.htm, accessed 27 September 2002.

Youth Link, *Vision*, http://www.youthlink.org.uk/index.cfm?id=4, accessed 4 April 2006.

Youth Link, *Which type of Course is for you?* http://www.youthlink.org.uk/which_course.htm, accessed 27 September 2002.

## SECONDARY SOURCES

### Books

Barkley, J. M., *Blackmouth and Dissenter* (Belfast: The White Row Press, 1991).

Bew, P. and Gilespie, G., *Northern Ireland: A Chronology of the Troubles 1968–1999* (Dublin: Gill and Macmillan, 1999).

Bliss, F. M., *Catholic and Ecumenical: History and Hope* (Wisconsin: Rowman and Littlefield, 1999).

Boyd, R., *Ireland: Christianity Discredited or Pilgrim's Progress?* (Geneva: WCC, 1988).

Brewer, J. D. with Higgins, G. I., *Anti-Catholicism in Northern Ireland 1600–1998: The Mote and the Beam* (London: Macmillan, 1998).

Brierley, P. (ed.), *UK Christian Handbook: Religious Trends 1998–99* (London: Christian Research, 1999).

Bruce, S., *God Save Ulster! The Politics and Religion of Paisleyism* (Oxford: Oxford University Press, 1986).

Cooke, D., *Peacemaker: The Life and Work of Eric Gallagher* (Peterborough: Methodist Publishing House, 2005).

Daly, C. and Worrall, S., *Ballymascanlon: An Irish Venture in Inter-church Dialogue* (Dublin: Veritas, 1978).

Davey, R., *A Channel of Peace* (London: HarperCollins, 1993).

Davey, R., *An Unfinished Journey An Anniversary Anthology of the Corrymeela Community 1965–1986* (Belfast: Corrymeela Press, 1986).

Ellis, I., *Vision and Reality: A Survey of Twentieth Century Inter-Church Relations in Ireland* (Belfast: IIS, 1992).

Elliott, M., *The Catholics of Ulster* (London: Penguin, 2000).

Fitzgerald, B., *Father Tom: An Authorised Portrait of Cardinal Tomas O'Fiaich* (London: HarperCollins, 1990).

Gallagher, E. and Worrall, S., *Christians in Ulster 1968–1980* (Oxford: Oxford University Press, 1982).

*Good News Bible* (London: The Bible Society/HarperCollins, 1994).

Grant, J., *One Hundred Years with the Clonard Redemptorists* (Dublin: Columba, 2003).

Hurley SJ, M., *Christian Unity: An Ecumenical Second Spring?* (Dublin: Veritas, 1998).

Kerr, C. *The Way of Peace: Peace Amidst the Conflict in Northern Ireland,* (London: Hodder and Stoughton, 1990).

Kinahan, T., *A More Excellent Way A Vision for Northern Ireland* (Belfast: Corrymeela Press, 1998).

Leichty, J. and Clegg, C., *Moving Beyond Sectarianism Religion, Conflict and Reconciliation in Northern Ireland* (Dublin: The Columba Press, 2001).

McGarry, J. and O'Leary, B., *Explaining Northern Ireland* (Oxford: Blackwell, 1995).

Megahey, A., *The Irish Protestant Churches in the Twentieth Century* (London: Macmillan, 2000).

Morrow, D., *The Churches and Inter-Community Relations* (Belfast: Centre for the Study of Conflict, 1990).

Radford, I., *Breaking Down Divisions, the Possibilities of a Local Church to Improving Community Relations* (Belfast: Community Relations Council, 1993).

Richardson, N. (ed.), *A Tapestry of Beliefs: Christian Traditions in Northern Ireland* (Belfast: Blackstaff, 1998).

Ruane, J. and Todd, J., *The Dynamics of the Conflict in Northern Ireland:*

*Power, Conflict and Emancipation* (Cambridge: Cambridge University Press, 1996).

Taggart, N. W., *Conflict, Controversy and Co-operation: The Irish Council of Churches and 'The Troubles' 1968–1972* (Dublin: The Columba Press, 2004).

Wells, R. A., *Friendship Towards Peace The Journey of Ken Newell and Gerry Reynolds* (Dublin: Columba, 2005).

Whyte, J. H., *Interpreting Northern Ireland* (Oxford: Clarendon Press, 1990).


## Articles and chapters in books

Barnes, L. P., 'Was the Northern Ireland Conflict Religious?', *Journal of Contemporary Religion*, 20 (2005), pp. 55–69.

de Burca, B., 'The Northern Ireland Conflict and the Christian Churches', *Doctrine and Life*, 23, 9 (1973), pp. 463–75.

Dawson, A., 'The Origins and Character of the Base Ecclesial Community: a Brazilian Perspective', in Rowland, C. (ed.), *The Cambridge Companion to Liberation Theology* (Cambridge: Cambridge University Press, 1999), pp. 109–28.

Dunlop, J. 'Reconciliation: Gift of God and Source of New Life', *One in Christ*, 33, 4 (1997), pp. 317–28, 322.

Elliot, M., 'Religion and Identity in Northern Ireland', in W. A. van Horne (ed.), *Global Convulsions Race, Ethnicity, and Nationalism at the End of the Twentieth Century* (New York: State University of New York Press, 1997), pp. 149–67.

Hickey, J., 'The Role of the Churches in the Conflict in Northern Ireland', *Studies*, Winter (1985), pp. 402–10.

Keogh, D., 'The Role of the Catholic Church in Ireland 1922–1995', in *Building Trust in Ireland: Studies Commissioned by the Forum for Peace and Reconciliation* (Belfast: Blackstaff, 1996).

Morrow, D., 'Church and Religion in the Ulster Crisis', in S. Dunn (ed.), *Facets of the Conflict in Northern Ireland* (London: Macmillan, 1995), pp. 151–67.

Morrow, D., 'Churches, Society and Conflict in Northern Ireland', in A. Aughey and D. Morrow (eds), *Northern Ireland Politics* (London: Longman, 1996), pp. 190–8.

Seldon, A., 'Interviews' in Anthony Seldon (ed.), *Contemporary History Practice and Method* (Oxford: Oxford University Press, 1998), pp. 3–16.

# Endnotes

## INTRODUCTION

1 John Hickey, 'The Role of the Churches in the Conflict in Northern Ireland', *Studies*, Winter (1985), pp. 402–10.

2 Peter Brierley (ed.), *UK Christian Handbook: Religious Trends 1998–99* (London: Christian Research, 1999).

3 NISRA, *Northern Ireland Census 2001 Key Statistics*, Table KS07a, http://www.nisra.gov.uk/census/pdf/Key%20Statistics%20ReportTables.pdf, accessed 26 July 2005.

4 For example since 1921, both the Presbyterian Church and COI have suffered a decline in their size of around 10% which 'had only been partly off-set by the rise in the number of those attached to smaller Protestant groups, who now make up 8 per cent of the population'. Duncan Morrow, 'Church and Religion in the Ulster Crisis', in S. Dunn (ed.) *Facets of the Conflict in Northern Ireland* (London: Macmillan, 1995), pp. 151–67, 156.

5 Hickey, 'The Role of the Churches in the Conflict in Northern Ireland', p. 403.

6 D. Morrow, 'Churches, Society and Conflict in Northern Ireland', in A. Aughey and D. Morrow (eds), *Northern Ireland Politics* (London: Longman, 1996), pp. 190–8, 194.

7 David Stevens, 'The Churches and Ten Years of the Peace Process', in *Beyond Sectarianism? The Churches and Ten Years of the Peace Process* (Belfast: Community Relations Council, 2005), p. 10.

8 Ken Logue cited in Marianne Elliott, 'Religion and Identity in Northern Ireland', in W.A. van Horne (ed.), *Global Convulsions Race, Ethnicity, and Nationalism at the end of the Twentieth Century* (New York: State University of New York Press, 1997), pp. 149–67, 158.

9 J. H. Whyte, *Interpreting Northern Ireland* (Oxford: Clarendon Press, 1990), p. 103.

10 For a fuller discussion of this issue see L. Philip Barnes, 'Was the Northern Ireland Conflict Religious?', *Journal of Contemporary*

*Religion*, 20 (2005), pp. 55–69, John McGarry and Brendan O'Leary, *Explaining Northern Ireland* (Oxford: Blackwell, 1995), Joseph Ruane and Jennifer Todd, *The Dynamics of the Conflict in Northern Ireland: Power, Conflict and Emancipation* (Cambridge: Cambridge University Press, 1996) or Whyte, *Interpreting Northern Ireland*.

11 Marianne Elliott, *The Catholics of Ulster* (London: Penguin, 2000).

12 McGarry and O'Leary, *Explaining Northern Ireland*, p. 212.

13 Geraldine Smyth, 'Peace Ten Years On: And Where Are the Churches Now?', in *Beyond Sectarianism?*, p. 30.

14 Eric Gallagher and Stanley Worrall, *Christians in Ulster 1968–1980* (Oxford: Oxford University Press, 1982).

15 Ian Ellis, *Vision and Reality: A Survey of Twentieth Century Inter-Church Relations in Ireland* (Belfast: IIS, 1992). Ellis was the secretary of the Church of Ireland's Church Unity Committee.

16 Norman W. Taggart, *Conflict, Controversy and Co-operation, The Irish Council of Churches and 'The Troubles' 1968–1972* (Dublin: Columba, 2004).

17 Ibid., p. 13.

18 See for example Dennis Cooke, *Peacemaker: The Life and Work of Eric Gallagher* (Peterborough: Methodist Publishing House, 2005) or Ronald A. Wells, *Friendship Towards Peace: The Journey of Ken Newell and Gerry Reynolds* (Dublin: Columba, 2005). In a similar vein, a recent history of the Clonard Monastery on the Falls Road in West Belfast also has a chapter dedicated to ecumenical activity there, James Grant, *One Hundred Years with the Clonard Redemptorists* (Dublin: Columba, 2003).

19 See for example Duncan Morrow, 'Church and Religion in the Ulster Crisis', in *Facets of the Conflict in Northern Ireland*, and Duncan Morrow, 'Churches, Society and Conflict in Northern Ireland', in *Northern Ireland Politics*.

20 Duncan Morrow, *The Churches and Inter-Community Relations* (Belfast: Centre for the Study of Conflict, 1994) and Inge Radford, *Breaking Down Divisions, the Possibilities of a Local Church to Improving Community Relations* (Belfast: Community Relations Council, 1993).

21 The Catholic Church, the Church of Ireland, the Presbyterian Church in Ireland and the Methodist Church.

22 *Author's interview with Maire Foley and Graeme Thomson*, Ploughshare, Bangor, Co. Down, 9 November 2005.

23 Oliver Crilly, 'The Catholic Church in Ireland', in Norman Richardson (ed.), *A Tapestry of Beliefs: Christian Traditions in Northern Ireland*, (Belfast: Blackstaff, 1998), pp. 23–44, 26.

24 John Erskine, 'The Presbyterian Church in Ireland', ibid., pp. 45–65, 52.

25 Ibid.

26 Ibid., p. 53.

27 *Catechism of the Catholic Church* (London: Geoffrey Chapman, 1994),

paragraph 822.

28  Erskine, 'The Presbyterian Church', p. 62.

29  These will not be discussed in this book as they work in an intra, rather than inter-church, manner.

30  John Morrow, 'Christian Reconciliation Movements', *A Tapestry of Belief* pp. 274–286, 274.

31  *Acts* 10: 34–5.

32  John Dunlop, 'Reconciliation: Gift of God and Source of New Life', *One in Christ*, 33, 4, (1997), pp. 317–28, 322.

33  Anthony Seldon, 'Interviews', in Anthony Seldon (ed.), *Contemporary History Practice and Method* (Oxford, 1998), pp. 3–16, 5.

CHAPTER ONE

1  Brian de Burca, 'The Northern Ireland Conflict and the Christian Churches', *Doctrine and Life*, 23, 9 (1973), pp. 463–75, 474.

2  John Barkley, *Blackmouth and Dissenter* (Belfast: The White Row Press, 1991), p. 164.

3  Cahal Daly and Stanley Worrall, *Ballymascanlon: An Irish Venture in Inter-church Dialogue* (Dublin: Veritas, 1978), p. 12.

4  Glenstal and Greenhills are annual inter-denominational theological conferences. The Glenstal Conference grew out of 'a mixed lay-clerical group of Dublin Catholic intellectuals interested in religion and theology' who, in 1963, began to develop contacts with members of the Church of Ireland clergy. Consequently, it was suggested by the Abbott of Glenstal that an ecumenical conference be held there in 1964 on the subject of the Liturgy. The first Greenhills Conference was held in January 1966 as a one-day inter-church conference and was initiated by the Rev Dr J. G.McGarry of Maynooth, who felt that the relative proximity of the location to Northern Ireland would be 'more readily accessible to participants from Northern Ireland [and] would ... be appropriate and meet a real need'. See Michael Hurley, 'The Preparation Years', in *The Irish Inter-Church Meeting: Preparation and Development* (Belfast: IICM, 1998), pp. 8–9.

5  For a full discussion of such dialogue see Gallagher and Worrall, *Christians in Ulster 1968–1980*, pp. 21–38 and 133–4.

6  Ibid., p. 26.

7  *Ecumenical Relations in Ireland* (Belfast: ICC, 1999).

8  Barkley, *Blackmouth and Dissenter*, p. 161. An assertion which is supported by Hurley when he says that the conferences 'paved the way for Ballymascanlon', 'The Preparation Years', p. 9.

9  This initial opposition was based upon the idea that the inclusion of the Presbyterian and Methodist Churches would hamper the progress already made between the Church of Ireland and the Catholic Church.

10  Hurley, 'The Preparation Years', p. 9.

11 Ibid.
12 Gallagher and Worrall, *Christians in Ulster*, p. 34.
13 Ellis, *Vision and Reality*, p. 118.
14 Taggart, *Conflict, Controversy and Co-operation*, p. 86.
15 These were the nature of the church, the renewal of the church and dialogue between the church and the modern world, Ellis, *Vision and Reality*, p. 117.
16 Cardinal Jan Willebrands, cited in ibid.
17 *Author's interview with Rev. Dr Ian Ellis*, Newcastle, 12 January 2000. Such a comment typifies the attitude of many Protestant clergy during this period towards the Catholic Church's apparent change of attitude towards ecumenical contact. They believed the Catholic Church to be moving towards their definition of ecumenical dialogue, which, although it contained some elements of a move towards church unity, was based upon a need to promote Christian belief, rather than reunite all the churches once more under Rome. As we shall see, this difference of definition was one of the main stumbling blocks preventing progress in ecumenical dialogue during this period.
18 This isolationist stance is a reflection of the dominant spirituality of the Catholic Church, which taught that in order to achieve holiness Catholics were expected to withdraw from the world, concentrating instead upon their interior life. For a fuller discussion of this see Frederick M. Bliss, *Catholic and Ecumenical: History and Hope* (Wisconsin: Rowman and Littlefield, 1999), pp. 25–9.
19 *Mortalium Animous*, 6 January 1928, cited in ibid.
20 *Ecclesia Catholica*, 20 December 1949, cited in ibid., p. 49.
21 *Decree on Ecumenism: Unitatis Redintegratio*, 21 November 1964 (Boston: Pauline Books and Media, 1964), p. 7.
22 Ibid., p. 8.
23 Bliss, *Catholic and Ecumenical*, pp. 100–1.
24 *Decree on Ecumenism*, p. 12.
25 Ibid., pp. 10–11.
26 Ibid., pp. 15–18.
27 Bliss, *Catholic and Ecumenical*, p. 101. For example, the Church of Ireland would be more likely to be viewed as a church because of its episcopal structure.
28 Gallagher and Worrall, *Christians in Ulster*, p. 132. However, both Taggart and Hurley argue that the Catholic attitude is mirrored by the Protestant Churches. 'If Rome thought of unity with non-Catholics only in terms of their "return" to the Catholic fold, Protestants envisaged closer relations with Catholics only on the basis of them turning their backs on Romanism and embracing the Reformation faith. For many on both sides there was no room for half measures.' Taggart, *Conflict, Controversy and Co-operation*, p. 85.

29 Gallagher and Worrall, *Christians in Ulster*, p. 131.
30 Professor Michael Ledwith, Secretary of the Commission on Ecumenism, cited in ibid.
31 Cited in ibid., p. 132.
32 Michael Hurley, cited in ibid., p. 141.
33 Cited in Taggart, *Conflict, Controversy and Co-operation*, p. 95.
34 Gallagher and Worrall, *Christians in Ulster*, p. 131.
35 Cited in Taggart, *Conflict, Controversy and Co-operation*, p. 94.
36 Hurley, 'The Preparation Years', p. 18. The first meeting took place on 31 January 1969.
37 Barkley, *Blackmouth and Dissenter*, p. 158.
38 At various times the Committee was known as 'Heads of Churches Consultative Committee', the 'Church Leaders Consultative Committee', and the '*ad hoc* Church Leaders Consultative Committee on Community Relations'.
39 Gallagher and Worrall, *Christians in Ulster*, p. 133.
40 Taggart, *Conflict, Controversy and Co-operation*, p. 97.
41 Ibid.
42 Commonly known as the 'Joint Group'. A full discussion of the Group's work can be found in ibid., pp. 99–110.
43 Gallagher and Worrall, *Christians in Ulster*, p. 134.
44 Hurley, 'The Preparatory Years', p. 19. Taggart also comments on the use of the term 'etc.': 'The inclusion of the "etc" in the joint announcement gave some hope of flexibility in interpreting the Group's terms of reference. Perhaps in the right circumstances, and as people grew in confidence and became more accustomed to this level and form of co-operation, it might prove possible to tackle other issues such as doctrine and causes of conflict within the community.' Taggart, *Conflict, Controversy and Co-operation*, pp. 99–100.
45 Cited in Hurley, 'The Preparatory Years', p. 20.
46 Cooke, *Peacemaker*, p. 236.
47 Ibid., p. 237.
48 *Violence in Ireland: A Report to the Churches* (Belfast: 1976), p. 8.
49 Ibid., p. 91.
50 However, this report did form the basis for the IICM's Discussion Document on Sectarianism, which was published in 1993.
51 Cited in Hurley, 'The Preparatory Years', p. 21.
52 *Belfast Telegraph*, 18 April 1972 cited in ibid. According to the *Irish Press* report (14 April 1972) of the Spring Meeting, the question of including the Catholic Church in the ICC had come up in discussion. Ibid., p. 37.
53 *Irish Times*, 29 September 1998.
54 Cited in Robin Boyd, *Ireland: Christianity Discredited or Pilgrim's Progress?* (WCC: Geneva, 1988), pp. 46–7.

55 That this protest against an ecumenical event was unusually muted is surprising, especially as Steve Bruce, in *God Save Ulster*, has argued that ecumenical contact between the Protestant and Catholic Churches had helped to solidify support for the Free Presbyterian Church and Paisley's DUP amongst conservative Protestants. This, he believes, is due to their conviction that Rome and terrorism were intrinsically linked, both through the WCC, and its programme to combat racism, and the negotiations between some Protestant clergy and the IRA to bring about a ceasefire during this period. 'Thus the conservative Protestant critic of the ecumenical movement can equate ecumenism and terrorism and, given that the ecumenical movement is on the road to Rome, Rome can be equated with the IRA.' Steve Bruce, *God Save Ulster! The Politics and Religion of Paisleyism* (Oxford: Oxford University Press, 1986), p. 124.

56 Gallagher and Worrall, *Christians in Ulster*, p. 78.

57 Daly and Worrall, *Dissenter*, p. 164.

58 John Barkley, *Blackmouth and Dissenter*, p. 164.

59 Cited in Hurley, 'The Preparatory Years', p. 3.

60 Cited in ibid.

61 *Irish News*, 22 January 1998.

62 Dermot Keogh, 'The Role of the Catholic Church in Ireland 1922–1995' in *Building Trust in Ireland: Studies Commissioned by the Forum for Peace and Reconciliation* (Belfast: Blackstaff, 1996), p. 162.

63 Ibid.

64 Boyd, *Ireland*, p. 47. For example, the *Irish Times* stated that 'the occasion should give the adherents of the ecumenical movement in Ireland an opportunity to put an end to a decade of timidity – a timidity which opponents have fastened on as a sign of weakness and a lack of conviction. If the situation in the North does not now provide the necessary degree of conviction and a sense of urgency, nothing else will.' Cited in Gallagher and Worrall, *Christians in Ulster*, p. 137.

65 *Irish News*, 22 January 1998.

66 Ian Ellis, 'The Period since 1973', *The Irish Inter-Church Meeting*, p. 40.

67 Daly and Worrall, *Ballymascanlon*, p. 33.

68 For the full details and discussion of these reports see ibid. and Ellis, 'The Years since 1973'.

69 Ellis, 'The Period since 1973', p. 53. Similar areas of convergence were also reached on the issue of the Eucharist, which are noted on p. 49.

70 Bishop Dermot Ryan speaking to the 1977 Meeting cited in ibid., p. 51.

71 Daly and Worrall, *Ballymascanlon*, p. 57. Indeed, 'those who think such meetings are cosy, ecclesiastical get togethers do not appreciate how painful it can be to discuss issues that go to the heart of all one believes with people who at times differ quite fundamentally'. Ellis, 'The Period since 1973', p. 41.

72 Daly and Worrall, *Ballymascanlon*, pp. 81–2.

73  These recommendations are dealt with in full in ibid., pp. 89–106.
74  Ibid., pp. 103–4.
75  The controversy concerning the Catholic Church's attitude to the issue of inter-church or mixed marriage has been dealt with in great depth in numerous publications, see, for example, Ellis, *Vision and Reality*, pp. 135–43, Worrall and Gallagher, *Christians in Ulster*, pp. 138–9 or Alan Megahey, *The Irish Protestant Churches in the Twentieth Century* (London: Macmillan, 2000), pp. 172–3.
76  Daly and Worrall, *Ballymascanlon*, p. 70.
77  Cited in Gallagher and Worrall, *Christians in Ulster*, p. 139.
78  Ibid., p. 130.
79  Although, it should be remembered that the talks between the Catholic and Protestant Churches under the auspices of the IICM have never been labelled as official.
80  As we have seen, it is evident that the Catholic Church, despite protestations otherwise, viewed any form of ecumenical dialogue as a route to eventual reunification between the Christian Churches whereas the Protestant Churches were more guarded in their approach, using inter-church relations as a means of promoting Christian belief and improving the welfare of their congregations.

## CHAPTER TWO

1  Gallagher and Worrall, *Christians in Ulster*, p. 211.
2  *Letter from David Nesbitt*, 19 March 2002.
3  *Author's interview with Fr. Padraig Murphy*, Director of Ecumenism, Archdiocese of Armagh, Armagh, 4 February 2000.
4  *Letter from Cardinal Cahal Daly*, 12 March 2002.
5  *Letter from John Dunlop*, 8 March 2002.
6  *Ecumenical Relations in Ireland*.
7  Eric Gallagher, 'Northern Ireland', in *Ecumenism in Ireland Experiments and Achievements, Survey Papers Commissioned for the Inter-Church Meeting at Ballymascanlon, Co. Louth, on 6 March 1980* (Dublin: A Joint Publication of the Irish Catholic Bishops' Conference and the Irish Council of Churches, November 1981), p. 35.
8  Michael Ledwith, 'Ecumenism in the Republic of Ireland', in ibid., p. 7.
9  Eric Gallagher, 'Northern Ireland', p. 33.
10  It would seem at this time that there were those who were arguing that the work of the Meeting should remain on a purely doctrinal level, working towards church unity, rather than spending time discussing matters associated with community relations issues.
11  Eric Gallagher, 'Northern Ireland', p. 34.
12  Both Gallagher and Ledwith stressed the need for relationships at a grass-roots level to be encouraged and nurtured, with Ledwith stating:

'The statements from Ballymascanlon or from a Church leader will be empty without that response at the grass-roots level.' Michael Ledwith, 'Ecumenism in the Republic of Ireland', p. 7. Gallagher takes a more pragmatic and practical approach, asking: 'If it is not the task of the Churches to provide a political blueprint of the new society, it is equally not their function to become the major co-ordinator or indeed facilitator of each and every agency in the field. But is it unreasonable to suggest that each of the Churches should encourage its members to be active in the field?' Eric Gallagher, 'Northern Ireland', p. 34.

13 *The Inter-Church Meeting Organisation and Structure*, form approved at Meeting of Inter-Church Committee, 5 December 1984. Nelson Papers, Library of the Irish School of Ecumenics, Dublin (ISE version.) The tone of the version which was eventually accepted by the member churches was much harsher, pointing out the agenda of the critics of the Meeting, stating: 'In recent years, the Conference has often been criticised, more often by those not involved directly, and who have been suspicious of all ecumenical dialogue, but also by those who have been disappointed by the slow progress made in some areas of disagreement and conflict between the Churches.' *The Inter-Church Meeting, Ballymascanlon.* Version of the Inter-Church Meeting Organisation and Structure presented to the Inter-Church Relations Board of the Presbyterian Church in February 1985 and subsequently reproduced in the *Report of the General Assembly of the Presbyterian Church* (Belfast: 1985), p. 115. This version does not mention the involvement of the media in criticising the Meeting, which indicates that, the criticism from both the media and the member churches centred upon the same areas of the Meeting's work.

14 The hunger strikes in 1981 created problems for those engaged in inter-church work by polarising the two communities even further, with, for example, O'Fiaich's perceived support for the hunger strikers galvanising an already growing conservative element within Presbyterianism. The IICM, in effect, ignored their existence and never held any discussion relating to them or their consequences for the relationships between the churches, further highlighting their reluctance to constructively engage with the political situation in Northern Ireland.

15 *Report of the General Assembly of the Presbyterian Church in Ireland* (Belfast: 1981), p. 78.

16 *The Inter-Church Meeting Organisation and Structure*, ISE Version, p. 2.

17 This committee was convened solely for the purpose of organising the IICM and its terms of reference were strictly constructed, which meant that it could not make statements or decisions without the approval of the Meeting.

18 *The Inter-Church Meeting, Ballymascanlon.* The Inter-Church Relations Board of the Presbyterian Church version, February 1985, p. 115.

19  *Author's interview with Dr David Stevens,* General Secretary of the Irish Council of Churches, Belfast, 13 February 2002.

20  Billy Fitzgerald, *Father Tom: An Authorised Portrait of Cardinal Tomas O'Fiaich* (London: Collins, 1990), p. 95.

21  *Author's interview with Cardinal Cahal Daly,* Belfast, 3 February 2000.

22  With the Catholic Church having nineteen members, the Church of Ireland and the Presbyterian Church five each, the Methodist Church two and the other denominations five5, one of whom would be a member of the inter-church committee. Finally the ICC would also be represented with three members. *The Inter-Church Meeting,* ISE version, p. 4.

23  Ibid., p. 3.

24  Ibid.

25  *Interview with David Stevens,* 2002.

26  Ibid.

27  *The Inter-Church Meeting,* ISE version, p. 3.

28  *Interview with David Stevens,* 2002.

29  *Report of the General Assembly of the Presbyterian Church in Ireland* (Belfast: 1986), p. 152.

30  *Ecumenical Relations in Ireland,* p. 5.

31  *Interview with David Stevens,* 2002.

32  *Author's interview with Rev. Norman McAuley,* Presbyterian Minister, Magherafelt, 6 October 2000.

33  *Report of the Working Party on Young People and the Church,* A Report to the Irish Inter-Church Meeting and its Department of Social Issues (Belfast: IICM, 1990), p. 4.

34  Ibid.

35  Ibid., p. 62.

36  Ibid., p. 68.

37  *Interview with David Stevens,* 2002.

38  Non-spiritual engagement of young people can be defined as any matter not directly re-lated to worship and other more traditional spheres of church influence, such as bible study. For example, non-spiritual engagement could be a community relations-based event or an unemployment advice centre.

39  *Young People and the Church,* p. 62.

40  Ibid., p. 43.

41  Ibid., p. 70.

42  Ibid., p. 72.

43  Ibid., p. 73. This they believed could be done by encouraging 'young people's wish to take positive action in respect of the divisions in Northern Ireland. They should enable young people to examine their own traditions as well as those of 'the other side' to overcome the major barrier for ignorance.' Ibid., p. 70.

44  Ibid.

45 Ibid., p. 72.
46 Ibid., p. 71.
47 'Youth Link is the Inter-Church Youth Service for Northern Ireland ... Youth Link is in a unique partnership of Churches which, through the training and development of youth workers, and the promotion of cross community activity, aims to empower young people to fulfil their potential, thereby promoting the peace of God in our divided community.' Youth Link, Home Page, http://www.youthlink.org.uk/ accessed 12 March 2002.
48 *Interview with David Stevens*, 2002.
49 *The Challenge of the City, A Report to the Churches* (Belfast: Department of Social Issues, 1990), p. 5. This report subsequently focuses on Dublin and Belfast urban areas.
50 Such an approach is perhaps providing us with the initial hints of a desire to develop a contextual theology for Northern Ireland. The report's analysis of the role of the church in society would bear such an assertion out, stating that:
We have already said that the Church's unique ability is that it can develop a framework of principles, values and responsibilities based on scripture and Christian tradition. It can elaborate themes of personal dignity, social justice, the common good and the responsible use of political and economic power. It can form a community of conscience in society. Christian values have played a decisive role in shaping Irish society. The role of the Church is to sustain these values, to articulate them when necessary, and seek to transpose them further into the structure of society. The Church combines this concern for moral values with active pastoral care in virtually every area of society. The Churches continue to offer moral insight and pastoral care together. In this they play a distinctive role in society.
Ibid., p. 71.
51 Ibid., p. 73.
52 Ibid., p. 71.
53 Ibid., p. 72.
54 Ibid., p. 76.
55 Ibid., p. 73.
56 *Author's interview with members of the Lamb of God Community*, Belfast, 12 February 2002.
57 This scheme was being carried out by Msg. Tom Toner, whose parish in West Belfast had links with a Presbyterian Church in Ballygilbert, North Down. This area is commonly known as Northern Ireland's 'stockbroker belt'. *Author's interview with Msg. Tom Toner*, Belfast, 1 February 2000.
58 *The Challenge of the City*, p. 74.
59 This perception of the church as a highly structured bourgeois organi-

sation is especially true amongst working-class Protestants, many of whom would argue that the church and religion have nothing to do with being a Protestant. *Author's interview with Rev. Jim Campbell*, Belfast, 6 October 2000.

60   *The Challenge of the City*, p. 75.

61   *Sectarianism: A Discussion Document: The Report of the Working Party on Sectarianism*, (Belfast: Department of Social Issues of the Irish Inter-Church Meeting, 1993).

62   *Violence in Ireland*, p. 72.

63   This working party operated through a series of meetings with one another and gathered some of the evidence for their report through letters received from the public.

64   *Author's interview with David Stevens*, General Secretary of the Irish Council of Churches, Belfast, 18 January 2000. He also adds that this issue has dominated inter-church relations in the 1990s leading to the creation of a programme designed by the ISE to combat sectarianism at a local level.

65   *Sectarianism: A Discussion Document*, p. 7.

66   Ibid., p. 8.

67   As it was argued that 'it is much easier to challenge people on the consequences of their beliefs or actions (which may be unintended) than to challenge their beliefs as wrong in themselves or to accuse them of hateful intentions. This, of course, does not mean that there are not wrong beliefs or hateful intentions that result in harmful action to others.' Ibid.

68   Ibid.

69   Ibid.

70   They also include Sectarianism and Violence, Law and Order, Education, North–South Links, The Republic of Ireland and dealing constructively with differences. See ibid., pp. 99–113.

71   Ibid., p. 105.

72   Ibid., p. 112.

73   The introductory paragraph to the recommendations for the churches states: 'The task of reconciliation, and not the maintenance of boundaries, is central for us in Ireland – for the credibility of the Gospel is at stake. What has happened in Northern Ireland society calls us to a profound change of heart (*metanoia*). It calls us to face reality and abandon our myths, to accept our part of the responsibility for what has happened and find new ways of living together.' Ibid., p. 100.

74   Ibid., pp. 100–1.

75   Ibid., p. 102.

76   Ibid.

77   Ibid., p. 104.

78   *Letter from David Stevens*, 15 March 2002.

79   *Interview with Rev. Ian Ellis*, 2000.

80 Joseph Leichty and Cecelia Clegg, *Moving Beyond Sectarianism Religion, Conflict and Reconciliation in Northern Ireland* (Dublin: The Columba Press, 2001), back cover. This report formed the basis of the Irish Inter-Church Meeting's agenda in 2002. It will be discussed in full in Chapter 5.

81 *Interview with David Stevens*, 2002.

82 This new name was adopted because 'The Inter-Church Committee on Social Issues is reasonably self-explanatory, whereas the Department name begged the question of "well what are you a department of ?" whereas the Inter-Church Committee on social issues doesn't.' *Author's interview with Rob Fairmichael*, Irish Inter-Church Meeting, Belfast, 11 November 2005.

83 *Ecumenical Relations in Ireland.*

84 *Interview with Rob Fairmichael.*

85 Ibid.

86 Such representations were usually made under the auspices of the Irish Council of Churches and have included a submission on *A Shared Future: A Consultation Paper on Improving Community Relations in Northern Ireland* (Belfast: OFMDFMNI, 2005) http://www.asharedfutureni.gov.uk/pdf_documents/irishcouncil.pdf, accessed 29 November 2005.

87 Ibid.

88 *Author's interview with Rev. Dr Johnston McMaster*, Irish School of Ecumenics, Belfast, 14 February 2002.

89 *Ecumenical Principles* (Dublin: Veritas, Department of Theological Questions, Irish Inter-Church Meeting, 1993).

90 *Salvation and Grace* (Dublin: Veritas, Department of Theological Questions, Irish Inter-Church Meeting, 1993).

91 Ibid., p. 5.

92 *Ecumenical Principles*, p. 5.

93 *Salvation and Grace*, p. 23.

94 Ibid., p. 24.

95 *Author's interview with Fr. Brian Lennon SJ*, Belfast, 26 January 2000.

96 Geraldine Smyth, a former Director of the Irish School of Ecumenics, Johnston McMaster, lecturer in the ISE in Belfast, and Brian Lennon SJ, commentator on Northern Ireland situation and founding member of Community Dialogue.

97 *Interview with Johnston McMaster*, 2002.

98 *Author's interview with Dr Geraldine Smyth*, Director of the ISE, February 1995–April 1999, Dublin, 7 March 2001.

99 Ibid.

100 *Letter from Rev. Robert Herron*, 12 March 2002.

101 *Freedom, Justice and Responsibility in Ireland Today* (Dublin: Veritas, Department of Theological Questions, Irish Inter-Church Meeting, 1997).

102 Ibid., p. 62.
103 Ibid., p. 61.
104 Ibid., p. 93.
105 Ibid. This analysis of the place of the church in Northern Irish society in comparison to the case of South Africa or Latin America is entirely valid: in the case of these two conflicts the churches were in a strong enough position to be agents of social change.
106 Ibid., p. 68.
107 Ibid., p. 71.
108 Ibid., p. 95.
109 This would mean a sharing of resources between Protestants and Catholics for those members of the laity who desired it.
110 Johnston McMaster points out that 'the reconciliation about which churches will speak its a very vertical kind of reconciliation, it's individualistic, it's the individuals relationship with God'. *Interview with Johnston McMaster*, 2002.
111 *Being Church in the New Millennium, A Discussion Document* (Dublin: Veritas, Department of Theological Questions, Irish Inter-Church Meeting, 2000), p. 9.
112 *The Dearest Freshness Deep Down Things, Papers from the Working Party on Spirituality* (Belfast: Irish Inter-Church Meeting, 2005).
113 *Being Church in the New Millennium*, p. 23.
114 *The Dearest Freshness Deep Down Things*, pp. 3–4.
115 *Being Church in the New Millennium*, p. 48.
116 *Author's interview with Michael Earle*, Executive Secretary of the Irish Council of Churches, Belfast, 11 November 2005.
117 *Interview with Johnston McMaster*, 2002.
118 Gerry O'Hanlon, *The Agenda of the Department*, 25 November 1992, Nelson Papers, Library of the ISE, Dublin.
119 *Author's interview with Rev. Robert Herron*, Convenor of the Presbyterian Church's Inter-Church Relations Board, Omagh, 24 January 2000.
120 *Review of the Irish Inter-Church Meeting, Report of the Review Group*, Appendix 1, *Report of the General Assembly of the Presbyterian Church* (Belfast: 1998), p. 109.
121 Ibid., p. 113.
122 Ibid., p. 110.
123 Ibid., p. 108.
124 Ibid.
125 Ibid., p. 112.
126 *Belfast Telegraph*, 26 May 1998.
127 *Review of the Irish Inter-Church Meeting*, p. 112.
128 *Interview with Robert Herron*.
129 *Review of the Irish Inter-Church Meeting*, p. 112.

130 Although it is unclear what they actually mean by doctrinal basis.

131 *Church of Ireland Gazette*, 28 May 1999.

132 *Interview with Cahal Daly.*

133 *Belfast Telegraph*, 1 August 1998.

134 *Annual Reports of the General Assembly of the Presbyterian Church* (Belfast:1999), p. 31.

135 *Interview with Norman McAuley.*

136 *Interview with David Stevens*, 2000.

137 *Author's interview with Rev. Tony Davidson*, Convenor of the Presbyterian Church's Irish Church Relations Board, Armagh, 13 January 2000.

138 *Author's interview with Rev. Harry Uprichard*, Ballymena, 9 October 2000.

139 *Letter from Rev. Stephen Nelly to the Presbytery of Dromore*, no date but part of a letter sent to author, 12 October 2000.

140 Due to the nature of authority within each of the ecumenically active Protestant Churches, the Ministers must be sensitive to their congregations' attitudes to contact with the Roman Catholic Church as they risk losing their jobs and homes if they aggravate the Conservative and Evangelical Members of their congregation.

141 Alexa Smith, 'Irish Presbyterians take a Principled Stand, Say Ecumenism Doesn't Extend to Catholics', *Presbyterian News Service*, 13 September 1999. http://www.pcusa.org/ pcnews/oldnews/1999/99300. htm, accessed 9 May 2002.

142 *Interview with Tony Davidson.*

143 *Author's interview with Rev. John Dunlop*, Former Moderator of the Presbyterian Church in Ireland, Belfast, 14 January 2000. However, an unprecedented 96 members of the Assembly felt compelled to record their dissent.

144 Ibid.

145 Biblical ecumenism is defined by the members of the Movement for Presbyterian Reform as somewhere 'Christians could have found a biblical basis together'. Such discussions would usually be with those churches who adhered to a reformed theology based upon 'the scriptures, through faith alone, by grace alone with Christ alone and would have been the Church as the company of those folk who were in that personal relationship with Christ.' Obviously Catholics, with their emphasis upon tradition and the sacraments, cannot be members of such a church. *Interview with Harry Uprichard.*

146 Ibid.

147 Ibid.

148 Campaign for Complete Withdrawal, *The World Council of Churches and Reformed Doctrine*, Pamphlet no. 1, c. 1979. (Original emphasis).

149 *Evangelical View*, May 1990.

150 W. M. Craig, 'Why I said "No" The PCI and the Proposed Conference of Churches in Ireland' *The Reformer, Magazine of the Movement for Presbyterian Reform*, Autumn 1999, vol. 4, no. 2, pp. 8–12, 9–11. Alexa Smith, 'Irish Presbyterians take Principled Stand'.

151 Ibid.

152 *Interview with Robert Herron.*

153 *Author's interview with Rev Ivan Neish*, Newtownabbey, 10 October 2000.

154 *Presbyterian Herald*, July/August 2000.

155 *Author's interview with Bishop Anthony Farquhar*, Auxiliary Bishop of Down and Connor and member of the Episcopal Commission on Ecumenism, Belfast, 26 January 2000.

156 *Author's interview with Rev. Dr Ian Ellis, Newcastle, Co. Down*, 23 June 2005.

157 *Annual Report of the General Synod of the Church of Ireland Committee for Christian Unity 2005* (Dublin: 2005), p. 220.

158 *Author's interview with Bishop Anthony Farquhar*, Belfast, 20 June 2005.

159 For example, in 2001 the report stated that: 'The Committee for Christian Unity views this situation with disappointment and regret and urges all traditions to re-examine the situation so that real movement can be made towards the establishment of one inclusive ecumenical body for Ireland.' *Annual Report of the General Synod Committee for Christian Unity 2000* (Dublin: 2000), p. 221. These issues are raised again in 2001 (see *Annual Report of the General Synod Committee for Christian Unity 2001* (Dublin: 2001), p. 279) and in 2005 (see *Annual Report of the General Synod Committee for Christian Unity 2005* (Dublin: 2005), p. 220).

160 *Church of Ireland Gazette*, 25 June 2004.

161 *Interview with Ian Ellis*, 2005.

162 *Author's Interview with Rev. Dr John Dunlop*, Retired Presbyterian Minister, Belfast, 16 June 2005.

163 *Irish Times*, 2 June 2004.

164 For example, calling the Pope 'Anti-Christ' and Rev. Newell 'traitor' and 'Judas'. *Irish Times*, 8 June 2004.

165 *Irish Times*, 12 June 2004. This article provides a full account of the reaction to the Archbishop's attendance, including the 'cunning' protest at a resolution proposed by Rev. Newell's nephew.

166 *Author's interview with Cardinal Cahal Daly*, Belfast, 22 June 2005.

167 Ibid.

168 *Interview with Anthony Farquhar*, 2005.

169 *Author's interview with Stephen Lynas*, Presbyterian Church's Information Officer, Belfast, 27 January 2000.

170 Ibid.

171 *Annual Report of the Irish Council of Churches* (Belfast: March 2005), p. 11.
172 *Interview with Ian Ellis*, 2005.
173 Ibid.
174 *Annual Report of the Irish Council of Churches*, p. 11.
175 O'Hanlon, *The Agenda of the Department*, 25 November 1992.
176 *Church of Ireland Gazette*, 30 January 2004.
177 *Letter from David Nesbitt*, 19 March 2002.

CHAPTER THREE

1   *Irish Times*, 15 May 1995.
2   The need for peace, especially before the ceasefires, has underlined all inter-church work and, on the most fundamental level, is based upon a rejection of violence. In addition to this, within local inter-church groups, it is also seen as a way of life through which Christians overcome division by using words and actions, such as their membership of a local ecumenical community, as a demonstration of their commitment to peace.
3   The concept of reconciliation is one of the most important ideas found in local inter-church relationships. It is based upon the idea that the Gospel emphasises reconciliation – see, for example, Matthew 5:23, Romans 5:9–11 and 2 Corinthians 5:11–6:2. It is defined, in the context of inter-church relations, as a need to actively overcome the barriers between Protestants and Catholics caused by sectarianism.
4   Two other concepts can also be added to this list – forgiveness and justice – as these are also central to the ethos of inter-church relations at a local level. Forgiveness is characterised as a two-way process in which both sides in the conflict need to forgive each other unconditionally. It is not expected to be an easy process but is, instead, presented as a painful one during which participants in inter-church groups are expected to examine their own role in the creation of barriers between the Protestant and Catholic communities. The concept of justice is based upon a concern for the rights of all rather than just the individual and is translated in the context of inter-church relationships into working against sectarian practices, such as religious discrimination, both at a local and national level (see, for example, Genesis 1:27 or Romans 3:21–6).
5   These projects, especially the discussion groups, were located in middle-class suburbs of Belfast and did not appear to have reached the inner cities. They were therefore unlikely to have a working-class membership.
6   This was the South Down Ecumenical Clerical Study Group.
7   Cahal Daly, *Ministering the Peace of Christ in a Divided Community*, Address in the Abbey Presbyterian Church, Dublin, 8 June 1983.
8   Community Relations Council Churches Advisory Group, *A Directory of*

*Cross-Community Church Groups and Projects in Northern Ireland 1999* (Belfast: Community Relations Council, 1999), p. 55.

9  *Letter from Fr. Michael Collins*, Roe Valley Clerical Study Group (founded 1973), 10 December 1999.

10  *Interview with Brian Lennon.* This view was supported by members of the South Belfast Clergy and Church Leaders Fellowship, who stated that: 'I find it very refreshing to be involved with people from so many traditions. I hear views which I have, perhaps, never thought about. They are a help to me in opening my mind.' 'Respecting diversity is quite rare. We are able to meet and share our concerns across the Churches in the community.' *Church of Ireland Gazette*, 29 June 2001.

11  *Interview with Anthony Farquhar.*

12  *Letter from Rev. John E. C. Rutter*, Bangor Clergy Fraternal, January 2000.

13  *Interview with John Dunlop.*

14  Ibid.

15  Ibid.

16  *Interview with Jim Campbell.*

17  Johnston McMaster, *An Inter-Church Directory for Northern Ireland* (Belfast: Community Relations Council, 1994), p. 7.

18  *Letter from Mrs Joan Hannon*, Women in Faith Group, Downpatrick, 9 December 2000.

19  McMaster, *Inter-Church Directory*, p. 23.

20  *Belmont District Council of Churches*, cited in *Directory of Cross-Community Church Groups*, p. 46. This group was the first lay inter-church group to be founded in Northern Ireland, coming into existence in 1971. It is based in an affluent suburb of Belfast close to Stormont.

21  *Ballymena Inter-Church Group*, cited in ibid., p. 45. This inter-church group was founded in 1995 in a place characterised by its deeply divided community and sectarian violence.

22  *Enniskillen Inter-Church Project* cited in ibid., p. 49. Enniskillen is close to the border with the Irish Republic and generally enjoys good community relations. This group was founded in 1988 in the aftermath of the Remembrance Sunday Bombing by the IRA in November 1987.

23  *Interview with Jim Campbell.*

24  *Interview with John Dunlop.*

25  *Author's interview with Rev. Tim Kinahan*, Church of Ireland Rector, East Belfast, Belfast, 14 January 2000.

26  Ibid.

27  An area's experience of violence and the presence of paramilitaries had a much stronger influence upon the foundation and experience of groups than the issue of class. Thus, as we shall see, they had to be more secretive in their meetings with one another and more work had to be put into building relationships during the initial stages of the group's existence.

This was due to the instinctive mistrust of the other community, which arose from their geographical proximity to a peaceline. However, once these barriers had been removed their contact was similar to that of their middle-class counterparts.

28 *Interview with Tim Kinahan.*

29 Protestants would have more to fear from their own paramilitary groups, as any ecumenical contact with Catholics would be unlikely to be tolerated. 'Some of the murals outside their churches really are frightening, stuff about liquidating your enemy and other blood-thirsty [imagery portrayed] in a semi-religious kind of way and that is the mixture that they are dealing with – the marriage of right-wing evangelical theology into right-wing military politics, the Paisley element.' *Interview with Tom Toner.*

30 Ibid. This dilemma has also been faced by others: 'In West Belfast you could meet in a neutral place but there was still a fear among many over what your own side would do to you. We would never meet on the others' territory as a first step and it was only when other people invited us to their territory that I would put it to people and they would say yea or nay.' *Interview with Tim Kinahan.*

31 Ibid.

32 The groups would concentrate upon issues of common concern, such as vandalism, rather than more contentious issues such as politics or theology.

33 A facilitator was someone who had been trained by a Peace and Reconciliation Education Initiative organisation to manage inter-church group meetings.

34 *Interview with Tom Toner.*

35 Ibid.

36 Campbell M. Young, *Draft History of the Belmont and District Council of Churches* (2002), p. 5.

37 *Author's interview with members of the Belmont and District Council of Churches*, Belfast, 10 November 2005.

38 Belmont and District Council of Churches response to the Shared Future Consultation, http://www.asharedfutureni.gov.uk/pdf_documents/belmont.pdf, accessed 27 December 2005.

39 *Interview with members of the Belmont and District Council of Churches.*

40 Young, *Draft History of the Belmont and District Council of Churches*, p. 6.

41 *Author's interview with Bishop James Mehaffey*, Bishop of Derry and Raphoe, Derry, 17 January 2000.

42 Social Action Projects make up a vital element of the model of programme work performed by most ecumenical communities.

43 McMaster, *An Inter-Church Directory*, p. 41.

44  This form of inter-church co-operation became largely redundant after 1994 when the Church Fora became the most prevalent new form of co-operation. Only one Social Action Project was founded after 1994, the Forthspring Inter-Community Group (est. 1996) and, as we shall see, this was as a result of the combination of the existence of two ecumenical communities in the area and the availability of suitable premises.

45  McMaster, *An Inter-Church Directory*, p. 44.

46  *A Directory of Cross-Community Church Groups and Projects*, p. 105.

47  Brian Tipping, *Parents and Kids Together, Lurgan, Final Evaluation Report* (March 1999), p. 6.

48  Central Community Relations Unit, *Project Directory entry for Forthspring*, http://www.ccruni.gov.uk/research/directory/srmcccc.htm, accessed 8 August 2002.

49  Email from Rev. Gary Mason to author, 8 August 2002.

50  Ibid.

51  *Author's interview with Sr. Noreen Christian*, Leader of the Currach Community, 21 October 1999.

52  *Author's interview with Rev. Ken Good*, Founding Member of PAKT, Lurgan, 5 October 2000.

53  Cited in David Williamson, Derek Brown and Gillian Irvine, *Dreams Judged on Delivery: A Report on the Work of Church Based Groups Supported by the Community Relations Council* (n.d.), p. 36.

54  Forthspring, *Application for Grant Aid* (n.d.).

55  Forthspring, *Vision-mission-aims*, http://home.btconnect.com/Forth spring/home.htm, accessed 4 January 2006.

56  Tipping, *Parents and Kids Together, Lurgan*, p. 7.

57  Ibid.

58  PAKT, 'Strategic Aims' http://www.paktlurgan.com/strat.html, accessed 4 January 2006.

59  *A Directory of Cross-Community Church Groups and Projects*, p. 109.

60  Ibid., p. 100.

61  Stephen Rourke, *PAKT Lurgan, Strategic Review of Activities and Operations: Summary of Conclusions and Recommendations* (May 2000), p. 1.

62  Central Community Relations Unit, *Project Directory entry for Forthspring*, http://www.ccruni.gov.uk/research/directory/srmcccc.htm. PAKT's management was founded upon a similar premise as 'the management committee was constructed of equal numbers drawn from the two communities'. Tipping, *Parents and Kids Together, Lurgan*, p. 6.

63  *Interview with Noreen Christian*, 1999.

64  Tipping, *Parents and Kids Together, Lurgan*, pp. 6–7.

65  Williamson *et al.*, *Dreams Judged on Delivery*, p. 36.

66  *Interview with Noreen Christian*, 1999.

67  *A Directory of Cross-Community Church Groups and Projects*, p. 107.

68  Ibid.
69  Rourke, *PAKT Lurgan, Strategic Review of Activities and Operation*, p. 2.
70  *Interview with Ken Good.*
71  Forthspring Inter-Community Group Ltd, *Annual Report 2001, The Community Together*, p. 5. It is interesting to note this theme of safety, which occurs frequently within the literature of both projects. For example, PAKT describe their children's programmes as developing the children 'in a safe and friendly environment'. PAKT (Lurgan), *6th Anniversary Report* (December 1999), p. 3. This is a theme which is central to all inter-church work, as a safe environment needs to be developed before difficult issues can be tackled.
72  Recruitment to these programmes is also structured with Forthspring's play workers visiting schools and local houses to promote a balance of Protestant and Catholic participants and PAKT's management monitoring their programme's intake to ensure a balance 'in relation to gender, religion and socio-economic background'. Rourke, *PAKT Lurgan, Strategic Review of Activities and Operation*, p. 3.
73  Forthspring, *Application for Grant Aid.*
74  Ibid.
75  Forthspring, *Annual Report 2001*, p.5.
76  PAKT, *6th Anniversary Report*, p. 3.
77  Rourke, *PAKT Lurgan, Strategic Review of Activities and Operation*, p. 19.
78  Ibid.
79  Single-identity work is a process whereby community workers engage with groups made up entirely of either Protestants or Catholics. They then take them through a programme designed to teach them more about their own cultural and religious identities. It is argued that this process makes the participants feel more secure and confident about their own identity and thus helps them to find it easier to engage with the other community during cross-community courses or in other areas, as they are able to answer questions about issues relating to their community and identity.
80  *Letter from Bernie Laverty*, Programme Co-ordinator of Forthspring, 15 August 2002.
81  Forthspring, *Annual Report*, 2002, p. 3.
82  Forthspring, *Annual Report*, 2004.
83  *The Hurt the Peace the Love and the War Living in West Belfast* (Belfast: Forthspring, 2004).
84  *Author's interview with Anne Doyle and Margaret Houston*, PAKT, Lurgan, 8 November 2005.
85  In one six-month period alone, PAKT increased the number of young people involved in its programmes by 19 per cent. PAKT, *10th Anniversary Report*, 2003.
86  Ibid.

87 Ibid.

88 Williamson *et al.*, *Dreams Judged on Delivery*, p. 37.

89 Rourke, *PAKT Lurgan, Strategic Review of Activities and Operation*, p. 4.

90 This development has been a matter of concern to those participating in PAKT, as many 'felt that the Christian ethos of PAKT Lurgan has been diluted and down played over the last six years and that more work needs to take place in identifying mechanisms through which the Christian focus of the project could be made more explicit and stronger'. Ibid., p. 19.

91 *Interview with James Mehaffey.*

92 For example, there are a number of Social Action Projects in Northern Ireland which provide similar services to those in Derry but on a much smaller scale, such as the Castlewellan Inter-Church Caring Project and the Downpatrick and Area Inter-Church Caring Project.

93 Those groups involved in this social action work do not undertake to provide formal courses in cross-community relationship building, such as single-identity work, as is the case in other Social Action Projects. However, there are other inter-church groups working in the city which provide this service to people, for example the Columba Community.

94 It will be known as the Churches Trust.

95 Although the Churches Voluntary Work Bureau and Churches in Co-operation maintain separate identities they are sister organisations, and their work post-1996 will be discussed in the next section on Church Fora.

96 *Interview with James Mehaffey.*

97 *Author's interview with George Glenn*, CEO of Churches in Co-operation and Churches Voluntary Work Bureau, Derry, 25 January 2000.

98 Prior to this 'Clergymen in the East Bank used to pick up problems from their parishioners and [George Glenn] used to take them over to the Catholic Advice Centre.' Ibid.

99 Action for Community Employment: 'Government Scheme for the long-term unemployed. Partially funded by the European Social Fund, it has become a semi-permanent feature of the Northern Irish economy. Each scheme is locally managed, often with Church involvement.' Cited in Morrow, *The Churches and Inter-Community Relationships*, p. 130.

100 Jim O'Neill, *My Faith, Our Faith Inter-Faith in Practice – An Overview. An Examination of Various Religious-Based Initiatives and Religious Faiths within Derry/Londonderry*, (Derry: Yes! Publications, Derry City Council, 1999), p. 20.

101 *Interview with James Mehaffey.*

102 O'Neill, *My Faith, Our Faith*, p. 18.

103 Ibid., p. 19.

104 McMaster, *A Directory of Cross-Community Church Groups and Projects*, p. 103.

105 O'Neil, *My Faith, Our Faith*, p. 20.
106 *Interview with George Glenn.*
107 Ibid.
108 Churches Voluntary Work Bureau and Churches in Co-operation, *Annual Report*, 1997–98.
109 Ibid.
110 Foyle Hill Environmental Group, cited in ibid.
111 Ibid.
112 *Interview with George Glenn.*
113 *Annual Report*, 1997–98.
114 The Ulster Project was founded in 1975 by Canon Waterstone, a COI Minister, after he felt that the attitudes of Northern Irish teenagers could be changed if they were able to experience the way in which other diverse societies live together. The Ulster Project operated in a slightly different way to Derry's Wider Horizons scheme. The young people, aged from 14 to 16, who were chosen by their teachers and clergy for their leadership potential, were taken to America for a month. During this period they lived with host families and met daily for organised activities, such as community service and socialising. By 1995, there were twenty-five such partnerships between areas in Ulster and America. The ethos of this project, in line with all projects promoting inter-church contact between Protestants and Catholics, was one of reconcil-iation and the creation of better relationships.
115 *Derry and Raphoe Vision*, Winter 1999.
116 It would seem that such an idea is successful, with 50 of those involved finding full-time employment. Churches Voluntary Work Bureau, *Annual Report*, 1998–1999, p. 6.
117 *Interview with George Glenn.*
118 *Annual Report*, 1997–1998.
119 Cited in Paul Bew and Gordon Gilespie, *Northern Ireland A Chronology of the Troubles 1968–1999*, (Dublin: Gill and Macmillan, 1999), p. 297.
120 *Dail Debates*, vol. 445, col. 1807, cited in ibid.
121 *CRC News*, February 2000, Issue 34.
122 Johnston McMaster and Cathy Higgins, *Churches Working Together – A Practical Resource* (Belfast: churches Advisory Group, Community Relations council, February 2001), pp. 5–17.
123 The Church Fora are run by the Churches in conjunction with the local Council's Community Relations Officer. They receive funding from the Community Relations Council and are therefore subject to certain con-straints and monitoring in a way in which many pre-1994 inter-church projects were not.
124 *A Directory of Cross-Community Church Groups and Projects*, p. 35.
125 *Author's interview with Rev. Doug Baker*, Mediation Network, Belfast, 4 October 2000.

126 Duncan Morrow, *'It's Not Everyone You Could Tell That To': A Report on the Churches and Inter-Community Relations to the Armagh Church Forum* (Belfast: Community Relations Council, 1997), p. 51.

127 *CRC News*, February 2000.

128 These were the Ards Churches Forum (*c.* 2005), Armagh Churches Forum (1996), Churches in Cooperation, Derry (1996), the Coleraine Borough Churches Forum (1998), the Cookstown Christian Churches Forum (2001), Dungannon Area Churches Forum (2002), Fermanagh Area Churches Forum (post 1999), Journey in Understanding, Carrickfergus (*c.* 1994), Larne Millennium Initiative (1997), Limavady Churches Forum (1999), Lisburn Inter-Church Project (1997–2003), Omagh Churches Forum (1996), Ploughshare, Bangor, Co. Down (*c.* 1994) and Strabane and District Church Forum (1998).

129 There are twenty-six CROs in Northern Ireland working for the Borough Councils (excluding Belfast). 'The Community Relations Officers in each Borough Council facilitates groups in the development of programmes that will increase cross-community contact and cooperation, improve mutual understanding and the fostering of relationships.' *Community Relations and the Churches, Conference Report,* Newtownabbey, 20 May 1998, p. 28.

130 Set up 'to support and advise the work of the council ... it consists of representatives from Clergy, laity and interested individuals'. *Author's Interview with Michaela Mackin,* Former Churches Officer, Community Relations Council, Belfast, 10 October 2000.

131 Ibid.

132 Ibid.

133 *Community Relations and the Churches, Conference Report,* Omagh, 27 May 1998, p. 4.

134 Tony Macaulay, Action Research Project: *Inter-Church and Church Community Relations in Newtownards* (April 2003), p. 28.

135 'The EU Programme for Peace and Reconciliation is a unique EU funded programme for all of Northern Ireland and the Border Regions of Ireland (Cavan, Donegal, Leitrim, Louth, Monaghan and Sligo). Its main aim is to promote reconciliation and help to build a more peaceful and stable society.' SEUPB, *Programmes,* http://www.seupb.org/prog.htm, accessed 29 December 2005.

136 *Author's interview with Kerry Nicholson,* Project Worker for Lisburn Inter-Church Project, Belfast, 12 February 2002. He states that 'There was particularly one minister, Gordon Grey – they had a cross-community group with St Patrick's Catholic Church, he was the minister of First Lisburn, and he thought "here is an opportunity, why not extend this whole idea of cross-community contact," and after a year of talking to the funders and having meetings with other clergy and lay people, they finally came up with the Lisburn Inter-Church Project.'

137 *Author's interview with an anonymous Community Relations Officer*, June 2005.
138 *Author's interview with Philip Clarke*, Community Relations Officer, Dungannon, Co. Tyrone, 28 June 2005.
139 Macaulay, *Inter-Church and Church Community Relations in Newtownards*, p. 28.
140 *Interview with Maire Foley and Graeme Thomson.*
141 *Interview with Tony Davidson.*
142 *Lisburn Inter-Church Project Newsletter*, Issue No. 2, Summer 1998.
143 Ibid.
144 *A Directory of Cross-Community Church Groups*, p. 36.
145 *Ploughshare's Aims* (2003/4).
146 *Lisburn Inter-Church Project Strategy 2002–2005*, p. 1.
147 *A Directory of Cross-Community Church Groups*, p. 38.
148 Ibid., p. 37.
149 Ibid., p. 40.
150 Lisburn Inter-Church Project, *Strategy 2002–2005*, p. 2.
151 Cookstown and District Inter-Church Forum, *Constitution* (May 2004).
152 *Author's interview with members of the Cookstown Christian Churches Forum*, Cookstown, Co. Tyrone, 10 November 2005.
153 *Interview with Padraig Murphy.*
154 *Interview with Philip Clarke.*
155 *Author's interview with Rev. Robert Herron*, Member of the Omagh Churches Forum, Omagh, Co. Tyrone, 7 November 2005.
156 Colraine Borough Council of Churches Forum, *Draft Summary of Origins, Aims and Progress of Colraine Borough Council of Churches Forum* (n.d.). 'This was similar to the experience of the Cookstown Forum which was established with 'a few meetings to get to know each other and we progressed with a facilitator to set up the Church Forum., *Interview with members of the Cookstown Christian Churches Forum.*
157 *Interview with Kerry Nicholson.*
158 *Interview with Maire Foley and Graeme Thomson.*
159 *Draft Summary of Origins, Aims and Progress of Colraine Borough Council of Churches Forum.*
160 *Interview with Padraig Murphy.*
161 *Interview with Robert Herron*
162 The Church Fora do not aim to provide physical resources to combat these problems such as the unemployment advice centres run by the SAPs or the addiction centres run by the ecumenical communities. Instead they aim to increase understanding of these problems in the area and provide the churches with coping mechanisms.
163 Joy McNally, Chairperson of the Larne Millennium Initiative, cited in McMaster and Higgins, *Churches Working Together*, p. 11.
164 These would be groups such as the Garvaghy Road Residents

Association, who campaign against Orange Marches through Catholic areas.

165 *Interview with Kerry Nicholson.*

166 *Interview with members of the Cookstown Christian Churches Forum.*

167 *Interview with Maire Foley and Graeme Thomson.*

168 Ibid.

169 *Interview with Kerry Nicholson.* He goes on to state that this is a crucial part of the Forum's work because 'most churches today are only involved in community work because they want to evangelise and get people back into the churches and it is trying to change that and get them to do it [together] because they are Christians'.

170 *Interview with Robert Herron,* November 2005.

171 See Ploughshare, *A Shared Future – Responses,* http://www.asharedfutureni.gov. uk/pdf_documents/ploughshare.pdf, accessed 30 November 2005.

172 *Interview with Maire Foley and Graeme Thomson.*

173 Gallagher and Worrall, *Christians in Ulster,* p. 177.


CHAPTER FOUR

1 McMaster, *A Directory of Cross-Community Church Groups and Projects,* p. 27.

2 Ray Davey, *A Channel of Peace* (London: HarperCollins, 1993), p. 63.

3 Bill Breakey cited in Colin Fowler, *The Corrymeela Community and its Programme Work: Part one, a description* (July 1995), p. 5.

4 Agape was established in Turin after the Second World War and, like Iona, is based upon a commitment to a holistic vision of Christianity.

5 Cited in Ray Davey, *An Unfinished Journey: An Anniversary Anthology of the Corrymeela Community 1965–1986* (Belfast: Corrymeela Press, 1986), Part One: Beginning the Journey.

6 Tullio Vinay, founder of the Agape Community, cited in ibid.

7 Ibid.

8 Fowler, *The Corrymeela Community,* p. 7.

9 David Stevens, *The Corrymeela Community: Way Forward* (1992).

10 As David Stevens comments, 'It gave special focus to the task of BREAKING DOWN the ENMITY and distrust. It expressed a sense of going on a NEW JOURNEY into new relationships and the hope that we might be a CATALYST for social and political change in Church and society.' Ibid.

11 Paraphrased from the Iona Information Leaflet.

12 Fowler, *The Corrymeela Community,* p. 9.

13 John Morrow, *Aims and Objectives of the Corrymeela Community* (Corrymeela Leaflet, n.d.) cited in Fowler, *The Corrymeela Community,* pp. 7–8. These were only two of the Community's aims and objectives,

there were five altogether which covered: developing new methods of community building within the Christian churches; working for social change and a more just society and alleviating the communal conflict in Northern Ireland.

14 John Morrow, *The Corrymeela Community*.

15 The Corrymeela Community, *The Corrymeela Community – Who we are*, http://www.corrymeela.org/Who_we_are/who_we_are.html, accessed 17 June 2002.

16 *Author's interview with Rev. Trevor Williams*, Leader of the Corrymeela Community, Belfast, 11 January 2000.

17 Ibid.

18 Ibid.

19 At which the members of the Community meet in their own locality in order to provide fellowship and support for one another.

20 Worrall and Gallagher, *Christians in Ulster*, p. 181.

21 Davey, *An Unfinished Journey*, Part VII.

22 Ibid.

23 Morrow, *The Corrymeela Community*, p. 3.

24 Fowler, *The Corrymeela Community*, p. 24.

25 Ibid., p. 25.

26 *Interview with Trevor Williams*.

27 Davey, *An Unfinished Journey*, Part VII.

28 The age range for participants was changed to 18–25-year-olds in the early 1990s. Potential participants for the seed groups are recruited from the members of the various youth and schools who have taken part in recent programmes.

29 Doug Baker, *Learning Together in Northern Ireland: The Seed Groups of the Corrymeela Community*, The Corrymeela Papers (Belfast: Corrymeela, 1984).

30 Ibid.

31 *Corrymeela Connections*, 5, 1 (2005), p. 14.

32 *Interview with Trevor Williams*

33 Susan McEwen, 'Protestants on the peace line', http://www.corrymeela.org/ Articles/protestant_the_peace_line.html, accessed 12 January 2006.

34 *Corrymeela Connections* (2005), p. 16.

35 Fowler, *The Corrymeela Community*, p. 14. Furthermore, 'the membership of the Community does not remain constant or static. Each member is asked to reflect at the end of each year upon their commitment and their ability to meet it in the coming year. Thus, there is often a number of people who do not rededicate themselves due to other current concerns in their lives.' Ibid., p. 12.

36 William Rutherford cited in Ray Davey, *An Unfinished Journey*, Part Two.

37  Fowler, *The Corrymeela Community*, p. 15.

38  Ibid.

39  These included Community Life, Corrymeela News, Corrymeela Press, Finance, Fund Raising, Staff Appointments, Volunteer Programme and Post-Review Groups.

40  These cover Christian Education work, Family and Community Work and Youth and Schools Work.

41  These groups are concerned with the Community's capital assets and services and oversee building/grounds, catering/housekeeping, maintenance and décor and transport.

42  Addressing the various aspects of the Community's Work such as bereavement, Community and Family, Summerfest and the Summer Programme and reporting on their progress.

43  A form of Christianity which places emphasis upon personal experience of the Holy Spirit in the life of the individual and community, often associated with various 'charismatic' phenomena, such as speaking in tongues.

44  Worrall and Gallagher, *Christians in Ulster*, p. 186.

45  Ibid.

46  The Charismatic Movement, through the Christian Renewal Centre, did have a small impact in the case of paramilitary activity but this was only achieved by the individual conversion of members of paramilitary groups through their contact with the group.

47  *Author's interview with Rev. Ruth Patterson*, Belfast, 21 October 1999. She argues that the origins of most of the inter-church initiatives founded at this time can be traced back to the Charismatic Renewal Movement.

48  Cecil Kerr, *The Way of Peace: Peace Amidst the Conflict in Northern Ireland* (London: 1990), p. 51.

49  *Church of Ireland Gazette*, 4 August 2000.

50  Cecil Kerr, *Reconciliation Breaking Down Divided Walls* (Christian Renewal Centre leaflet, n.d.), p. 2.

51  *Church of Ireland Gazette*, 4 August 2000.

52  Christian Renewal Centre, *Our Vision*, www.crc-rostrevor.org, accessed 12 January 2006.

53  John Morrow, 'Christian Reconciliation Movements', in *A Tapestry of Beliefs*, pp. 274– 86, 280.

54  Christian Renewal Centre, *Prayer for Ireland*, http://www.crc-rostrevor.org/ pr_4_irl.htm, accessed 21 June 2002.

55  Ibid.

56  Kerr, *The Way of Peace*, p. 91.

57  This involved some form of religious ceremony whereby the member makes a solemn vow to take part in the life of the Community for a year.

58  *Letter from Harry Smith*, 13 November 2001.

59 Ibid.
60 *Author's interview with Mr Tom Hannon*, Director of the Cornerstone Community, 28 January 2000.
61 *Questionnaire on the Experiences of the Ecumenical Communities: The Lamb of God Community, Belfast*, 11 September 2001.
62 Although this Community does not actually operate on a peaceline its methods and ethos are similar enough to its Belfast counterparts to be included here.
63 As one of their founding members later stated, the Community was founded there in order to 'avoid undue pressure from either side, it was necessary that we should be situated on neutral ground, [although] we are very near to both Protestant and Catholic troubled areas and hope increasingly to be able to serve both communities across the divide'. Eileen Mary Lyddon writing to *Encounter and Exchange*, 1986, reprinted in *We Plough the Fields and Scatter*, Booklet produced by the Columbanus Community of Reconciliation in *c.* 1994.
64 Margaret Carey and Carmel Roulston, *The Cornerstone Community, A Report for the Annual Review* (University of Ulster, September 1996), p. 6. The Malone Road is a predominantly Protestant, middle-class area situated in South Belfast close to Queen's University.
65 Ibid., p. 5.
66 *Interview with Noreen Christian*, 1999.
67 *Interview with the Lamb of God Community.*
68 *Questionnaire: the Lamb of God Community.*
69 *Interview with the Lamb of God Community.*
70 Ibid.
71 *Questionnaire: the Lamb of God Community.*
72 Ibid.
73 *Author's interview with Mr Liam Cluskey*, Lamb of God Community, Belfast, 9 November 2005.
74 Ibid.
75 *Questionnaire: the Lamb of God Community.*
76 *Interview with the Lamb of God Community.*
77 The prayer ministry and meetings have been a continuous part of the Community's work.
78 *Interview with the Lamb of God Community.*
79 Ibid.
80 Lamb of God Community, *Shalom House*, Information Leaflet (n.d.).
81 *Questionnaire: the Lamb of God Community.*
82 *Author's interview with Therese Gallagher*, Lamb of God Community, Belfast, 14 October 2005.
83 *Interview with the Lamb of God Community.*
84 Andrew Dawson, 'The origins and character of the base ecclesial community: a Brazilian Perspective', in Christopher Rowland (ed.), *The*

*Cambridge Companion to Liberation Theology* (Cambridge: 1999), pp. 109–28.

85 Neal Carlin, *Freedom to the Captives* (1983), p. 20.

86 The Columba Community, *Columba House,* Information Leaflet (n.d.).

87 Ibid.

88 Columba Community, *Good Friday Repentance Service,* (1985), p. 1.

89 *Author's interview with Alex Bradley,* Reconciliation Officer, Columba Community, Derry, 17 January 2000.

90 *Author's interview with Members of the Columba Community,* Derry, 17 June 2005.

91 Ibid.

92 *Author's interview with a Member of the Columba Community,* Derry, 14 February 2002.

93 *Interview with Alex Bradley.*

94 *Interview with Columba Community,* June 2005.

95 Columba Community, *White Oaks Centre for the Treatment of Individuals Addicted to Drugs or Alcohol,* http://www.columbacommunity.home-stead.com/ files/wobrochurenew.htm, accessed 8 February 2006.

96 *Interview with Columba Community,* June 2005.

97 Columba Community, *White Oaks Centre for the Treatment of Individuals Addicted to Drugs or Alcohol.*

98 *Letter from Tommy McCay,* 10 February 2002.

99 *Cornerstone Contact,* December 2001.

100 *Interview with Tom Hannon,* 2000.

101 *Letter from Geraldine Connolly,* Administrative Officer of the Cornerstone Community, 10 December 2001.

102 Cornerstone Community, Information Leaflet (n.d.).

103 Ibid.

104 Cornerstone Community, *Strategic Plan* (October 2001), p. 5.

105 *Letter from Geraldine Connolly.*

106 This is seen in Cornerstone's partnership with Forthspring.

107 *Cornerstone Contact,* 1986.

108 *Interview with Tom Hannon,* 2000.

109 *Cornerstone Contact,* Winter 1999.

110 *Cornerstone Contact,* 1986.

111 Carey and Roulston, *Cornerstone Report,* p. 14.

112 *Author's interview with Mrs Bridie Cotter,* Cornerstone Community Worker, Cornerstone Community, Belfast, 9 November 2005.

113 Carey and Roulston, *Cornerstone Report,* p. 11.

114 It was not until 2001 that they decided to put some sort of formal structure in place.

115 Carey and Roulston, *Cornerstone Report,* p. 10.

116 Ibid., p. 10.

117 Ibid., p. 11.

118 For example, Tom Hannon illustrates the comfortable relationship that the members of the Community have with the people in the surrounding area, as young children knock on the door when they want someone to help them cross the road or if they need help mending their bicycles. *Interview with Tom Hannon,* 2000.

119 *Author's interview with Rev. Glenn Barclay,* Leader of Columbanus 1998–2002, 15 February 2002.

120 Michael Hurley SJ, 'Columbanus Community of Reconciliation: the Feasibility Study, 1981–3', reprinted in *We Plough the Fields and Scatter.*

121 Ibid., pp. 8–9.

122 Ibid., p. 17.

123 The Columbanus Community of Reconciliation was modelled upon a number of European examples of Ecumenical Community, such as Taize.

124 Columbanus Community of Reconciliation, *An Introduction* (leaflet, n.d. but *c.* 1994).

125 *Eileen Mary Lyddon writing in Encounter and Exchange, 1986* reprinted in *We Plough the Fields and Scatter,* p. 32.

126 *Eileen Mary Lyddon,* reprinted in ibid., p. 35.

127 *Anne Ord writing for 'Quaker Monthly' May 1994,* cited in ibid., p. 68.

128 *Eileen Mary Lyddon,* reprinted in ibid., p. 34.

129 *Michael Hurley writing for PACE,* Summer 1992, reprinted in ibid., p. 23.

130 *Interview with the Lamb of God Community.*

131 Columbanus, *An Introduction.*

132 *Interview with Glenn Barclay.*

133 Ibid.

134 *Interview with Glenn Barclay.*

135 Ibid.

136 Columbanus Community of Reconciliation, *Draft Copy of an introductory leaflet about the Columbanus Community* (n.d.).

137 *Interview with Noreen Christian,* 1999.

138 *Author's interview with Noreen Christian,* Belfast, 13 February 2002.

139 *Interview with Noreen Christian,* 1999

140 *Interview with Noreen Christian,* 2002.

141 Ibid.

142 *Cornerstone Contact,* Spring 1999.

143 *Interview with Noreen Christian,* 2002.

144 Ibid.

145 *Cornerstone Contact,* 1983.

CHAPTER FIVE

1 Whilst these agencies are not entirely focused upon working with churches, they do have a specific Church Unit aimed at promoting co-operation.

2   *A Directory of Cross-community Church Groups*, p. 9.
3   This is not linked to the integrated education movement but provides inter-church courses on reconciliation and theological issues.
4   This was a joint initiative by the Irish Council of Churches and the Irish Commission for Justice and Peace involving the publication of materials on reconciliation for schools and adult Christian education movements.
5   Michael Hurley, 'An Ecumenical Institute: The Origins of the Irish School of Ecumenics', in *Christian Unity: An Ecumenical Second Spring?* (Dublin: Veritas, 1998), pp. 266–70.
6   Ibid., p. 275.
7   However, the funding was withdrawn shortly after it was granted; this was because of the ISE's links with the World Council of Churches and its Campaign to Combat Racism, which allegedly gave money to terrorist organisations in Zimbabwe. As the Irish Flour Millers Association was a predominantly Quaker organisation, and therefore pacifist in nature, it was unable to provide funding for an organisation with even the most tenuous links to terrorism.
8   These were Bishop John W. Armstrong (Church of Ireland ), Rev. Prof. John M. Barkley (Presbyterian Church in Ireland), The Very Rev. Cecil McGarry SJ (Catholic) and Rev. Robert A. Nelson (Methodist).
9   Irish School of Ecumenics, *Postgraduate Programmes* (2005), p. 1.
10  Although the ISE is an island-wide body, this section will concentrate upon its work in Northern Ireland.
11  Michael Hurley, 'An Ecumenical Institute', p. 271.
12  Ibid.
13  Irish School of Ecumenics, *Annual Report, 1999–2000*, back cover.
14  Courses facilitated by ISE staff in Northern Ireland and the border regions of the Republic, on theological and reconciliation issues.
15  ISE, *Learning Together: Education for Reconciliation* (information leaflet, 2000).
16  Students on this course had the option of studying either for an M.Phil. Degree or a Diploma.
17  Michael Hurley, 'An Ecumenical Institute', p. 270.
18  Irish School of Ecumenics, *Ecumenical Studies Programme: M.Phil. Degree and Diploma Programme*, http://www.tcd.ie/ise/degree_diploma/esp/index.html, accessed 10 September 2002.
19  Ibid.
20  Michael Hurley, 'An Ecumenical Institute', p. 287.
21  John Morrow, 'Christian Reconciliation Movements', in *A Tapestry of Beliefs*, pp. 274–86, 281.
22  The first group to take part in this were six shop stewards from the Irish Congress of Trade Unions. However, although further sessions of this nature were envisaged, they did not take place.
23  Hurley, 'An Ecumenical Institute', p. 281.

24  Ibid.

25  Ibid., p. 282.

26  Irish School of Ecumenics, *A Report on Graduates* (April 1999), pp. 4–5.

27  'Being church' is a term frequently used by more liberal members of the clergy to signify the application of their Christian beliefs to the situation in which they are living. So, in the Northern Irish context, this, for example, would lead them to actively challenge sectarianism through engaging in inter-church initiatives.

28  Johnston McMaster, 'Reconciliation: The Irish Experience', paper given at *Church and Peace Conference*, Amerdoun, June 2000.

29  Irish School of Ecumenics, *Reconciliation Studies Programme: MPhil Degree and Diploma Programme*, http://www.tcd.ie/ise/degree_diploma/rs/index.html, accessed 10 September 2002.

30  *Author's interview with Johnston McMaster*, Belfast, 27 January 2000.

31  Irish School of Ecumenics, *Reconciliation Studies Programme: MPhil Degree and Diploma Programme*.

32  ISE, *Annual Report*, 1999–2000, p. 18.

33  McMaster, 'Reconciliation: The Irish Experience'.

34  Liechty and Clegg, *Moving Beyond Sectarianism*.

35  ISE, *Annual Report*, 1999–2000, p. 22.

36  Liechty and Clegg, *Moving Beyond Sectarianism*, p. 22.

37  ISE, *Annual Report*, 1999–2000, p. 22.

38  Liechty and Clegg, *Moving Beyond Sectarianism*, p. 23. This attitude survey was later abandoned.

39  Ibid.

40  ISE, *Annual Report*, 2003–2004, p. 8.

41  Irish School of Ecumenics, *The Achievements   You Are Promoting Through the Irish School of Ecumenics* (n.d.).

42  ISE, *Annual Report*, 2003–2004, p. 8.

43  *Author's interview with Alwyn Thompson*, Research Officer, ECONI, 16 May 2001.

44  *Interview with Brian Lennon*.

45  Inter-Church Group on Faith and Politics, *Breaking Down the Enmity Faith and Politics in the Northern Ireland Conflict* (Belfast: 1993), p. 13.

46  Although the publications were widely distributed, the group themselves do not know how much use was made of their work in this regard. *Interview with Brian Lennon*.

47  Faith and Politics, *Breaking Down the Enmity*, p. 22. They go on to say that they invite interested parties to discuss and respond to their publications to determine if 'they can accept the text as it stands, or, failing that, suggest alternative ways in which the links between faith and politics might be made more appropriately', pp. 22–3.

48  Johnston McMaster, 'Churches and Politics', in *A Tapestry of Beliefs*, pp. 298–313, 307.

49  *Breaking Down the Enmity* (1985), *Understanding the Signs of the Times* (1986), *Towards an Island that Works: Facing Divisions in Ireland* (1987), *Towards Peace and Stability: A Critical Assessment of the Anglo-Irish Agreement* (1988), *Remembering Our Past: 1690 and 1916* (1991), *Burying Our Dead: Political Funerals in Northern Ireland* (1992), *The Things that Make for Peace* (1995), *Liberty to the Captives? The Early Release of Politically Motivated Prisoners* (1995), *Forgive us our Trespasses …? Reconciliation and Political Healing in Northern Ireland* (1996), *Doing unto Others Parity of Esteem in a Contested Space* (1997), *New Pathways Developing a Peace Process in Northern Ireland* (1997) and *Self-righteous Collective Superiority as a Cause of Conflict* (1999).

50  *Authors interview with Fr. Brian Lennon SJ*, Community Dialogue, Armagh, 7 November 2005.

51  *Interview with Brian Lennon.*

52  *Breaking Down the Enmity*, p. 28.

53  Ibid.

54  'true politics … being the nourishing of humanness in corporate life and of finding ways of human beings living with each other'. Ibid., p. 10.

55  'Towards Peace and Stability' in *Breaking Down the Enmity*, p. 111.

56  Ibid., p. 140.

57  *Remembering Our Past* in *Breaking Down the Enmity*, p. 147.

58  *The Things that Make for Peace*, p. 3.

59  *Forgive us our Trespasses …?*, p. 19.

60  *New Pathways*, p. 21.

61  Ibid., p. 22.

62  McMaster, 'Churches and Politics', p. 310.

63  Johnston McMaster, *The Churches and Cross-Community Work with Young People* (Youth Link: 1993), p. 13.

64  Ibid.

65  Ibid.

66  Ibid., p. 14.

67  Williamson *et al.*, *Dreams Judged upon Delivery*, p. 30.

68  Youth Link, *Vision*, http://www.youthlink.org.uk/index.cfm?id=4, accessed 4 April 2006.

69  Johnston McMaster, *The Churches and Cross-Community Work with Young People* and Doug Baker, *A Biblical Basis for Cross-Community Work* (1994).

70  Johnston McMaster, *Young People as the Guardians of Sectarian Tradition: The Challenge to the Churches* (1993), Patrick K. White, *The Needs of Young People in Northern Ireland* (1993) and Johnston McMaster, *Cross-Community Goals and Personal Development* (1993).

71  Johnston McMaster, *Historical Perspectives on a Divided Community* (1994) and Johnston McMaster, *Living Through the Troubles* (1994).

These will not be dealt with as they make no real contribution to Youth Link's development. All my booklets were published in Belfast.

72  McMaster, *The Churches and Cross-Community Work with Young People*, p. 9.

73  Ibid., p. 12.

74  Ibid.

75  Baker, *A Biblical Basis for Cross-Community Work*, p. 3.

76  McMaster, *Young People as the Guardians of Sectarian Tradition*, p. 3.

77  Ibid.

78  McMaster, *Cross-Community Goals and Personal Development*, p. 15.

79  McMaster, *Young People as the Guardians of Sectarian Tradition*, p. 10.

80  *Link:Up*, January 2001, Issue 1.

81  Ibid.

82  Ibid.

83  Youth Link, *New Opportunities for Young People and Youth Workers*, http://www.youthlink.org.uk/ylni_courses.htm, accessed 27 September 2002.

84  This is the phase's current name. Youth Link, *Kairos Menu*, http://www.youthlink.org. uk/index.cfm?id=35, accessed 4 April 2006.

85  Cathog is 'the Catholic training agency, Cathog has a responsibility to foster and facilitate the development of youth ministry in the province. Cathog is aiding the development of a youth ministry training strategy throughout the five northern dioceses.' Youth Link, *New Opportunities for Young People and Youth Workers*, http://www.youthlink.org.uk /ylni_courses.htm, accessed 27 September 2002.

86  'The Churches' Youth Service Council is an agency sponsored by the Church of Ireland, Methodist and Presbyterian Churches, established in 1943 as a response to the needs of those working with young people at that time. That is still the vision today as the Council concentrates on more informal day conferences and training in your local church. Working in partnership with the Church, CYSC endeavours to equip youth workers both spiritually and practically in their ministry with young people.' Ibid.

87  Youth Link, *Cathog*, http://www.youthlink.org.uk/cathog.htm, accessed 27 September 2002.

88  Ibid.

89  Ibid.

90  Youth Link, *Which type of Course is for you?* http://www.youthlink. org.uk/ which_ course.htm, accessed 27 September 2002.

91  Youth Link, *Further Steps … Exploring Difference and Diversity*, http://www.youthlink.org. uk/kairos.htm, accessed 27 September 2002.

92  *Link:Up*, January 2001.

93  McMaster, *Cross-community Goals and Personal Development*, p. 4.

94  Johnston McMaster, *Building Confidence – A Single Identity Programme for Church-based Groups* (Youth Link, n.d.), p. 2.

95 Ibid.

96 *Link:Up*, January 2001.

97 Ibid.

98 Ibid.

99 Williamson *et al.*, *Dreams Judged Upon Delivery*, p. 31. This was the latest figure available for programme participation as Youth Link were unable to provide more recent information.

100 *Fortnight*, February 2000, p. 18.

101 Ibid.

102 Ibid., p. 19.

103 Mediation Network, *Home Page*, http://www.mediation-network.org. uk/, accessed 5 April 2000.

104 Ibid.

105 Mediation Network, *Annual Report*, 1997/1998, http://www.media-tion-network.org. uk/html/programme_of_the_m_n_.html, accessed 5 April 2000.

106 Mediation Network, *Services*, http://www.mediation-network.org.uk/ html/services.html, accessed 24 September 2002.

107 *Fortnight*, February 2000, p. 20.

108 *Interview with Doug Baker.*

109 Ibid.

110 Mediation Network, *Training for Conflict Transformation*, http://www. mediation-network.org.uk/html/training.html, accessed 24 September 2002.

111 Ibid.

112 Ibid.

113 Ibid. This course was run in conjunction with the ISE's Moving Beyond Sectarianism Project.

114 *Interview with Doug Baker.*

115 Ibid.

116 Discussed p. 174.

117 *Interview with Doug Baker.*

118 Ibid.

119 This letter from St Paul to the Ephesians is particularly relevant to the Northern Irish experience due to its use of imagery: 'For Christ himself has brought us peace by making Jews and Gentiles one people. With His own body He broke down the wall that separated them and kept them enemies.' *Ephesians* 2:14.

120 *Interview with Doug Baker.*

121 *A Directory of Cross-community Church Groups*, p. 10.

122 *Interview with Michaela Mackin.*

123 Ibid.

124 They 'would direct them to some of those organisations and the church may come to us for the funding to pay for the course, we provide sup-

port in the way of advice, direction, signposting and the finance as well'. *Author's interview with Derek Matthews*, Churches' Project Officer, Community Relations Council, 10 October 2000.

125 Inge Radford, *Breaking Down Divisions*, pp. 66–7.

126 McMaster, *Churches Working Together – A Practical Guide for Northern Ireland.*

127 Ibid., p. 9.

128 Ibid., p. 10.

129 The examples put forward were mainly clergy and lay inter-church fellowships.

130 McMaster, *An Inter-Church Directory for Northern Ireland.*

131 *Interview with Derek Matthews.*

132 Indeed they only offered two publications aimed at promoting inter-church groups.

133 *Interview with Michaela Mackin.*

134 I was unable to gain access to material that might have provided an exposition of the development of the funding criteria as this was not available to researchers.

135 For example in 1997/8 34 groups received Core Funding. Community Relations Council, *Annual Report*, 1998–1999.

CONCLUSION

1   Ellis, *Vision and Reality*, p. 153.

2   Through the use of the word peacemaking they were arguing for church involvement in the creation of better relationships between the Protestant and Catholic communities.

3   *Author's interview with a project worker for an inter-church group*, February 2002.

4   See for example *Colossians* 1:20.

5   *Letter from Rev. David Chillingworth*, 7 March 2002.

6   Liechty and Clegg, *Moving Beyond Sectarianism*, p. 281.

# Index